Library of
Davidson College

Philosophy of Logic

Philosophy of Logic

Papers and discussions by:
J. P. CLEAVE
MICHAEL DUMMETT
FREDERIC B. FITCH
ROBERT J. FOGELIN
P. T. GEACH
R. GILES
IAN HACKING
JAAKKO HINTIKKA
CZESŁAW LEJEWSKI
JOHN McDOWELL
RUTH B. MARCUS
TIMOTHY C. POTTS
DAG PRAWITZ
DANA SCOTT
T. J. SMILEY
DAVID WIGGINS

Edited by
STEPHAN KÖRNER

UNIVERSITY OF CALIFORNIA PRESS
Berkeley and Los Angeles 1976

UNIVERSITY OF CALIFORNIA PRESS
Berkeley and Los Angeles, California

ISBN: 0-520-03235-7
Library of Congress Catalog Card Number: 76-6020

© Basil Blackwell 1976

All Rights Reserved. No part of this publication may be reproduced, stored in a retrieval system, or transmitted, in any form or by any means, electronic, mechanical, photocopying, recording or otherwise, without prior permission from the publisher.

Printed and bound in Great Britain

TO THE MEMORY OF ABRAHAM ROBINSON

Contents

Preface	ix
I Ontology and Logic	
CZESŁAW LEJEWSKI	1
Comment: MICHAEL DUMMETT	28
Comment: DAG PRAWITZ	43
Reply: CZESŁAW LEJEWSKI	48
II Does Many-Valued Logic Have Any Use?	
DANA SCOTT	64
Comment: T. J. SMILEY	74
Comment: J. P. CLEAVE	88
Comment: R. GILES	92
III Identity, Necessity and Physicalism	
DAVID WIGGINS	96
Comment: RUTH B. MARCUS	132
Comment: IAN HACKING	147
Reply: DAVID WIGGINS	159
IV The Relation between Natural Languages and Formalized Languages	
FREDERIC B. FITCH	183
Comment: P. T. GEACH	191
Comment: JOHN MCDOWELL	196
Reply: FREDERIC B. FITCH	201
V Quantifiers in Logic and Quantifiers in Natural Languages	
JAAKKO HINTIKKA	208
Comment: ROBERT J. FOGELIN	233
Comment: TIMOTHY C. POTTS	243
Reply: JAAKKO HINTIKKA	254
Index	271

Preface

The papers, comments and replies contained in this volume constitute the Proceedings of the Third Bristol Conference on Critical Philosophy, held under the auspices of the Society for the Furtherance of Critical Philosophy—the sponsors of *Ratio*—and the University of Bristol. The aim of the conference, as of its predecessors, was the discussion of a central philosophical theme by philosophers who would make a worthwhile contribution to it. My thank are, once again, due to the contributors, the two supporting institutions and to my colleagues Mr. David Hirschmann and Mr. Michael Welbourne who helped me in all matters connected with the organization of the conference and the publication of its results.

STEPHAN KÖRNER

1/Ontology and Logic

Czesław Lejewski

> *Vix aliud hodie contemtius*
> *est nomen quam Ontologiae.*
>
> *Christian Wolff*

The title of my paper can be taken to presuppose that there is something which is called ontology, and that there is something which is called logic. It can also be taken further to presuppose that between the two there is a certain relationship which calls for clarification and discussion; but from the title alone it is by no means clear what I mean by 'ontology' or what I mean by 'logic'. Thus I propose to begin my paper by first outlining the traditional conception of ontology, because it is in accordance with this conception that the term will be used in what follows. Secondly, I shall state and examine a very simple ontological doctrine in order to see what sort of logical problems it raises. In the third place, I shall be concerned with the contribution logic has made, and can still make, to ontological studies. This is the general strategy to be adopted, but there will be a number of specific problems which will arrest our attention as we proceed.

The term 'ontology', or to be more precise its Greek counterpart ὀντολογία, does not occur in the writings of ancient Greek philosophers. Its Latin version has been traced back to Goclenius, but it was Aristotle who, in his *Metaphysics*, Book Γ (4), at 1003^a 21, first claimed that 'there is a science (ἐπιστήμη) which investigates being as being (τὸ ὂν ᾗ ὄν) and the attributes which belong to it in virtue of its own nature'.

And in *Metaphysics*, Book E (6), at 1025ᵇ 3 he confirms that he is engaged in 'seeking the principles and the causes of the things that are (τὰ ὄντα), and obviously of them *qua* being (ᾗ ὄντα)'. Aristotle has no special name for this new science of his. He sometimes seems to refer to it very generally as *wisdom* (σοφία) or simply as *philosophy* (φιλοσοφία), and on a few occasions he calls it *first philosophy* (πρώτη φιλοσοφία). But he seems to be quite clear in his mind as to what sort of science the science of being should be. Its principle characteristic, according to him, is universality. The science which investigates being as being, points out Aristotle, is not the same as any of what we call special sciences; for none of these special sciences treats universally of being as being; they cut off a part of being and investigate the attributes of this part. This is what mathematical sciences do, and physics is in the same position as mathematics (see *Metaphysics*, *Γ* (4), 1003ᵃ 17–26, K (11), 1061ᵃ 25–33). Due to its universality the science which investigates being as being is farthest removed from the senses. It is an abstract discipline and consequently it is the hardest for men to master (see *Metaphysics*, A (1) 982ᵃ 23). Finally, in Aristotle's view the science which investigates being as being is more exact than other disciplines as it deals with fewer principles (see *Metaphysics*, A (1) 982ᵃ 25).

Centuries later the science of being as being was named ontology and the term established itself in the philosophical vocabulary owing to the writings of Christian Wolff (1679–1754) and Alexander Gottlieb Baumgarten (1714–1762), one of Wolff's pupils and followers. The full title of Wolff's principal ontological work, first published in 1729 with a second new edition following seven years later, reads as follows: *Philosophia Prima, sive Ontologia, Methodo Scientifica Pertractata, qua Omnis Cognitionis Humanae Principia Continentur*. Thus Wolff identifies ontology with Aristotle's first philosophy, subjects it to a treatment which in his view complies with the rigours of scientific method, and emphasizes the discipline's universal nature. In the dedication of the book to King Frederick of

Sweden, Wolff writes that just as a long time ago Euclid reduced into a system the principles of all mathematical science so that their unshattered truth might become obvious, so he, Wolff, following Euclid's example, has now reduced into a similar system the first principles of all human knowledge. This system, continues Wolff, contains the foundations of all science as well as the foundations of mathematics itself.

Wolff's conception of ontology does not seem to differ significantly from Aristotle's conception of the science of being *qua* being. In fact, it can be described as a restatement of the latter. This does not mean, however, that the two philosophers implemented their respective conceptions in the same way.

Although we are not primarily interested in Aristotelian ontology, or in Wolffian ontology for that matter, it may be helpful to say a few words about some of the problems which Aristotle and Wolff believed to be ontological problems. In his *Metaphysics*, Book B (3), Aristotle gives us a list of fourteen such problems. At least the following four have a direct bearing on the theme of the present paper:

(i) should the science of being also study the principles of demonstration?
(ii) whose business is it to study *same* and *other*, *like* and *unlike*, and the other topics of dialectical discussion?
(iii) is there anything apart from individual objects?
(iv) are the objects of mathematics substances?

It is interesting to note that to the first question listed above Aristotle's answer is 'yes', and as regards the second question, it is, in his view, the business of the science of being to study the topics of dialectical discussion, and this on account of the universality of these topics. Concerning the principles of non-contradiction and of excluded middle Aristotle points out that they are true of everything that exists and not only of a certain subclass of what there is.

All these problems and topics are also discussed by Wolff in his *Ontologia*, but, as I have already said, our main concern is not with the way in which Aristotle or Wolff implemented their conception of the science of being. Suffice it to note that Wolff devotes a great deal of space to the discussion of the significance of ontological principles for an inquiry into the foundations of mathematics.

To turn to philosophers of the twentieth century, G. E. Moore in Chapter I of his *Some Main Problems of Philosophy* tells us that the first and the most important problem of philosophy is to give a general description of the whole universe. According to Moore a description of this sort should provide the answer to the following fundamental question: What kinds of things are there? By 'things' Moore does not understand material 'things'. Whatever there is is a thing for Moore, and echoing Aristotle he maintains that there is no other science which is concerned to establish that such and such kinds of entities are the only kinds of entities that there are.

An ontology which was not inspired by Moore's fundamental question, yet provides an answer to it, has been propounded for almost half a century by Tadeusz Kotarbiński, the doyen of contemporary Polish philosophers. The doctrine has been called by him reism, or pansomatism, or concretism. It consists of the following theses:

(i) an entity is a thing if and only if it lasts and is bulky; in other, less concrete words, an entity is a thing if and only if it is extended in time and in space;

(ii) only things exist; there are no other kinds of entities apart from material things, that is to say, apart from entities that last and are bulky; living beings, perceiving beings, intelligent beings are all material things; strictly speaking there are no properties or attributes; there are no relations; there are no classes; there are no numbers; there are no facts or states of affairs; in brief, if one can be forgiven for making what may turn out to be an illicit generalization, there are no abstract entities of any kind;

(iii) statements which appear to be true and at the same time appear to imply the existence of abstract entities of one kind or another, are to be treated as a sort of metaphor and can, as a rule, be rephrased without any loss of relevant content, so as to have no existential implications or so as to imply the existence of material things only.

(iv) statements which appear to imply the existence of abstract entities of one kind or another, and are claimed by their proponents to be in need of no paraphrase, are to be rejected as false.

Now, the theses listed above characterize reism in its unrepentant form. The wording of the theses slightly differs from the original wording proposed by Kotarbiński, but the spirit of the doctrine is the same. I mention this because, as a result of the criticism levelled at reism by Ajdukiewicz, Kotarbiński made a number of concessions and worked out weaker forms of reism. As far as I can judge Ajdukiewicz's criticism was not entirely justified, nor was Kotarbiński's retrenchment really necessary. But this is another story.

Of the four theses of reism the first two are ontological theses. In fact the first thesis is a definition. One could do without it if one preferred to reformulate the second thesis in an obvious fashion. The second thesis consists of two parts: a hardly controversial positive part and a negative part, which to some philosophers is palpably unacceptable. Theses (iii) and (iv) are, in a sense, consequential to the first two theses. They are not really ontological, but can be said to belong to the reist's theory of meaning as applied to ordinary language. Although it is the justification of the third thesis that has exercised Kotarbiński's mind for the most part, we shall focus our attention on the ontological theses of reism. In fact it will be possible to illustrate the problems these theses raise by examining in detail the following three propositions:

1   there are material things,
2   there are classes,
3   there are no classes.

Propositions (1) and (3) are, of course, parts of the reistic doctrine. Propositions (1) and (2) are held by some opponents of reism. But formulated as they are, in terms of ordinary language, the three propositions are by no means unambiguous. Proposition (1) is perhaps the least controversial. It means that something is a material thing, that is to say, that

4   for some a, a is a material thing.

And by 'material thing' we understand something that is extended in space and time. In other words, we assume that the following equivalence holds:

5   for all a, a is a material thing if and only if both a lasts and a is bulky.

Propositions (2) and (3) are not as simple as proposition (1). Thus, for instance, someone who asserts proposition (2) may mean to say that classes form a subclass of what there is whereas material things form another such subclass. In accordance with this interpretation we can say that all material objects are entities and that all classes are entities, provided of course we agree that whatever exists is an entity. Since no class is a material thing, we can describe classes as abstract entities. And an ontologist who asserts proposition (1) and understands it in the way just mentioned, and who regards any other abstract entities as forming subclasses of what there is, can be described as a unicategorial Platonist. He is a Platonist because he accepts the existence of abstract entities; but he is a unicategorial Platonist because for him there exists only one kind of entities. They divide into various subclasses of which one is formed by classes.

Thus to both, the reist and the unicategorial Platonist, the proposition which says that

4   for some a, a is a material thing or a is a class,

is entirely acceptable. Both agree that it is implied by (1). And according to the reist, who admits (3), (4) is equivalent to (1).

However, (4) will have to be rejected as meaningless by an ontologist who regards classes as differing in kind from material things. He maintains that the notion of existence which is made use of in (1) differs from the notion of existence in (2), but the difference is somewhat obscured by the inaccuracy of ordinary language. According to him the expression 'there are', which occurs in (1) and (2), is ambiguous just as the expression 'the lion' is found to be ambiguous when we consider the following propositions:

5   the lion is asleep
6   the lion is a species.

In (5), which can be regarded as a remark made by a visitor to a zoo, the expression 'the lion' is a singular name referring to a particular animal, which happens to be asleep, whereas in (6) it is a singular class expression referring, in a somewhat different sense of referring, to a class, viz., to the class of lions. According to ordinary grammar singular names are nouns or noun expressions and so are singular class expressions. In other words a singular name is supposed to be the same part of speech as a singular class expression. If this were really the case, our ontologist would argue, then a singular name could be substituted for a singular class expression in a meaningful context without destroying the syntactical cohesion of the context. But this sort of substitution does not seem to work. Consider, for instance, the following propositions:

7   the sun is a heavenly body
8   the class of lions is a species.

On replacing 'the sun' in (7) by 'the class of lions' and, conversely, on replacing 'the class of lions' in (8) by 'the sun' we get:

9   the class of lions is a heavenly body
10   the sun is a species.

Now, in our ontologist's view (9) and (10) are syntactically incongruous, meaningless expressions. And so is (4) according to him. He rejects the unicategorial Platonist's suggestion that (9) and (10) should be regarded as somewhat odd but otherwise meaningful false propositions, and maintains that in meaningful expressions of the form 'a is a heavenly body' or 'a is a material thing' the variable 'a' can stand only for singular names, whereas in meaningful expressions of the form 'a is a class' or 'a is a species' the variable 'a' stands for singular class expressions. The same type of variable cannot stand for both singular names and singular class expressions, and (4) should be amended to read thus:

11   for some a and α, a is a material thing or α is a class.

An ontologist who interprets (1), (2) and (4) in the manner outlined above can be described as multicategorial Platonist. He is a Platonist because he asserts the existence of abstract entities, albeit this is not the same mode of existence as the one attributed to abstract entities by the unicategorial Platonist. He is a multicategorial Platonist because unlike the unicategorial Platonist, who envisages one universe of entities a subclass of which is formed by abstract entities, he assumes at least two separate universes of entities: one universe consisting of entities of which material things are a subclass, and another universe consisting of classes. If he happens to assume exactly two different universes then he can be said to be a bicategorial Platonist.

The two interpretations of proposition (2), the one favoured by the unicategorial Platonist and the one propounded by his multicategorial friend, are by no means the only possible interpretations. In fact there seem to be contexts where classes should be understood as aggregates or collections of material things, collections which themselves are material things. Thus, for instance, by the class of stars which form Ursa Major we may be invited to understand the constellation itself which is a material thing. And again some philosophers make statements which appear to imply (2), although such implication is not intended. To avoid misunderstanding they often warn the reader or the audience that such statements should not be taken in their literal sense but should be treated as a sort of convenient *façon de parler* which does not carry with it any commitment to abstract entities. Understood in this way proposition (8) may be said to mean no more than the proposition which says that

12   lions form-a-species.

Here the functor 'form-a-species', which is to be treated as logically not analysable, is the same part of speech as the functor 'exist' in 'lions exist' or the functor 'intermarry' in 'Europeans intermarry'. There is no need to mention that with these last two ways of interpreting statements, which seemingly imply the existence of abstract entities, the reist has no quarrel.

Our discussion so far has mentioned an answer to Moore's fundamental question, but the answer manifestly falls short of the conception of ontology entertained by Aristotle or by Wolff. We have considered various interpretations of the ontological statement asserting the existence of classes and distinguished three points of view, that of the unicategorial Platonist, that of the bicategorial Platonist and that of their opponent, the reist, but we can hardly expect credit for establishing in a convincing way that ontology is a universal, precise discipline, amenable as Wolff hoped to a system resembling, as regards its structure, the system of Euclid. If we want to convince ourselves that Wolff's conception of ontology is not a dream, we have to turn to the achievements of those philosophers who are better known to us as logicians. This may appear to be a puzzling suggestion and in need of explanation. As we remember Aristotle argued the universality of his science of being from its subject matter. In accordance with his argument a science or a theory T_1 can be said to be more general than a theory T_2 if the entities that constitute the subject matter of T_2 are among the entities that constitute the subject matter of T_1. On this account zoology is more general than anthropology, and ontology, whose subject matter contains everything that exists, is a most general, that is to say, a universal theory. However, the claim to universality can be supported by certain linguistic considerations. A theory T_1 can be said to be more general than a theory T_2 just in case the vocabulary exhibited in the theses of T_1 has to be used in the theses of T_2 together with the vocabulary characteristic of T_2. Now, every science makes use of terms such as 'if . . . then', 'and', 'or', 'it is not the case that', 'object' or 'entity', 'is identical with' or 'is the same as', 'is', 'exists', 'the class of', 'everything', 'something', to mention only a few. Thus a science or a theory which, given this vocabulary and definitions, requires no further terms to formulate its theses is more general than any other science or theory, that is to say, it is universal.

Several logicians would claim that logic is such a science, and if logic's claim to universality is conceded, then logic and ontology are one or, at least, they overlap one another. Examining our sample of logical vocabulary again, we can hardly fail to notice that all the theses of the Logic of Propositions can be formulated with the aid of 'if . . . then', 'it is not the case that', and quantification, the remaining required vocabulary being made available through definitions. Consequently, the Logic of Propositions, which exhibits the use of 'if . . . then', 'it is not the case that', and the derivative vocabulary emerges as a discipline more general than logic, in the wider sense of the term, comprising what is commonly described as the Theory of Quantification with Identity. It may be agreed that the notion of identity constitutes a strong link between ontology and logic. But is there any such link between ontology and the Logic of Propositions? Should we distinguish a sort of 'Propositional Ontology' and identify it with the 'Logic of Propositions'? Or should we say that ontology presupposes the Logic of Propositions just as the Theory of Quantification with Identity does? It seems to me that the second course may recommend itself as preferable whereas the first one appears to be groundless. Yet without committing myself one way or the other I should like to make the following comments. First, I admit that it is impossible to determine the subject matter of the Logic of Propositions. In this respect it seems to differ from any other theory. It exhibits the use of certain vocabulary but it has no means of referring to anything. Secondly, although the Logic of Propositions cannot claim any entities as its subject matter, some of its statements strike one as true or false. Now how can they be true or false if they are entirely unrelated to what there is? It has been suggested that they are true, or false, by virtue of their form, but this does not seem to be the case. As far as I understand the notion of form, in complete abstraction from meaning, the propositions which say, respectively, that

13   for all p, p if p
14   for all p, p and p

are of the same form. Yet, (13) is true and (14) is false. Some may say that when one maintains that the statements of the Logic of Propositions are true or false by virtue of their form, one really means to point out that they are so by virtue of the meaning we attach to the constant terms occurring in them. (13) is true and (14) is false because the constant term 'if' is understood or interpreted in one way and the constant term 'and' is understood or interpreted in quite another way. Consider, however, the following two propositions:

15   for all p, q, and δ, if (p if and only if q) then (if $\delta(p)$ then $\delta(q)$)
16   for some p, q, and δ, ((p if and only if q) and $\delta(p)$ and it is not the case that $\delta(q)$)

Proposition (15) is a consequence of the law of extensionality for propositions, and (16) is a denial of (15). Now, some logicians assert (15) as true, others assert (16) as true, although either side will agree that the constant terms occurring in both propositions are used in the same sense. Finally, it may be suggested that although mistakes in asserting or rejecting certain propositions within the framework of the Logic of

Propositions are not excluded, the true propositions within this framework can still claim a special status because, unlike true propositions in other disciplines, they are true in 'all possible worlds'. As regards this point, it seems to me that the discovery of many-valued logics has shown that even at this highest level of generality there is scope for alternative views and an opportunity for making a mistake. However, I leave it an open question as to whether or not our choice between two-valued logic and one of the many-valued logics involves ontological consideration.

Our references to logic in the preceding paragraphs presuppose a certain conception of logic which will not be approved by those who favour a formalistic approach to the discipline. For a formalist, logical systems which he constructs and examines are purely formal systems devoid of interpretation. Thus, instead of meaningful expressions he has well-formed formulae, instead of axioms conceived as unproved true propositions he has arbitrary postulates, which need not have any interpretation, and instead of rules of inference he has rules of transformation, which enable him to derive—not to deduce or conclude—certain well-formed formulae, provided certain other well-formed formulae are already in the system. It is true that a certain formal system may lend itself to an ontological interpretation, but this is incidental and of little interest to the formalist. The subject matter of logic as he understands it is not the totality of what there is but a small portion of it, namely that portion of it which contains certain formal systems.

According to yet another conception of logic, logicians should be preoccupied not with everything that exists, not with certain formal systems, but with arguments or inferences. Conceived in this way logic becomes a theory of inference. Its subject matter is inferences. It exhibits the use of a vocabulary which comprises such terms as 'is a consequence of', 'implies', 'is necessary', 'is a deductive system' and their definitional derivatives, and it presupposes the Logic of Propositions with its vocabulary of 'if... then', 'and', 'or', and 'it is not the case that', and in addition it presupposes the Theory of Quantification with Identity or an alternative theory such as Leśniewski's Ontology. Since a theory of inference is about certain linguistic entities, it is itself metalinguistic, and while among metalinguistic theories it has a claim to a high degree of generality, it is not as general as ontology.

Although he was primarily concerned with the foundations of mathematics, the logical theories of Frege seem to have a distinctive ontological content, as witnessed by his use of the notion of reference and 'Gegenstand'. And the same can be said about the theories of Georg Cantor, who tried to see everything that exists in terms of sets and their elements. However, Frege's scheme and Cantor's scheme suffered a setback through the discovery of set theoretical antinomies and, in Frege's case, through Russell's antinomy of the class of all those classes that are not elements of themselves. The antinomies seem to have had a two-fold effect on the development of logic. They gave a boost to formalism on the one hand and, on the other, they convinced some logicians of the need for re-thinking the conceptual foundations of their theories. As regards Cantor's set theory, efforts were made to axiomatize it in the first place and by doing so to make the reconstruction of antinomies impossible. And indeed Zermelo's axiomatization of set theory has proved to be successful in the sense that so far no one has shown it to be inconsistent, but the originally intended interpretation of the notion of set seems to have been lost in the process of axiomatization. Today set theoreticians of world-wide repute openly admit that they do not know what sets are. They do not even know whether there are any sets or not. Their theory has been disinterpreted. It has become a purely formal system.

Faced with the problem of antinomies some logicians preferred to follow a line of inquiry different from the one adopted by Zermelo and his successors. Russell, for instance, explained the antinomies by our failure to give expression in our language to the immense variety of logical types. At first it was not quite clear whether by expounding his theory of logical types Russell wanted to classify, in a certain way, the kinds of entities that there are in the world; in other words, it was not clear whether his theory was meant to be an ontology or whether he wanted to classify the variety of logical parts of speech in a logically standardized language. No such ambiguity affects Leśniewski's theory of semantic categories which is in fact a sort of grammar of a logically standardized language. In developing his theory of semantic categories Leśniewski was inspired on the one hand by certain remarks by Husserl and, on the other, by Russell's theory of logical types in its simplified form, rejecting of course its ontological interpretation. Without going into details the principal idea of the theory of semantic categories can be outlined as follows: all constant expressions of a logically standardized language divide into classes called semantic categories, the term 'semantic category' being a technical term for what, with reference to ordinary language, could be described as a part of speech; now the notion of semantic category is extended to include variables of which the relevant constant expressions are said to be substituends; all variables are bindable, that is to say quantifiers are available in the language but these stand outside the classification of expressions in terms of semantic categories; every meaningful compound expression begins with a quantifier or consists of a finite number of arguments, which in concatenation with a functor form the compound expression in question; expressions belonging to certain semantic categories can only be used as arguments, never as functors, but functors can also be used as arguments; the semantic category of a functor differs from that of each of its arguments as well as from that to which the expression formed by the functor belongs; only expessions belonging to the same semantic category can be replaced by one another in a meaningful context without destroying its meaningfulness.

In the light of these comments we can now go on to state a more formal definition of the notion of forming a semantic category:

D1   Propositions, i.e. declarative sentences, form a semantic category with respect to a's; a's form a semantic category with respect to a's; if every member of the sequence $e_1, \ldots, e_m, e_{m+1}$ forms a semantic category with respect to a's, so does the class of functors each of which, in concatenation with expressions belonging to $e_1, \ldots, e_m$ respectively and employed as arguments, forms an expression belonging to the semantic category e_{m+1}.

The definition is recursive and, for the sake of generality, relativized to certain expressions. By specifying these expressions we can define the notion of forming a semantic category in application to a logically standardized language. Thus if by a's in D1 we mean singular referential names, i.e. proper names or definite descriptions that do not fail to describe something then D1, so interpreted, characterizes a language which out of respect for history could be called Frege–Russellian. And if by a's in D1 we mean general names, whether referential or not, then D1, so understood, becomes applicable to Leśniewskian language. There is an important difference to be noted between these two types of language. Frege–Russellian language is not ontologically neutral. The mere use of singular referential names commits one to an ontology with entities which are named by singular referential names. Now the mere use of general names carries with it no ontological commitment because there are general names which do not designate anything. Moreover in Frege–Russellian language quantifiers which bind variables whose substituends are singular referential names have existential import, whereas in Leśniewskian language quantifiers binding nominal variables have no such import since the variables take as their substituends any general names whether referential or not.

This last remark may be in need of substantiation but, for simplicity's sake, I prefer to offer it with reference to another ontologically neutral language which, in a sense, comes between

Frege–Russellian language and the one worked out by Leśniewski. The notion of forming a semantic category in application to this new type of language (I shall refer to it as L'), is obtained by interpreting a's in D1 as singular names irrespective of whether they are referential or non-referential.

The meaning of the quantifiers in that part of Quantification Theory with Identity, formulated in Frege–Russellian language, which is sometimes described sa the First Order Predicate Logic, can conveniently be explained in terms of so-called expansions. On the assumption that the universe is not empty but consists of a finite number of objects, say n, the meaning of the quantifier can be read off from the following equivalences:

17    $(a).Fa. \equiv .Fa_1.Fa_2. \ldots .Fa_n$
18    $(\exists a).Fa. \equiv .Fa_1 \vee Fa_2 \vee \ldots \vee Fa_n$

In these equivalences, which are held to be true for the assumed universe, the conjunction and the alternation are expansions of the universal and the particular quantifiers respectively, and 'a_1' ... 'a_n' are singular referential names each naming an object in the universe. Thus '$(a).Fa$' means the same as 'each object a is such that Fa', and '$(\exists a).Fa$' means 'there exists an object a such that Fa'. Obviously this interpretation of the quantifiers is warranted by the meaning of the respective expansions. Having grasped the meaning of the quantifiers for a non-empty universe with a finite number of objects we can now drop the assumption as to the 'size' of the universe and replace (17) and (18) by

19    $(a).Fa. \supset .Fa_n$
20    $Fa_n. \supset .(\exists a).Fa$

where 'Fa_n' stands for any expression that may qualify as a conjunct or as an alternant in an expansion applicable to any finite part of the universe. On this interpretation it is correct to hold that the quantifiers have existential import, that is to say, carry with them ontological commitment since their use presupposes the existence of entities named by the names in the possible conjuncts or alternants in the corresponding expansions. The entities are said to constitute the universe of values of the variables whose substituends are singular referential names. And it makes no difference if this universe happens to be finite or not.

This conclusion seems to be in harmony with certain theses obtainable within the framework of the traditional Theory of Quantification with Identity. First of all it is 'tautologically true that for all a, a is the same object as a. In symbols:

21 $(a).a=a$

Now, the notion of identity can be used to define the notion of individual existence by asserting the following equivalence:

22 $(a):ob(a). \equiv .a=a$

where '$ob(a)$' means the same as 'a is-an-individual' or 'a is-an-object' or 'there-exists-exactly-one a'.

From (21) and (22) we can infer that

23 $(a).ob(a)$

and

24 $\sim(\exists a).\sim(ob(a))$

Proposition (23) means that everything is an object or that everything exists, and implies

25 $(\exists a).ob(a)$

which says that there exists an a such that it exists, always in the sense of individual existence. And if we define the notion of individual non-existence with the aid of an equivalence which says that:

26 $(a):nonob(a), \equiv . \sim(ob(a))$

then to say that there exists an a such that it does not exist, that is to say, to assert that

27 $(\exists a).nonob(a)$,

amounts, in view of (23), to asserting a contradiction. And indeed the notion of existence embedded in the quantifier '($\exists a$)' seems to be incompatible with the notion of non-existence embedded in the constant term 'nonob'.

So far so good. One may sympathize with Russell's view that the possibility of deriving, within a system of logic, an existential proposition such as (25) is a defect in logical purity, but one cannot deny that the quantifiers binding variables whose substituends are singular referential names carry with them existential connotation. But do quantifiers binding variables whose substituends are expressions other than singular referential names carry with them existential connotation? Some logicians have been arguing that they do. In their view, all quantifiers, with the exception of the quantifiers binding variables in the Logic of Propositions, involve ontological commitment to a universe of entities of one kind or another. Thus, for instance, quantifying variables whose substituends are one-place predicates presupposes the universe of attributes or classes.

Let us subject this contention to a closer scrutiny, and let us begin by considering ontological implications of the proposition which says that

28   Socrates is-a-philosopher

It would appear that (28) commits us to an ontology with individual objects only. The singular referential name 'Socrates' names exactly one such object and the predicate 'is-a-philosopher' is true of, or applies to, at least one such object. There is no suggestion, at least *prima facie*, that the predicate *names* an attribute or that an attribute or another kind of abstract entity is somehow referred to by (28). Now, (28) implies

29   $(\exists F).F(\text{Socrates})$

and (29), we are told, commits us to the universe of values of the quantifiable variable 'F'. The realm of these values is not identical with the universe of individual objects; it is supposed to consist of attributes or classes. Clearly, if (29) carries with it this sort of ontological commitment then either the inference from (28) to (29) is not valid or there are certain unstated assumptions involved, which make it valid. The second horn of the dilemma can be substantiated if we assume that (28) implies

30   Socrates is an element of the class of philosophers

which, in turn, implies

31   $(\exists a).$ Socrates $\epsilon\, a$

or rather, if we assume, more generally, that

32   $(F):(\exists a):(a): a \,\epsilon\, a. \equiv .Fa$

The variable 'a' in (31) and (32) is a class variable; its substituends are singular referential class expressions, which cannot be significantly replaced by singular referential names or by expressions of any other semantic category available in Frege–Russellian language as characterized earlier. In fact class expressions presupposed by (32), which will be recognized as the axiom of abstraction, form a new primitive semantic category. In meaningful expressions they can occur as arguments, never as functors. Proposition (32) extends the traditional Theory of Quantification with Identity into a Theory of Quantification with Identity and Classes. In order to characterize the language of the extended theory we first modify D1 to read as follows:

D2   Propositions, i.e. declarative sentences, form a semantic category with respect to a's and b's; a's form a semantic category with respect to a's and b's; b's form a semantic category with respect to a's and b's; if every member of the sequence $e_1, \ldots, e_m, e_{m+1}$ forms a semantic category with respect to a's and b's then so does the class of functors each of which in concatenation with expressions belonging to $e_1, \ldots, e_m$, respectively and employed as arguments, forms an expression belonging to the semantic category e_{m+1}.

By assuming that a's and b's in D2 are singular referential names and singular referential class expressions respectively, we obtain the definition of the notion of belonging to a semantic category as applied to the language of the Theory of Quantification with Identity and Classes. As regards the existence of classes the language is not ontologically neutral. The mere use of singular referential class expressions commits us to the existence of classes in the sense of existence required by the bicategorial Platonist. We saw earlier that the notion of individual existence can be defined in terms of identity. Now, the notion of class existence is defined in terms of class identity, which in turn is defined in terms of class membership, the relevant definitions being as follows:

33    $(\alpha\beta) \therefore \alpha = \beta . \equiv :(a): a \,\epsilon\, \alpha . \equiv . a \,\epsilon\, \beta$
34    $(\alpha): Cl(\alpha) . \equiv . \alpha = \alpha$

And it is easy to see that (33) and (34) between them imply that

35    $(\alpha) . Cl(\alpha)$

which means that everything, or rather *every-class* (if you can tolerate this sort of pronoun or, I should have said, pro-class expression) is a class. This tallies with the meaning of the quantifiers '(α)' and '$(\exists \alpha)$' as determined by appropriate expansions analogous to those given above in connection with the problem of quantifying name variables.

Now, within the framework of the Theory of Quantification with Identity and Classes one can perhaps claim that quantifying predicate variables commits one to an ontology with classes. This is evident from the axiom of abstraction (32). And at the same time it is evident that the use of such a predicate as 'is-a-philosopher' in (28) implies the existence of the class of philosophers. There is, however, one thing, which must be pointed out, namely that in the theory of quantification just outlined predicate variables and class variables, that is to say variables belonging to two different semantic categories, would have one and the same realm of values. It is not surprising that some logicians suggest attributes, differing in kind from classes, as values of predicate variables. But this problem would take us beyond the scope of the present paper.

While the Theory of Quantification with Identity and Classes, and the doctrine of ontological commitment based on it are acceptable to the bicategorial Platonist, his unicategorial opponents would not be slow in raising objections. Their principal objection is that in the language proposed by the bicategorial Platonist it is not possible to deny the existence of classes just as it is not possible to deny the existence of individual objects. If they wish to use that language at all, without making themselves open to the charge of inconsistency, they must avoid using class vocabulary and they must avoid quantifying variables other than name variables. In other words they cannot use the language of the bicategorial Platonist to state their own ontological views. For if they tried to deny the existence of classes they would have to use class vocabulary and this commits them to the existence of classes.

A way out of this predicament would be to devise an ontologically neutral language acceptable to those who assert the existence of classes as well as to those who deny it, and this is what will occupy us for the rest of the paper.

The first step consists in admitting the use of singular names which are not referential, including definite descriptions which fail to describe anything. Ordinary language makes use of singular non-referential names without impairing the meaningfulness of expressions in which such names occur. And if we want to express our views as regards the existence or non-existence of classes as a special kind of what there is, we have to admit the use of class expressions which do not name or designate, in an appropriate sense of naming or designating, any class at all. Such class expressions are not readily available in ordinary language but the following examples are likely to help our intuition:

36 'the class of philosophers' names or designates the class of philosophers
37 'the class which has no elements' names or designates the empty class
38 'the class which has and has not elements' names or designates no class at all

I may mention at this stage that eventually a singular non-referential name and a singular non-referential class expression can be introduced into the language by definition.

Anticipating certain results which are still to be established, we can now say that the notion of forming a semantic category in an ontologically neutral language L'_u, which is sufficient for the positive part of unicategorial ontology, can be defined by interpreting a's in D1 as singular names irrespective of whether they are referential or not. Similarly, the notion of forming a semantic category in an ontologically neutral language L'_b, which is sufficient for the positive part of bicategorial ontology, can be defined by interpreting a's and b's in D2 as singular names and singular class expressions respectively. As we shall see later, it is this sort of ontologically neutral bicategorial language that will enable the unicategorial ontologist to deny the existence of classes.

Before we turn to the problem of quantifiers in L'_u and in L'_b, which is an extension of L'_u, we shall adopt the following conventions: we shall use the symbol 'Λ' to mean the same as 'the object which does not exist', and the symbol 'Δ' to mean 'the class which does not exist'. Now, assuming that the number of individual objects in the universe is finite, the meaning of the universal quantifier binding name variables could be determined with the aid of the following equivalence:

39 $\quad [a].Fa. \equiv .Fa_1. \ldots .Fa_n.F(\Lambda)$

And assuming that the universe of classes is finite the meaning of the universal quantifier binding class variables is determined analogously, as follows:

40    $[a]:\Phi a. \equiv .\Phi a_1. \ldots .\Phi a_n.\phi(\Delta)$

The corresponding equivalences for the particular quantifier read thus:

41    $[\exists a].Fa. \equiv .Fa_1 \vee \ldots \vee Fa_n \vee F(\Lambda)$
42    $[\exists a].\Phi a. \equiv .\Phi a_1 \vee \ldots \vee \Phi a_n \vee \Phi(\Delta)$

Generalizing the meaning of these quantifiers by dropping the assumption as to the size of the relevant universe, which in the limiting case may be empty, should present little difficulty to our intuition. There are, however, certain consequences of our reinterpretation of the quantifiers which deserve to be noted. Thus, on purely intuitive grounds, propositions which say that

43    $ob(\Lambda)$
44    $Cl(\Delta)$

are false. Consequently the following propositions are true:

45    $\sim[a].ob(a)$
46    $[\exists a].\sim(ob(a))$
47    $\sim[a].Cl(a)$
48    $[\exists a].\sim(Cl(a))$

If this is so then the quantifiers, in this sense of the term, have no longer any existential import. In our re-interpretation the notion of quantification has been separated from the notion of existence, which has been left to be embedded in certain constant terms. Since the traditional notion of quantification does not allow for the use of singular non-referential names (or singular non-referential class expressions) I once called it *restricted* and opposed to it the *unrestricted* notion of quantification which makes the use of non-referential names possible, and which, as far as I know, was first introduced into logical language by Leśniewski. It has been suggested that the difference between the two notions of quantification goes deeper, and that it would be more appropriate to describe the traditional interpretation as *referential* and to label Leśniewski's notion of quantification and, *a fortiori*, the one presented just now, as *substitutional*. For, so the argument goes, proposition (23) means the same as 'each entity is such that it is an individual object' and this contains a reference to what there is, whereas (45) should be understood as meaning the same as 'it is not the case that each result of substituting a singular name for "*a*" in "*ob*(*a*)" holds'. It seems to me that the argument has missed the point and is misleading. Equally well we can argue that (45) should be understood as meaning that it is not the case that both each entity is such that it is an individual object and the object which does not exist is an individual object whereas (23) means the same as 'each result of substituting a singular referential name for "*a*" in "*ob*(*a*)" holds'. To my mind it is not the case that one notion of quantification is referential and another one is substitutional, but it is true that in explaining the meaning of either we may wish to refer to what there is, or we may prefer to talk about substitutions. Clearly, there is nothing 'substitutional' in propositions of the form '$F(\Lambda)$' where 'F' stands for a proposition forming functor for one argument which is a singular name. For instance, there is nothing 'substitutional' in the false proposition which says that

49   the object which does not exist is a philosopher.

Now, if this much is conceded, then, on the assumption that the universe is not empty, the following equivalences can be said to determine the meaning of unrestricted quantification in terms of the traditional quantification:

50   $[a].Fa. \equiv :(a).Fa:F(\Lambda)$
51   $[\exists a].Fa. \equiv :(\exists a).Fa.\vee.F(\Lambda)$

It remains for me briefly to characterize a system of Quantification Theory with Identity and Classes, formulated in ontologically neutral language $L'b$, and this I will do by giving a short list of theses which hold in that system:

Czesław Lejewski 25

T1	$[ab]:a=b. \equiv .[\exists c].c=a.c=b$	(axiom)
T2	$[ab]:a=b. \supset .b=a$	(theorem)
T3	$[abc] \therefore a=b.b=c. \supset .a=c$	(theorem)

T2 and T3 between them imply and are implied by T1.

T4	$[ab] \therefore a \cong b. \equiv :[c]:c=a. \equiv .c=b$	(definition)
T5	$[ab] \therefore a = \Lambda. \equiv :a=a:[b]: \sim(b=b). \equiv .a=b$	(definition)
T6	$[a]. \sim (a=\Lambda)$	(theorem)
T7	$\Lambda \cong \Lambda$	(theorem)
T8	$[a]: \sim (a=a). \equiv .a=\Lambda$	(theorem)
T9	$[ab] \therefore [c]:c=a. \equiv .c=b: \equiv :[F]:Fa. \equiv .Fb$	(extensionality)
T10	$[abF]:a=b.Fa. \supset .Fb$	(theorem)

It is easy to convince oneself that the set of presuppositions consisting of

52   $[a\alpha]:a \in \alpha. \supset .a=a.Cl(\alpha)$
53   $[a\alpha]:a \, \acute{\epsilon} \, \alpha. \equiv .a \in \alpha.\lor.a \cong \Lambda.Cl(\alpha).[b]. \sim (b \in \alpha)$

is inferentially equivalent to the set of presuppositions consisting of

54   $[\alpha]:Cl(\alpha). \equiv .[\exists a].a \, \acute{\epsilon} \, \alpha$
55   $[a\alpha]:a \, \acute{\epsilon} \, \alpha. \equiv .a \, \acute{\epsilon} \, \alpha.a=a$
56   $[ab]:a \, \acute{\epsilon} \, \alpha.b \, \acute{\epsilon} \, \alpha.a=a. \supset .b=b$

The functor '$\acute{\epsilon}$', which gives expression to the notion of weak class membership, can be used as an undefined term, and in our system we can have

T11	(=(56))	(axiom)
T12	(=(54))	(definition)
T13	(=(55))	(definition)
T14	(=(52))	(theorem)
T15	(=(53))	(theorem)

The axiom of abstraction takes the form of the following expression:

T16 [aα]:·:a ∊ α. ⊃ ::[F]::[∃β]::[b]::b ∊ β. ≡ ∴Fb∴.
[c]:Fc. ⊃ .c=c:v:[c]:Fc. ⊃ . ~(c=c)   (axiom)

The antecedent in T16 secures ontological neutrality of the axiom, which can now be strengthened either by the bicategorial Platonist's additional assumption to the effect that

57   [∃aα].a ∊ α

or by the negation of this assumption, which says that

58   [aα]. ~(a ∊ α),

and is welcome to unicategorial ontologists.

The directives of the system consist of the usual rules of inference by substitution, quantification, and detachment, the rules of definition adapted to the three primitive semantic categories: propositions, singular names, and singular class expressions, and the rules of extensionality similarly adapted.

And now, let me close with a brief summary.

There is a conception of ontology according to which ontology is a universal theory of what there is. Terms such as 'is identical with', 'is', everything', 'something', and their definitional derivatives such as 'exists', 'object' or 'entity', among many others, are ontological terms. According to some logicians these terms belong to logic. Thus ontology and logic overlap. There is a tendency on the part of logicians to keep logic ontologically neutral, whereas ontologists seem to have no objections to existential assumptions. An ontologically neutral system of logic contains no existential theses. An ontologically neutral language is the language of an ontologically neutral logic. Such a language makes it possible meaningfully to negate any existential proposition. Ontological neutrality of language is of particular importance for minimalistic ontologies such as reism. It has been suggested that the ontological commitment of a theory is encapsulated in the use of quantification. If you quantify a variable then you commit yourself to asserting the existence of the universe of values of that kind of variable, unless the quantification can be analysed out. If you want to avoid committing yourself to the existence of a universe of values, you must avoid quantifying corresponding variables. But if you desire to negate the existence of a universe of values then all you can do, on this view, is to suppress your desire. Now, this doctrine of ontological commitment seems to be untenable. The view that to every semantic category of quantifiable variables there corresponds a universe of entities which are said to be the values of the variables is as unwarranted as the view that every significant expression must name something. Some significant expressions name things, others do not. Similarly, some quantifiable variables have values, others do not. If we have reasons for believing that in addition to individual objects there are entities of quite another kind, classes for instance, and if we wish to give expression to this belief, then we have to expand our language by introducing a new primitive semantic category. It is in this way that the traditional theory of quantification has been expanded, by the adoption of the axiom of abstraction, into a theory of quantification with identity and classes. But the theory so expanded is not ontologically neutral. If one accepts it, one can deny neither the existence of individual objects nor the existence of classes. Thus the problem of ontologically neutral logic arises, a logic which ontologists of different persuasion, the unicategorial ontologist and the bicategorial ontologist for that matter, could use and expand, in their own way, by adopting axiomatically existential assumptions of a positive or negative nature. In the present paper I tried to outline a possible solution to this problem.

Another problem is this: on the assumption that individual objects and classes are the only possible kinds of entities, is the vocabulary of the Theory of Quantification with Identity and Classes as formulated in $L'b$ sufficient for the purpose of ontology as the theory of what there is? The answer is 'no'. Clearly an ontologist will wish to make certain existential assumptions concerning parts of objects and totalities of objects, or concerning their temporal and spatial characteristics, and he may expect logicians to have worked out a deductive theory of part-whole relations, and theories of time and space. Indeed, systems of mereology, which is a theory of part-whole relations, are in existence; work on theories of time is in progress while a theory of spatial characteristics of objects is likely to attract the attention of logicians in the years to come. But is it correct to include all these theories within the scope of logic? There does not seem to be a simple answer to this question. If the Theory of Quantification with Identity is part of logic then I do not know on what grounds other than arbitrary the discipline should not include mereology.

The main difference between the ontologist and the logician seems to be this. The ontologist is anxious to justify, with the aid of informal arguments, his existential answers to the fundamental question: what kinds of entities are there? The logician is not concerned with these arguments. The theories he develops do not imply, in the logical sense of 'imply', the existence of anything or should not imply the existence of anything, if he cares for logical purity. His theories tell us about reality as much, some would say as little, as would be true even if nothing existed. Yet, when expanded by existential assumptions they seem to implement the traditional conception of ontology as the most general science of what there is, and as regards the rigour of proof they would certainly satisfy the expectations of Wolff. For in this respect they surpass Euclid.

Comment

BY MICHAEL DUMMETT

Professor Lejewski is opposed to the idea that the ontological commitments of an individual, or of a theory, are to be gauged by the existential assertions made by the former, or by the existential statements provable in the latter. Here, of course, 'existential statement' is a tendentious expression: it would be better to say 'statement whose main operator is an existential quantifier'. Thus Professor Lejewski discusses the statement

28 Socrates is a philosopher.

He allows that this statement carries a commitment to the existence of an object—the denotation of 'Socrates'; he does not expressly connect this with the possibility of inferring from it

28a $(\exists a).a$ is a philosopher,

but I do not think he would regard it as wrong to do so. By contrast, he denies that (28) carries any commitment to the existence of a property or attribute. As he remarks, there are two versions of this denial. One is to deny that (28) implies

29 $(\exists F).F(\text{Socrates})$;

the other is to allow this inference, but to deny that (29) itself carries any ontological commitment. The latter course is that followed by Professor Lejewski. According to him (29) does not, in itself, carry any ontological commitment, but does so only when taken in conjunction with a further thesis, one which may be formulated, and, when formulated, equally well denied as asserted. This further thesis is

32 $(F):(\exists a):(a): a \,\epsilon\, a. \equiv .F(a).$

(32) together with (29) of course yields

31 $(\exists a).\text{Socrates} \,\epsilon\, a,$

and Professor Lejewski *does* think that (31) carries ontological commitment.

 Professor Lejewski does not make any explicit contrasts between his own views on this matter and those of other named philosophers; but, when the doctrine that 'to be is to be the value of a variable' is discussed, thoughts naturally turn towards Quine, and I will here draw the contrast between

Professor Lejewski's views and those of Quine. We have to distinguish between the earlier, and simpler, version of Quine's doctrine and the later, and subtler, one. According to the earlier version, a sentence carries *direct* ontological commitment if and only if it is existential in form, i.e. its main operator is an existential quantifier. Hence (28) has no direct ontological commitment, whereas (28a), (29) and (31) all do. A sentence may have indirect ontological commitment if it implies one with direct ontological commitment; but this cannot be told from the sentence itself, depending, as it does, on the surrounding theory. Most people, including Quine himself, would sanction the inference from (28) to (28a), and thus allow that (28) carried indirect ontological commitment to the existence of an object; but Quine would reject the inference from (28) to (29), and thus deny that (28) carried any indirect ontological commitment to the existence of a property. Quine thus embraced the first horn of Professor Lejewski's dilemma, rejecting the validity of the inference from (28) to (29) rather than denying that (29) carries ontological commitment. This is not, however, because Quine held (29) to be well-formed, but capable of being false while (28) is true: the inference from (28) to (29) is rejected because second-order quantification is itself rejected as obscure in meaning, and hence (29) cannot even be formulated in a language constructed in accordance with Quine's wishes. Thus, on Quine's original view, the ontological thesis that there are properties cannot be straightforwardly denied in a language in which it can be formulated; if it can be formulated at all, it will come out as a truth of logic. What does duty for it, and what can be significantly (and, on Quine's view, correctly) denied is the metalinguistic statement that our language contains, or that it ought to be construed as containing, second-order quantifiers. As for (31), Quine allowed, originally with some reluctance, that it is well-formed and does follow from (28); (28) thus *indirectly* carries ontological commitment to the existence of a class.

On Quine's later, modified, doctrine, an existential statement carries ontological commitment only if the quantification is explained in the classical manner, rather than substitutionally. (Quine calls the classical type of explanation, in terms of a domain of quantification, 'objectual', while Professor Lejewski uses the word 'referential'; I prefer the term 'ontic', regarding the alternatives as question-begging in different ways, but will here follow Professor Lejewski's terminology.) A form of quantification can be explained substitutionally if we can specify a set of terms in the language none of which is empty and which, between them, denote all the elements of the intended domain. We ought, I think, to say that the possibility of explaining a given type of quantification substitutionally does not change the ontological significance of quantification of that kind if we need to appeal to a notion of denotation, applied to those terms, in order to explain the truth-conditions of the substitution instances; and Quine's modified doctrine appears to allow for that. Hence, on this later doctrine, we could ascribe an ontological significance even to a sentence, such as (28), which contained no quantification, if a term contained in it, such as 'Socrates', had to be understood as denoting an object; and we could do this even if we thought that individual quantification, as in (28a), could be explained substitutionally. On the other hand, we could admit a restricted form of second-order quantification, and thus allow the inference from (28) to (29), and still make no commitment to the existence of properties, provided that we explained such quantification substitutionally.

There is thus an important divergence between Professor Lejewski and Quine, both in the earlier and in the later phases of Quine's thought on this topic, namely over whether (29), at least when the quantifier is explained referentially, involves any ontological commitment: it certainly does not arise, however, over whether (28) involves any commitment to properties. It is possible, on the other hand, that Professor Lejewski has Frege more in mind as the object of his implied criticism. Certainly Frege held that (28) involves reference both to an object and to a concept. In this he was undoubtedly in some disagreement with the earlier doctrine held by Quine, according to which quantification, and not reference, is the point at which ontological commitment enters. However, even this disagreement should not be made too sharp. For one thing, Frege had no qualms about either first- or second-order quantification, and thus held that both (28a) and (29) followed from (28): he was thus operating within a theory according to which (28) involved, by Quine's original criterion, *indirect* commitment to the existence both of an object and of a concept (property). Furthermore, the thesis that a given expression stands for a concept cannot even be expressed without (implicitly) using second-order quantification, and hence the very terminology presupposes the theory which Frege in fact held, under which such quantification is permissible and the inference to (29) consequently indisputable. As for whether Frege should be viewed as in disagreement with Quine's later doctrine, that depends upon what is meant by saying that (28) involves reference to a concept. It might be argued that it does not, on the ground that, in order to give the semantics of sentences such as (28), we need ascribe to the predicate only the feature that it is determinately true or false of each object, taken separately, in the relevant domain, and do not need to associate any one entity with that predicate. But, against this, it might be argued that to ascribe such a feature to the predicate just *is* to associate a concept with it, since a concept, as Frege thought of it, has no more to it than just the fact that each object determinately either falls under it or fails to do so. If it be replied that there is no necessity to think of any *one* thing as being that which, as it were, determines whether or not the predicate is true or false of each object in turn, this might be countered by observing that, while the truth or falsity of (28) depends only upon the local application of the predicate, the falsity of (28a) depends upon its global application. It would not be unreasonable to take, as clinching the matter, the fact that there does not seem to be anything analogous, for predicates, with the *identification* of an object with the bearer of a name, either in relation to a sentence like (28) or to one like (28a). The fact of the matter remains, however, that the relation of concept to predicate is not supposed by Frege to resemble more than analogically the relation of object to proper name, and that Frege is not specific about the details of the analogy. There can therefore be no determinate answer to the question whether the standard classical semantics for a quantificational language involves associating concepts with the one-place predicates, in Frege's sense of 'concept'; nor, consequently, to the question whether Quine's revised doctrine represents a complete rapprochement between his views and Frege's.

The primary disagreement between Professor Lejewski and Quine thus relates to sentences such as (29). Quine holds that, if we admit second-order quantification, and accordingly hold (29) true, and if we interpret such quantification non-substitutionally, then we are committed to the existence of properties: Professor Lejewski holds that, even in such a case, we are involved in no ontological commitment, unless we go further and deduce such a sentence as (31), say by appeal to (32). Professor Lejewski's reason for this is that he sees ontological commitment as relating only to *objects* of one sort or another. An existentially quantified statement in which the quantified variable is an individual variable, in a one- or a many-sorted language, for instance (28a) or (31), does involve ontological commitment, on his view; but one in which the quantification is of second or higher order, such as (29), involves no ontological commitment.

I confess puzzlement why Professor Lejewski should think this: he gives no argument for it. Where second-order quantification is interpreted substitutionally, then, as already remarked, the question turns on the delicate point whether sentences containing predicates involve reference to properties: but if second-order quantification is not so interpreted (say because we wish to allow impredicative substitution instances), I find myself baffled to see on what grounds it can be maintained that no ontological commitment is involved. This is especially perplexing in view of the fact that the distinction between quantifying over properties and functions and quantifying, in a many-sorted language, over abstract objects correlated with them often appears as little more than a matter of notation. The distinction becomes significant only when (as in Frege's formalism) we have a one-sorted language which admits of no differentiation of category between objects, and hence no restrictions in the formation rules upon which objects can appear as arguments for the first-order predicates and function symbols; but Professor Lejewski expressly allows the use of many-sorted languages, with, apparently, what restrictions we wish upon the formation rules. Russell thought it of importance to be able to explain classes in terms of propositional functions, and Professor Lejewski would, it seems, agree that such an explanation effected an important ontological reduction. But, by contrast, for Frege, class-variables, taken as subject to a theory of types, would already be mere disguised variables over concepts of different levels; while, for Quine, quantification over propositional functions involves as heavy an ontological commitment as quantification over classes, being merely somewhat more obscure. It seems to me that Frege and Quine are in the right in this matter as against Russell and Professor Lejewski. We can go backwards and forwards between a theory of propositional functions, subject to simple or to ramified type theory, and a theory of classes and relations in extension, subject to the same type structure; and a semantics for either can with ease be converted into a semantics for the other: it is hard to understand why, in the process, the degree of our ontological commitment should be thought to alter so radically.

This ingredient in Professor Lejewski's doctrine—that higher-order quantification has no ontological significance—allows him to hold that existential statements such as (29) do not carry ontological commitment: but this still leaves ones like (28a) and (31) as doing so. Professor Lejewski is not happy with this situation, partly because he does not want ontological commitment to be a matter of the existential statements that are asserted, but also for a more general reason: the line of distinction between logic and ontology. Professor Lejewski holds that logic and ontology are both sciences of the greatest possible generality, and both expressible by means of the same vocabulary. He does not, however, conclude that ontology is a branch of logic, since he thinks that ontological theses have different epistemological justifications from logical ones: logic should be powerless to assert any ontological theses, whether affirmative or negative ones. If, however, we adopt a standard classical logic, we shall be unable to draw a clean line of distinction between logical and ontological theses, since classical logic permits the derivation of such theses as

25a $(\exists a).a=a,$
25b $(\exists a):Fa.\mathrm{v}.\sim Fa$

and

25c $(\exists a):Fa.\supset .(b).Fb.$

Such theses do carry ontological commitment, and hence logic should be purified of the principles which permit their derivation. Our logical symbolism should be such that all ontological theses, whether affirmative or negative, can be formulated within it; but logic itself should be ontologically neutral, not allowing the derivation of any such theses.

This proposal sounds at first like those previously made, and well explored, to reformulate logic so that the provable theses become valid in all domains, including the empty one, thus obtaining the so-called 'free logic'. However, that is not exactly Professor Lejewski's strategy. It would, I think, accord with his desire to separate logic from ontology, but not with his subsidiary purpose of 'separating the notion of quantification from that of existence', as he puts it, i.e. of using even first-order quantifiers in such a way that existential statements no longer carry ontological commitment. To this end, he introduces a new kind of quantifiers as primitive, which he indicates by the use of square brackets, as opposed to the round brackets which he uses for the quantifiers of classical logic; I shall speak of 'square quantifiers' and 'round quantifiers'. When this new type of quantification is in question, it becomes misleading to speak of an 'existential statement', or of the quantifier which is the main operator in such a statement as an 'existential quantifier', since the whole point is that a statement of the form '$[\exists a].Fa$' will carry no ontological commitment and will not assert the existence of anything: so, when speaking of the square quantifier corresponding to '$(\exists a)$', I shall follow Professor Lejewski's practice and speak of the 'particular quantifier'.

Within Professor Lejewski's formalism, the square quantifiers can be distinguished from the round ones, and, whichever type is taken as primitive, the other type can be defined in terms of it, given other parts of the formalism; as already remarked, Professor Lejewski's intention is that the square quantifiers be taken as primitive. Furthermore, within that formalism, the round quantifiers do not obey exactly the same laws as in classical logic; for instance, we shall not have the thesis

25d $\quad (a).Fa: \supset :(\exists a).Fa.$

In fact, the round quantifiers will, I think, obey just the laws that hold in free logic. But, in order to appreciate the significance of the formalism, we have to be able to apprehend the distinction between Professor Lejewski's square quantifiers and the round quantifiers of standard classical logic; otherwise we might identify the two, and arrive at a quite unintended interpretation, missing the whole point of Professor Lejewski's construction. However, virtually the *whole* work of making this distinction is thrown upon the explanations of the two types of quantifier, and not upon the logical theory itself, since, as far as I can see, formally speaking, almost all the classical theses and principles go through unchanged. (That is to say, in Professor Lejewski's system, the square quantifiers obey nearly the same laws as the round ones do in classical logic.) It is true that we do not have

46a $\quad [\exists a].a=a,$

since the theory of identity is somewhat weakened, and we therefore do not get

45a $[a].a=a.$

But we shall have

46b $[\exists a]:Fa.\mathrm{v}.\sim Fa,$
46c $[\exists a]:Fa.\supset.[b].Fb$

and

46d $[a].Fa:\supset:[\exists a].Fa;$

that is, the first-order logic without identity will, formally speaking, be entirely classical. Hence, in order to recognize that, nevertheless, we are no longer within classical logic, we need to appeal to the intuitive explanations of the square quantifiers.

The explanations which Professor Lejewski actually gives invoke the use of a symbol 'Λ' for the non-object, and, where quantification over classes is concerned, of a symbol '$\varDelta$' for the non-class; more prosaically, 'Λ' is a name recognized to be empty, and '$\varDelta$' a class-term also so recognized. The symbol 'Λ' is not taken as primitive in Professor Lejewski's actual system, but is introduced by a 'definition' T5 which, when the square quantifiers are read as ordinary ones, says that something is identical with the non-object just in case it is identical with itself but identical with nothing that is identical with itself. This contextual definition does not expressly provide for the occurrence of 'Λ' in any context other than an identity-statement, and, in any case, presupposes an understanding of the square quantifiers, and so cannot be appealed to in an explanation of them. An explanation of them that adverts to the symbols 'Λ' and '$\varDelta$' therefore assumes as given a stipulation of the truth-values of atomic sentences (or satisfaction conditions of atomic formulas) containing these symbols. The natural supposition is that every such atomic sentence is to be considered false: actually, this is not quite accurate, since 'ϵ' is primitive and '$\Lambda \epsilon \emptyset$' is true; but, in any case, *some* suitable stipulation is presupposed. Given such a stipulation, the condition for the truth of '$[a].Fa$' is that condition U should be fulfilled, and that, in addition, '$F\Lambda$' should be true, where condition U is whatever condition we should regard as necessary and sufficient for the truth of '$(a).Fa$', allowing the possibility that the domain may be empty; and, likewise, the condition for the truth of '$[\exists a].Fa$' is that either condition E should be fulfilled or '$F\Lambda$' should be true, where condition E is whatever condition we should regard as necessary and sufficient for the truth of '$(\exists a).Fa$'. I have put the matter in this clumsy way, in terms of the conditions U and E, partly in order to avoid specifying exactly how we should want to state the truth-conditions of sentences involving the round quantifiers, and partly in order to avoid saying that we explain the square quantifiers in terms of the round ones, since I do not mean to suggest that there is anything wrong in taking the former as primitive.

Now Professor Lejewski voices a strong objection to its being said that the round quantifiers are explained in a referential, but the square quantifiers in a substitutional, manner. We may readily agree that, if conditions are suitable for it, it may be possible to explain the round quantifiers substitutionally. We may further agree that, wherever we cannot explain the round quantifiers substitutionally, we cannot explain the square quantifiers in a purely substitutional manner either. The fact remains, however, that, at just that point in the explanation where the difference in the interpretation of the square quantifiers from that of the round ones comes out, the explanation has recourse to the notion of a (very special kind of) substitution instance; in so far as the meanings of the two kinds of quantifier differ, the difference is explained substitutionally. The significant question is whether there is any *other* method of explaining the difference between them; if there is, Professor Lejewski has not told us what it is.

Given this explanation, it is plain that we cannot credit every statement of the form '$[\exists a].Fa$' with existential force: but, if we are to be able to make a clear distinction between logical principles and ontological ones, we must be able to say which sentences, of Professor Lejewski's formalism, do carry ontological commitment. For instance, the sentence

46e $[\exists a] . \sim a = a$

and the sentence

46f $[\exists a] . \sim a = \Lambda$

do not, but the sentence (46a) does. This is by no means an entirely trivial matter. In working with Professor Lejewski's system, there is a persistent temptation to read the (square) particular quantifier in an existential sense. For instance, one might raise the question whether

48   $[\exists \alpha] . \sim Cl(\alpha)$

can be proved from T11, T12 and T16, without invoking a 'definition' of 'Δ' analogous to T5. The answer is that one can, provided that the laws of the system enable us to derive, by basic logical principles,

48a $[\exists \alpha] . Cl(\alpha) : \mathrm{v} : [\exists \alpha] . \sim Cl(\alpha).$

The temptation is to say, 'We are able to infer the existence of Δ': (48) is equivalent to

48b $[\exists \alpha] . [b] . \sim b \, \hat{\epsilon} \, \alpha,$

which says that, for some α, α does not, for any b, weakly contain b, and this looks on the face of it like a piece of existential information.

It is easy to frame the objection to this, from Professor Lejewski's standpoint, namely that it derives from illicitly construing '$[\exists a]$' as if it were '$(\exists a)$'. However justified this retort may be, it remains a necessity for Professor Lejewski to characterize those sentences which do carry ontological commitment; and I can see no way of doing so save by saying that they are those which are, or are equivalent to, sentences whose main operator is the round existential quantifier (binding an individual variable of some sort). But, now, it seems to me, not very much has been achieved in the direction of replacing the old criterion, in terms of existential quantification, for when a sentence carries ontological commitment; in the direction, that is, of satisfying Professor Lejewski's subsidiary aim of separating quantification from ontology. It is true that the new criterion does not relate in the same simple way as the old one to the form of the sentence in the primitive notation. But the fact is that, given the explanation which is supplied for the square particular quantifier, and the definition of the round existential quantifier in terms of it, we arrive very quickly at the standard explanation of the round quantifier, to which our new criterion for ontological commitment relates; we therefore have, in effect, just the very same criterion for ontological commitment as before, arrived at by an only slightly more roundabout route. We have not really found any way of liberating ourselves from the alleged illusion that a statement with existential force is one which starts with an existential quantifier; on the contrary, we are relying on it. Moreover, we have arrived at no criterion for when a sentence should be regarded as expressing a *negative* ontological thesis. If we want logic to be neutral with respect to such negative theses, as well as to the affirmative ones, we cannot admit every sentence beginning '$\sim (\exists a) \ldots$' as expressing such a thesis, for there will be sentences of this form which can be proved in our logic.

However this may be, Professor Lejewski's principal aim is undoubtedly achieved: in this manner we have arrived at a logical formalism in which all affirmative and negative ontological theses may be expressed, but which the logic itself is unable to prove or disprove. But is this really an advantage? Let us go back to the question whether (28) carries ontological commitment to the existence of an object, and consider it in our new framework. It is certainly true that, in general, in the new formalism, a sentence of the form '$A(t)$' does not imply '$(\exists a).A(a)$', but only '$[\exists a].A(a)$'. However, in the particular case (28), the implication from it to (28a) still goes through, because '*a* is a philosopher' is being tacitly treated as atomic; in fact, Professor Lejewski explicitly informs us that

49   *A* is a philosopher

is false. We are thus in the position that, while our logic does not, by itself, allow us to derive the truth of the ontological thesis that there are objects (individuals), the formalism does allow us to derive that thesis from certain sentences which, on non-logical grounds, we should normally consider true. Now what are ontological disputes about? Professor Lejewski leaves this question rather murky. As typical examples, we may take the questions whether there are events and whether there are facts. (I believe that the *philosophical* question whether there are subatomic particles is ultimately of the same character, but shall not argue this.) Someone who asserts that there are events, or that there are facts, is maintaining that, in giving a semantics for certain sentences of natural language, we should have to represent those sentences as involving quantification over or reference to events, or facts, and that, even if it is possible to explain quantification of that kind substitutionally, we should be unable to dispense with the notion of reference in explaining the substitution instances. The dispute is therefore one which does not relate, at any rate in the first instance, to the *truth* of certain sentences of natural language, perhaps of sentences like 'There are events' or 'There are facts'; it relates, rather, to the kind of semantics that can be given for other sentences of natural language, sentences like 'He went for a walk' and 'Something surprising happened', or 'He saw that the post had arrived' and 'One fact proved a serious obstacle to their efforts'. It is not of importance to the participants in ontological disputes whether their rival theses can be framed within natural language as it stands, or demand that a technical vocabulary be devised; the disputes arise, not within natural language, but at the level where we are concerned with the analysis and semantic explanation of natural language. It will be recalled that I remarked that, for Quine, affirmative ontological theses are such that, if they can be intelligibly framed within the language, they cannot reasonably be denied—they will in fact then be truths of logic for him: all that can intelligibly be denied are corresponding metalinguistic statements, that is, statements about the semantics of natural language. And this view seems to me to accord with the nature of the case: the difference between ontology and logic is not a difference in generality, but a difference in the *level* at which one is speaking. (That is, when 'logic' is interpreted as Professor Lejewski interprets it, as referring to the logical theory itself, and not to its metatheory.)

But how do matters stand when they are put within the framework recommended by Professor Lejewski? He wants to frame his formal language so that all ontological theses can be expressed within it, and then affirmed or denied according to taste, and without any constraints imposed by logic. In order to be able in this way to state the theses that there are events and that there are facts, we should have to introduce suitable sorts of variables, variables ranging over events and variables ranging over facts. The same would hold for every type of entity which any philosophical ontologist has ever asserted to exist; in a version of Professor Lejewski's formalism truly adequate to its assigned task, there would be very many different sorts of individual variables—object-variables and class-variables constitute only a small sample to enable us to get the general idea. Since we should admit empty event-terms and empty fact-terms, corresponding to 'Λ' and to 'Δ', we should not be able, as a matter of pure logic, to prove the two affirmative theses; we should similarly have an empty term for every different sort of variable, and so should be unable to give logical derivations of any affirmative ontological thesis. Nevertheless, it appears to me that, in this framework, the upholder of the affirmative theses would already have all that he could ask for: for the explanations of the event-variables and the fact-variables would necessarily be such that sentences involving genuine ontological commitment to events and to facts—sentences beginning with round existential quantifiers—would be able to be derived from various quite ordinary sentences of natural language which we should normally consider true, in just the way that (28a) is derivable from (28). The opponent of the affirmative ontological theses would thus have the ground cut from under his feet. He wanted to propose, for those sentences of natural language, analyses which would not involve any even ostensible quantification over events or over facts, and in that way to justify barring any such quantification from the formal language which he employs to analyse natural language. But he is unable to do this, since such quantification has already been admitted into the formal language, in order to allow him to express, within it, his denial of the ontological theses. He can, indeed, express it; but only at the price of committing himself to the falsity of a large number of sentences of natural language which are obviously true. This is a hollow triumph: his whole point was that he could admit the truth of those sentences without admitting the affirmative ontological theses.

Comment

BY DAG PRAWITZ

Like the first commentator I am not quite sure about what the main intentions are in Professor Lejewski's paper. Therefore, I shall start by summarizing how I have understood his main points.

I should like to divide Lejewski's paper into four parts.

1. In the first part, Lejewski discusses what ontology is or should be. Quoting Aristotle, Wolff, and Moore, he suggests an ontological discipline which is characterized by two traits:

(i) The first one concerns the subject matter. Ontology is to deal with questions of existence, questions about what kind of entities there are and what properties they have in their capacity as entities.

(ii) The second trait concerns the way in which this subject matter is to be treated. Lejewski's idea is that the discipline in question should be, firstly, universal or as general as possible and, secondly, rigorous, presented in a way resembling Euclid's system.

He briefly discusses three examples of ontological doctrines: reism, unicategorial Platonism and bicategorial Platonism.

2. The second part of the paper is concerned with logic. Lejewski contrasts three views of logic:

(i) Logic as the most general discipline.
(ii) Logic as the study of formal systems.
(iii) Logic as the metalinguistic study of inferences.

The expression 'most general' in (i) is explained by saying that a discipline T is more general than T' if the notions of T occur also in T', but not vice versa. Lejewski argues for view (i).

3. The third part of the paper discusses the relationship between ontology and logic. Here Lejewski seems to be a little ambiguous. On the one hand, he argues that in order to develop ontology we have to turn to logic and that 'logic and ontology are one or, at least, they overlap one another'. On the other hand, discussing a fragment of Russell's simple type theory, called quantification theory with identity and classes, Lejewski makes the claim that this logic is not ontologically neutral since it implies the existence of certain entities.

4. The fourth and final part then outlines how this quantification theory could be revised so as to become ontologically neutral.

I shall now comment upon these four parts in order. To start with I want to question the whole idea of an ontology as suggested by Lejewski. With the risk of sounding very unphilosophical, I want to ask why one should be interested in ontology.

Such questions as whether classes really exist (denied by reism) or, granted that they exist, whether or not they exist in the same way as material objects (unicategorial or bicategorial Platonism) do not in themselves seem very thrilling. We know of course that ontological questions can be important in connection with certain other questions. The discussions raised by intuitionism may serve as an example. But Lejewski seems ready to discuss the ontological questions exemplified above in complete isolation from other questions; indeed, his idea of ontology is of an abstract and most general science that in some way comes before other sciences. I am afraid that such discussions will be rather fruitless and that it will be difficult to make a choice between rival ontological principles without bringing them into a much richer context.

However, it is not difficult to suggest a rather general situation in which ontology becomes of some importance. To use Bertrand Russell's picture of the difference between (ordinary) mathematics and mathematical philosophy, we may say that both start from some generally accepted beliefs, but while mathematics works upwards proving new theorems on the basis of the given beliefs, mathematical philosophy works downwards in order to derive these accepted beliefs from some more basic principles. If we are engaged in this latter activity, as, e.g., Frege and Russell were, then of course we may have to answer certain ontological questions when stating our basic principles. And then we also have a standard for judging proposed principles, namely the extent to which they are suitable for the derivation of the accepted beliefs.

Although Lejewski has not told us why we should be interested in ontology, I shall assume that he has in mind some general situation of the kind just suggested, i.e. that we are concerned with ontology as a basic and general discipline needed in the axiomatic systematization of other sciences such as mathematics.

On this assumption, I agree with Lejewski that ontology and logic have something in common; indeed, logic may naturally be looked upon as a basic and general discipline just in this way. But as we have seen, Lejewski is not satisfied with this state of affairs. What must be taken as the main thesis of his paper is the claim that logic should be divided into two parts: one called pure logic in which no ontological commitments are made and the other comprising ontological principles.

Also here Lejewski does not say much about the interest of such a separation. His main idea seems to be that in order to discuss or already in order to be able to state conflicting ontological views, we need a language and a logic which are ontologically neutral and which thus allow us to deny that expressions belonging to certain semantical categories refer to anything. But this seems to me to be a very weak argument for what Lejewski calls logical purity. The comparison between different ontologies seems best carried out in a metalanguage. One can there compare whole mathematical systems based upon different ontologies. It is not to be expected that these systems can be obtained from a common ontologically neutral logic by either asserting or denying existential principles. Indeed, it seems very awkward or extremely luxurious first to introduce a semantical category and then deny that it refers to anything. This kind of situation is exemplified in the last part of Lejewski's paper.

For the sake of the discussion, let us nevertheless assume that for some reason we are interested in separating the ontological principles from the 'purely logical' ones and let us then turn to the last part of the paper.

There is one kind of existential assumption which can easily be avoided in logic, viz. the assumption that there exist individuals. There are many ways known from the literature of doing this. One natural way is to restrict at least one of the rules of universal instantiation and existential generalization. Lejewski's way is different—at least, it is so on the surface. He makes use of two new kinds of quantifiers within square brackets, [a] and [∃a], and assume the ordinary rules for them. In addition, he introduces an expression for 'the object which does not exist' and another expression for 'the class which does not exist'. The quantified variables are now to be understood as ranging also over these 'objects'. Finally, he expresses 'real' existence of individuals and classes by special predicates '*ob*' and '*Cl*' respectively. Thus, if $A(a)$ is a tautology, $[\exists a]A(a)$ holds in Lejewski's system but is not to be interpreted as asserting the existence of anything. This would be asserted by $[\exists a](ob(a)$ & $A(a))$, which does not become a logical principle by the mere fact that $A(a)$ is a tautology since it is possible that $\sim [\exists a]ob(a)$.

I am in some doubt about the value of this unorthodox way of constructing a logic without an existence assumption. If I am not mistaken, it is possible to define the ordinary quantifications of so-called free logic within Lejewski's system; they will then satisfy the usual restricted rules of universal instantiation and existential generalization. Since the system anyway contains this more orthodox construction of an existence-free logic, it is difficult to see the value of introducing the extra apparatus with such strange notions as 'the object that does not exist'.

More seriously, however, I do not see how Lejewski is to build up a theory of classes without assuming the existence of classes. Perhaps this is not his intention. His purpose may only be to state a language of set theory in which one can consistently deny the existence of sets. (This can of course easily be accomplished, e.g., in the same way as for individuals.) As far as I can see, one can have no further use for the notions of sets in Lejewski's system if one denies the existence of sets; e.g. Lejewski's axiom of abstraction is formulated as a conditional whose antecedent asserts the existence of sets. But to restate my earlier remark, it seems to be a strange ontological system in which the language of set theory is introduced only to deny the existence of sets. In fact, although Lejewski shows some appreciation of the doctrine of reism that there are no abstract entities, this doctrine appears in Lejewski's presentation as a very eccentric alternative to the theory which asserts the existence of classes. To discuss seriously the thesis that there exist no classes, the important thing is not to develop a system in which this existence can be denied but, as I have argued above, to develop a system in which this existence is not asserted and which nevertheless is sufficient for the needs of science.

Reply to Comments

BY CZESŁAW LEJEWSKI

I wish to begin by expressing my gratitude to both commentators for drawing my attention to a number of points in my paper that evidently call for clarification if not for substantial expansion. I am particularly impressed by Mr. Dummett's detailed, and for the most part correct, exegesis of my views on quantification. This I gladly interpret as indicating that although I may have failed to convince him of their validity, I at least have succeeded in making some of my ideas clear. However, in one or two places Mr. Dummett's comments seem to be based on presuppositions that are in need of some qualification, and I shall attend to this matter in the course of my reply. Some criticism coming from Dr. Prawitz appears to be of a very general nature and, consequently, it is perhaps appropriate for me to discuss his objections first, before turning to the more specific criticism offered by Mr. Dummett.

In my reply I shall try to be as brief as possible, even if this means leaving some minor criticisms unanswered.

I

1. On reading my paper Dr. Prawitz remains uncertain as to what my main intentions were. It seems to me that there are several passages in the paper, the concluding summary for instance, which, one would think, reveal my principal aims by implication. However, I may be wrong; so let me say now what

it really was that I wanted to achieve. First, I wanted to show that there is a certain conception of ontology, originating with Aristotle and held by some modern and contemporary philosophers, a conception in accordance with which ontology should be a rigorous and most general theory of what there is. Secondly, I set out to argue that the best implementation of such a conception is to be found in deductive systems of interpreted logic, whose vocabulary, as I tried to point out, is ontological. Since ontological disputes are usually about existence or non-existence of various kinds of entities, I wanted, thirdly, to vindicate the notion of pure or ontologically neutral logic, that is to say the notion of logic within the framework of which there is no room for existential theses. A theory may be ontologically committed because it is formulated in terms of ontologically committed language, or it may be ontologically committed because it rests on certain existential presuppositions although its language is ontologically neutral. On Russell's own admission the logic of *Principia* exemplifies the former case. As far as I know Leśniewski was the first to devise an ontologically neutral language, and use it for the purpose of formulating systems of his logic. It is ontological commitment resulting from the use of ontologically committed language that is the main target of my objections. For the use of such a language in an ontological dispute condemns some participants to silence. This is why, in the fourth place, I wanted to show how, on re-interpreting the quantifiers in the light of certain constant terms, one can construct an ontologically neutral language not only for the purpose of unicategorial ontology, but also for the purpose of bicategorial ontology with individuals and classes as two kinds of entities, or for the purpose of any other multicategorial ontology. Finally, I intended to outline the foundations of a system of pure logic for bicategorial ontology.

2. So much about my intentions. Now let me turn to Dr. Prawitz's criticism. To him ontological questions do not in themselves seem very thrilling, and he asks why one should be

interested in ontology. He takes me to task for not anticipating and answering that last question. He then continues by assuming that in my view we should be concerned with ontology as 'a basic and general discipline needed in the axiomatic systematization of other sciences such as mathematics'. Surely, I have given in my paper enough reason for the reader to make this very assumption, and I am glad that Dr. Prawitz has not failed to make it.

3. It is on this assumption that Dr. Prawitz agrees with me that ontology and logic have something in common, but he is unhappy about my general discussion of the relationship between these two disciplines, and in particular he takes exception to the notion of logical purity. The general view that I advocate is that logic and ontology are one or, at least, they overlap each other. Admittedly the notion of overlapping leaves a few options open, and in this one can rightly detect a modicum of ambiguity. So I may be allowed to elaborate my view a little.

Once ontology has been given the form of a deductive system without any restrictions as regards the use of definitions then the vocabulary of such a system does not differ from the vocabulary of logic as I understand it. Thus on this assumption ontology and logic are one or, if one wants them to differ, then the difference must be placed in their presuppositions. I cannot think of any logical presupposition that might prove to be unacceptable to ontology, and the only ontological presuppositions that logic may prefer doing without appear to be existential presuppositions. But even if we let logic contain existential statements and become identical with ontology, the question whether in such a theory an ontologically neutral part can be distinguished or not seems to be of interest for the following reason. The language of a logic (or ontology) whose every thesis implies that entities of such and such kind exist is an ontologically committed language. And in terms of such a language, whose mere use commits one to an ontology with entities of certain kinds, one cannot consistently deny the existence of entities of any of these kinds. And if that is the case then, it seems to me, the language in question is not suitable for the purpose of ontological discussion. Dr. Prawitz seems to suggest that ontological disputes should be carried out in metalanguage, but he does not show how this can be done. I must admit that whenever I venture into the realm of metalogic, I invariably find that metalogical vocabulary contains the vocabulary of logic, which is not surprising since metalogic is less general than logic. Now, if the language of the logic which is presupposed by metalogic is not ontologically neutral then in discussing ontologies of various systems we may find ourselves wishing to say something that cannot be said in an ontologically committed metalanguage. Thus we are back to square one.

4. In Dr. Prawitz's view 'it seems very awkward or extremely luxurious first to introduce a semantic category and then deny that it refers to anything'. Indeed, I should readily agree with this view, were it the case that the first to develop multi-categorial ontologies are those philosophers who in fact believe that reality is unicategorial. What usually happens is this. A philosopher or a logician who believes, for instance, that there are two kinds of entities—individuals and classes—proposes a system of ontology or logic, which in his view provides a very general description of what there is. More often than not such a description contains or implies statements which carry with them commitment to the existence of individuals, and statements which carry with them commitment to the existence of classes. Moreover, and this is a crucial point, more often than not our philosopher's description of reality is couched in terms of an ontologically committed language. And if this is the case then the unicategorial ontologist is placed in a hopeless situation. For if he tries to deny any of the statements that carry with them commitment to the existence of classes, he is told that this cannot be done because his denial implies other statements which, in turn, carry with them commitment to the existence of classes. He finds little consolation in the advice that he can avoid committing himself to the existence of classes if he refrains from employing the class vocabulary altogether.

In this situation, it seems to me, an attempt at constructing an ontologically neutral language, which on the one hand enables the multicategorial ontologist to commit himself to the existence of as many kinds of entities as he may have reason to countenance, and on the other, makes it possible for his opponent significantly to deny the existence of any kind of entities, can hardly be regarded as a luxurious extravagance.

5. Assuming, for the sake of discussion, that we are concerned in constructing a system of pure logic, Dr. Prawitz criticizes my way of constructing it. He finds it unorthodox yet differing from what he regards as an orthodox approach, only on the surface. My unorthodox approach is supposed to consist in making use of a *new* kind of quantifiers and assuming *ordinary* rules for them, and, the horror of horrors, in introducing such strange notions as the object which does not exist. 'Square' quantifiers without any existential import yet subject to the ordinary rules were first used by Leśniewski. My 'square' quantifiers differ from his in that the substituends for the lowest order variables in Leśniewski's language are general names (or common nouns) whether referential or not, singular names being treated as if they were general ones, whereas the substituends for the lowest order variables in my system are singular names be they referential or not, there being no provision for the use of general names. As regards the strange notion of *the object which does not exist*, one is at liberty to replace this expression by any other singular name, simple or compound, provided it fails to name or designate anything. Ordinary language offers a wide choice of such singular names. Take, for instance, the singular name 'Pegasus' which was found a long time ago not to name or designate anything. The offending expression 'the object which does not exist' is in fact synonymous with the name 'Pegasus' in the sense that whatever is designated by the name 'Pegasus' is also designated by the name expression 'the object which does not exist', and vice versa, there being nothing that is designated by either. The use of singular names that do not designate does not affect the range

of values of nominal variables, if by values of a variable we understand entities outside the language, and in no place in my paper have I said that a quantified variable is to be understood as ranging over, among other things, the object which does not exist or over the class that does not exist. For there is no such object as the object which does not exist, nor is there any such class as the class which does not exist. And this is provable in the proposed system. The innovation, which for Leśniewski would be no innovation, consists in including among the substituends of nominal variables the expression 'the object which does not exist' and among the substituends of class variables the expression 'the class which does not exist'. And these expressions are definable in the system.

6. Dr. Prawitz's argument against my system of pure logic, and for the systems of pure logic developed by the advocates of so-called free logic, seems to amount to this. There is no value in constructing a system like mine since in it one can get everything that is obtainable in systems of free logic. As far as I can see, it is true that whatever is obtainable in the system worked out by Karel Lambert is obtainable in mine, but is this a weakness in my system? The argument establishes that my system is not weaker than Lambert's. I should worry, indeed, but only if Dr. Prawitz succeeded in showing that there are some theses provable in systems of free logic but unobtainable within the framework of the system proposed in my paper.

7. A system of pure logic, System A, based on T1 as a single axiom was published in my 'A Theory of Non-Reflexive Identity and its Ontological Ramifications', *Grundfragen der Wissenschaften und ihre Wurzeln in der Metaphysik*, ed. Paul Weingartner, Salzburg-München, 1967, pp. 65-102. It at once attracted the attention of Karel Lambert, who in collaboration with Thomas Scharle published a paper ('A translation theorem for two systems of free logic', *Logique et analyse*, 10 (1967), pp. 328-41), in which he related a first order fragment of my system with his own system FL and found that the latter was weaker. To equal the former in deductive power it had to be

strengthened with the aid of additional axioms. Quite naturally, Lambert discusses the fragment of System A in the light of his system FL and its extensions. What still remains to be done is to examine systems of free logic in the light of pure logic as exemplified by System A, which is a part of the system outlined in my paper under the present discussion. Dr. Prawitz's comments have convinced me that this is a worthwhile project, but it calls for a separate paper.

8. Dr. Prawitz's comments on my supposed view concerning set theory appear to be due to some misunderstanding. I say, explicitly, in my paper that although the original intuitions of Cantor bear on ontology, the axiomatized set theory seems to defy any ontological interpretation and, until an acceptable interpretation is found, can best be treated as an uninterpreted, purely formal system. Like some distinguished set theoreticians I do not know what sets are, or what they are supposed to be.

9. In his concluding paragraph Dr. Prawitz writes: 'To discuss seriously the thesis that there exist no classes, the important thing is not to develop a system in which this existence can be denied but, as I have argued above, to develop a system in which this existence is not asserted and which nevertheless is sufficient for the needs of science.' Surprisingly enough this remark almost coincides with my own view, which I would put in this way: to deny significantly the existence of classes, the important thing is not to work out a language the mere use of which implies in one way or another that there are no classes but, as I have insisted in my paper, to develop a system in terms of an ontologically neutral language, a system in which the existence of classes is neither asserted nor in any way implied and which nevertheless is sufficient for the needs of science. The system based on T_1, T_{11}, and T_{16} and developed in accordance with the directives mentioned in the paper is, as far as I can see, such a system. Its language is ontologically neutral. It neither asserts nor denies the existence of individuals or the existence of classes. It can be extended by assuming, axiomatically, the existence of individuals and the existence

of classes. Alternatively, it can be extended by assuming
the existence of individuals only, or by coupling this latter
assumption with the assumption that there are no classes.
Finally, it would yield no contradiction if it were extended
by assuming that there are no classes and that there are no
individuals.

II

As I have already said in the beginning of my reply, Mr.
Dummett's comments contain no evidence that he has
misunderstood any of my views. With negligible qualifications
he summarizes them correctly, he seems to have found no
glaring mistakes in them, but he says that some of them are
just stated, without any argument to support them. He concludes
by evaluating the system of logic proposed in my paper and
doubts whether the supposed advantages of it justify the effort
involved in constructing it.

1. The first major problem, discussed by Mr. Dummett, is
that of ontological commitment. It is true that in my paper I
did not make any explicit contrasts between my own views on
this matter and those of Quine, and that I referred to Quine
indirectly by mentioning his doctrine. This I did because the
term 'ontological commitment', so it appears, has come to be as
good a means of referring to its originator as his own name. And
I did not involve myself in comparing my views on quantification
with those of Quine because I had discussed this question
at some length on three earlier occasions. (See my 'Logic and
Existence', *The British Journal for the Philosophy of Science*, 5
(1954/55), pp. 104–19; reprinted in *Logic and Philosophy*, ed.
Gary Iseminger, New York, Appleton-Century-Crofts, 1968,
pp. 167–82; 'The Problem of Ontological Commitment',
Fragmenty Filozoficzne (Third Series), PWN Warszawa, 1967,
pp. 147–64; 'Quantification and Ontological Commitment',
Physics, Logic and History, eds. W. Yourgrau and A. D. Breck,
Plenum Press, New York, 1970, pp. 173–81.)

Mr. Dummett's account of my views, with reference to the

interpretation of propositions (28), (28a), (29), (31) and (32), is correct. I take it that when he says that according to me (29) involves no ontological commitment, he really means that it involves no ontological commitment other than that to the existence of individual objects. For this last commitment is effected by the use of a singular referential name 'Socrates' and confirmed by the fact that from (29) we can validly infer

29a $(\exists x)(\exists F).Fx.$

However, Mr. Dummett is puzzled why I should interpret (29) as carrying with it no ontological commitment to the existence of properties or attributes or classes, and expects some argument in support of such an interpretation. Well, the argument which happens to convince me could be outlined as follows: the meaning of second order quantification can be explained in terms of expansions analogous to those which explain first order quantification. Now, consider equivalences of the following forms:

17a $(F).Fa. \equiv F_1a.F_2a \ldots F_na$
18a $(\exists F).Fa. \equiv .F_1a \vee F_2a \vee \ldots \vee F_na$

According to Quine, none of the conjuncts (or alternants) $F_1a, F_2a, \ldots F_na$ carries with it a commitment to the existence of properties or attributes or classes. To think that each of them does, that it 'names', in some sense of naming, a property or an attribute or class would be, as Quine puts it, confusing meaning with naming. With this I entirely agree. Moreover, and still according to Quine, if our expansions consisted of a finite number of conjuncts (or alternants) then, again, they would carry no ontological commitment over and above the commitment affected by the use of the singular referential name 'a'. In such cases second order quantification would be free from ontological commitment, since in fact such quantification could be analysed out in favour of appropriate expansions. And with this I entirely agree. But Quine goes on to urge that the situation radically changes if in order to analyse out second order quantification we needed expansions with infinitely many conjuncts or alternants. For we cannot have such expansions. True, we cannot have conjunctions with infinitely many conjuncts, or alternations with infinitely many alternants. True, in such cases second order quantification could not be analysed out. But I still fail to see how all this implies that in such cases second order quantification becomes ontologically committed. I would admit the presence of ontological commitment if, for instance, instead of a non-finite alternation, which I cannot have, I were offered just one alternant of which one could plausibly claim that it carried with it commitment to the existence of a property or attribute or class. But in accordance with an earlier assumption in the argument there are no such alternants. The view that quantification of any order carries with it commitment to the existence of the corresponding values, would be justified if those who hold it approved of what Gilbert Ryle once called 'Fido'—Fido semantics. But to this sort of semantics Quine strongly objects. And so do I.

2. Another problem of mine to which Mr. Dummett devotes a considerable section of his comments is that of 'separating the notion of quantification from that of existence'. Again his account of my 'square' as opposed to 'round' first order quantifiers, as he conveniently calls them, appears to require only a few minor amendments and, perhaps, a little elaboration on my part. Thus, for example, a further reason for wishing to separate the notion of first order quantification from that of existence could be added. In multicategorial languages the first order quantifiers which take objects of one kind as their values are analogous as regards their meaning and use to the first order quantifiers which take as their values objects of any other kind. Now, hardly any difficulty arises if the universe of discourse presupposed by first order quantification contains objects known to us from experience. For few philosophers, if any, would argue that such a universe is empty. But when it comes to considering the universe which is supposed to contain

classes or objects of any other kind then the situation is different. Unicategorial ontologists will be inclined to hold that the universe of this latter sort is empty. It is thus important for them that any first order quantification used by their multicategorial opponents should be divorced from existential connotation. And for the sake of preserving analogy in the use of first order quantification throughout one's language it appears to be desirable to free from existential import even those quantifiers among the values of which we count objects known to us from experience. Concerning the relationship between the square quantifiers and the round ones, Mr. Dummett writes that in my language whichever type of quantifiers 'is taken as primitive, the other type can be defined in terms of it'. I think that in my paper I am a little less categorical. Referring to equivalences (50) and (51) I only claim that they determine the meaning of the square quantifiers for a non-empty universe. (51) holds for an empty universe, too, but this cannot be said about (50). If I understand him well, Mr. Dummett would like me to make the distinction between the two types of quantifiers within the framework of a system of logic rather than base it on less formal foundations. This is an entirely legitimate suggestion but it would take me well outside the scope of my original paper. And this is why I preferred a recourse to intuitive explanations. A more formal approach can be found only in my mentioning some of those theses which relate the square quantifiers to certain constant terms such as '$=$', 'ob', and 'Λ'. My general strategy was in fact this. In what Mr. Dummett calls classical logic the provable theses involving round quantifiers are true in every non-empty universe of discourse. Some of them, however, do not hold in the case of the empty universe. The proponents of the so-called free logic try to weaken the system so as to make all provable theses obtain in every universe including the empty one. They achieve it by weakening the theses which determine the uses of the round quantifiers without affecting their original intuitive meaning. The formal aspect of the theory of identity in free logic is preserved, but the notion of identity is now interpreted as free of existential import. My proposal involves no formal changes in that part of classical logic which determines the use of quantifiers without relating their meaning to constant terms other than the constant terms of the logic of propositions, but I interpret the quantifiers in such a way as to make that part of logic obtain even in the case of the empty universe. I preserve the original meaning of the notion of identity, but I weaken its axiomatic characterization by abandoning the law of absolute reflexivity. Unlike the proponents of 'free logic' I make in my system, no use of schematic letters, whose relationship to quantifiable variables is, in my view, by no means clear.

3. When mentioning my definition of 'Λ' Mr. Dummett remarks that it 'does not expressly provide for the occurrence of "Λ" in any context other than an identity-statement'. It seems to me that my explicit inclusion of the rule of inference by substitution among the directives of the system implicitly supplies the required provision. From the definition we learn that 'Λ' is a singular name and that consequently it becomes a legitimate substituend for a nominal variable in any context. True, I appeal to 'Λ' in my *explanation* of the square quantifiers, but the explanation is not part of the proposed deductive system, in which square quantifiers occur as undefined primitive notions. It is part of presystematic informal preparations for the setting up of a deductive system. In such preparations circularity, however vicious, is no sin provided the meaning of the notions involved has been successfully conveyed. And Mr. Dummett's comments, I am delighted to say, provide hardly any evidence in support of the view that my explanation of the square quantifiers has failed. This brings me to another comment of Mr. Dummett. He writes that I voice 'strong objection to its being said that the round quantifiers are explained in a referential, but the square quantifiers in a substitutional, manner'. This strikes me as a case of misunderstanding. What I strongly object to is the substitutional *interpretation* of the square quantifiers. For it has been suggested

that the square quantifier, say in '[a].Fa', should be read: *each object or entity a is such that Fa*, whereas the proper reading of '[a].Fa' should be: *for all substitutions for 'a' in 'Fa', 'Fa' holds*. My view is, and I think I make it clear in the paper, that either type of quantifiers can be explained in a referential manner or in a substitutional manner, but that it is entirely wrong to interpret or read the square quantifier in the way mentioned above. Mr. Dummett maintains that my referential explanation of the square quantifiers involves a substitutional element. He may be right. However, I wish to point out that my objections are directed not against any manner of explaining the meaning of the square quantifiers but against the substitutional manner of interpreting or reading them. Mr. Dummett continues by asking whether there is any other method of explaining the difference between the round and the square quantifiers. As far as I can judge, the one which appeals to the notion of the universe of discourse, may turn out to be helpful. It proceeds as follows: consider the universe consisting of human beings only, and suppose that a predicate 'F' applies to every object in that universe. On these presuppositions, which are stated, informally, outside our 'system of anthropology', we can state within the framework of the system that (i) for all a, Fa. If we wanted to incorporate our presuppositions into the system then we should replace (i) by: (ii) for all a, if a is human then Fa. Now, it may happen that the predicate 'F' applies to every object in a larger universe, say, the universe consisting of animals. Thus we can strengthen (ii) by weakening its antecedent and asserting: (iii) for all a, if a is an animal then Fa. In some cases we may find that the predicate 'F' applies to everything that exists, in other words, that it applies to every object in the largest possible universe. Consequently, we can strengthen (iii) by weakening its antecedent in this way: (iv) for all a, if a exists then Fa. (23), which is derivable in the traditional theory of quantification with identity, means the same as (v) for all a, a exists, and from this latter proposition and (iv) we infer that (vi) for all a, Fa. And (vi) means the same as (vii) $(a).Fa$. The universe consisting of everything that exists cannot be enlarged, but we can still weaken the antecedent in (iv) and obtain: (viii) for all a, if (a exists or it is not the case that a exists) then Fa. Now, in the case of the non-empty universe consisting of everything that exists (viii) is stronger than (iv), and since the antecedent in (viii) is a tautology we can infer: (ix) for all a, Fa, but this time (ix) does not mean the same as (vii). It means the same as: (x) $[a].Fa$. A corresponding explanation of the particular quantifiers can easily be worked out.

4. In Mr. Dummett's view it remains a necessity for me to characterize those sentences which do carry ontological commitment and this, according to him, can only be done by appealing to the use of the round existential quantifier binding an individual variable of some sort. I note that in this remark ontological commitment has been attributed to a round quantifier of the first order. In fact, I have never denied that first order quantification carries ontological commitment. Its weakness, in my view, is that it is not adequate for the purpose of registering a negative ontological commitment. Square quantification suffers from no such weakness and this is the reason why I find it preferable. It is with the aid of square quantification supplemented by appropriate constant terms, which may be primitive or defined, that one can provide the characterization of ontologically committed statements. A statement can be said to carry positive ontological commitment to the existence of objects or classes if and only if it implies (i) $[\exists a].ob(a)$ or (ii) $[\exists a].Cl(a)$. And a statement can be said to carry negative ontological commitment if and only if it implies (iii) $[a].\sim(ob(a))$ or (iv) $[a].\sim(Cl(a))$. Propositions (i) and (ii) can be replaced, respectively, by propositions (v) $(\exists aF).Fa$ and (vi) $(\exists a\Phi).\Phi a$. But no corresponding formulae with round quantification seem to be available to replace (iii) or (iv). Round quantification can be introduced into the system of logic proposed in my paper, but I do not know how to introduce square quantification into a system of classical logic. Square quantification alone does not carry any ontological commitment.

In order to carry such commitment it has to be supported by constant terms strong enough to define the notion of existence for objects of a given kind. This is what I had in mind when I talked about separating the notion of quantification from that of existence. Propositions (i) and (ii), as opposed to (v) and (vi), illustrate my point.

5. I am afraid I may have missed some important points in the last section of Mr. Dummett's comments, where he gives his final assessment of the framework of logic and language recommended in my paper. Having correctly summarized my intentions he points out that, in his view, the upholder of theses with positive ontological commitment would already have, in this framework, all that he could ask for, whereas his opponent would have the ground cut from under his feet. In the first place it was my intention to give the upholder of any ontologically committed positive thesis all that he may need. And I also intended to give his opponent all that he may need. The upholder of a thesis with positive ontological commitment can have his first order round quantification to express his thesis, which can also be expressed with the aid of square quantification and appropriate constant terms. It is in this latter form that the thesis can be denied. According to Mr. Dummett, if I understand his argument, the predicament of the objector to theses with positive ontological commitment consists in this, that he can express the denial of such theses, 'but only at the price of committing himself to the falsity of a large number of sentences of natural language which are obviously true'. In this connection I have to refer Mr. Dummett to the reistic interpretation of proposition (8) in my paper. Speaking generally, one must admit that in the body of common knowledge formulated in ordinary language we find a great number of statements, which *appear* to imply propositions with ontological commitment to objects of various kinds. The denial of such propositions does not always amount to the denial of the premiss. It often indicates that the premiss calls for rephrasing. In numerous instances it is possible to give a paraphrase of the original premiss without

altering its truth value and without losing any relevant content, a paraphrase which no longer implies the offending proposition with a positive ontological commitment. If no such paraphrase is acceptable to the upholder of the original premiss then his opponent must give up and gracefully agree to disagree.

II / Does Many-Valued Logic Have Any Use?

Dana Scott

INTRODUCTION

I have often asked the question of the title, but seldom have I heard anyone attempt a serious answer. So I shall try again to provoke some discussion. But before looking into details let me ask an historical question: how did Łukasiewicz come to propose his many-valued truth tables? As far as I can make out he said very little in print about the genesis of the idea. And once an idea like this is put forward, it has a life of its own with no one ever asking what right it has to travel so far or where its intellectual visa is. To go far it needs two principal qualities: first, it must be rather simple-minded so as not to tax the patiences of the people it will meet; and in the second place. it must stand in opposition to something 'classical' so we can all have the thrill of the break-through or revolution. None of us wants to be remembered for his bad review of a Beethoven. Speculation in ideas is as risky as speculation in land, but unfortunately the punishment does not come as quickly, and bad shares are still thick on the market.

Among non-classical logics, intuitionism certainly had the second of the two principal virtues, but alas not the first. In cases like this, the plan generally is to fall back on a state of near-religious mysticism in order to make people feel guilty that they are unable to ascend to that higher consciousness. But please do not misunderstand me: even though the intuitionistic logic is not as straightforward as the many-valued brand, I definitely consider it a good investment and only hope to see soon a more attractive and glossier brochure than those currently available. I think that intuitionism can be brought down to earth and will be found solid, but I am not all that sure about many-valued logic. A quick review of the situation will bring out the weak point that could lead to collapse.

Take the first example of the three-valued system. The table for implication is usually written thus:

$\rightarrow$	1	$\frac{1}{2}$	0
1	1	$\frac{1}{2}$	0
$\frac{1}{2}$	1	1	$\frac{1}{2}$
0	1	1	1

The value $\frac{1}{2}$ is especially piquant. We deny that propositions are to be just *true* or *false*. Pandora's box is open! Where to turn in the face of such uncertainty? And then all of a sudden here is $\frac{1}{2}$ sitting exactly in the middle. What excellent symmetry—surely something classical in that! Now this *is* an idea. But hold; why just *one* intermediate value? why not more? Did Pandora's box contain only one creature? Of course not. This was only a quick snapshot. If you want to see the rest, here they are:

$\rightarrow$	1	$\frac{5}{6}$	$\frac{2}{3}$	$\frac{1}{2}$	$\frac{1}{3}$	$\frac{1}{6}$	0
1	1	$\frac{5}{6}$	$\frac{2}{3}$	$\frac{1}{2}$	$\frac{1}{3}$	$\frac{1}{6}$	0
$\frac{5}{6}$	1	1	$\frac{5}{6}$	$\frac{2}{3}$	$\frac{1}{2}$	$\frac{1}{3}$	$\frac{1}{6}$
$\frac{2}{3}$	1	1	1	$\frac{5}{6}$	$\frac{2}{3}$	$\frac{1}{2}$	$\frac{1}{3}$
$\frac{1}{2}$	1	1	1	1	$\frac{5}{6}$	$\frac{2}{3}$	$\frac{1}{2}$
$\frac{1}{3}$	1	1	1	1	1	$\frac{5}{6}$	$\frac{2}{3}$
$\frac{1}{6}$	1	1	1	1	1	1	$\frac{5}{6}$
0	1	1	1	1	1	1	1

You see; there *are* lots. Clearly anything as exact as that must be correct. And if you *still* want more, all of these systems are subsystems of an infinite-valued system. Please don't be afraid of the maths, since it is all quite easy with simple rules of calculation.

No doubt you are annoyed by my sarcasm, but I do ask this:

Before you accept many-valued logic as a long-lost brother, try to think what these fractional truth values could possibly mean. And do they have any use? What is the conceptual justification of 'intermediate' values? This is the weak point of the programme, because we tend to become so fascinated with the patterns and possibilities. Certainly modal logic also suffers from an over-developed formalism. The literature on many-valued systems is ridiculously large,[1] but I am sure it does not match in waste of time that on modalities. I suppose the reason is that the many-valued systems are more rigid, while modal systems permit greater variation. But before we let the formalism run wild, we should ask whether there is any point to it all. A slight nod towards probabilities will definitely not be sufficient for justification either, for it only takes a moment's thought to see that the probability of $[p \to q]$ *cannot* be a function of the probabilities of p and q. We must seek elsewhere for sensible reasons for considering this new 'logic'. Two directions of investigation will be described.

I A LOGIC OF ERRORS

I do not mean an erroneous logic, though I am prepared to hear people argue that the idea is wrong. What I am asking is whether we can distinguish some kind of *degrees* of truth. The answer is likely to be 'No' if we expect these degrees to combine with one another in little truth tables. Surely error is connected with both *knowledge* and *belief*; and (Professor Hintikka and the other possible worlders notwithstanding) until we have a coherent logic of these notions, we shall probably not have a convincing treatment of error. But before we are too critical, let us try a little experiment in formalization so that we might get a better grasp of where the difficulties lie.

For simplicity consider a 'model' language with atomic propositional symbols $p, q, r, \ldots$ and one binary connective $\to$. I have complained before about the presuppositions behind such formal systems,[2] but for this discussion we should put these worries aside. If A is a well-formed formula of this language, we are going to attempt to explain what could be meant by saying '*the statement* A *is true to within degree of error* i'. An ideographic way of writing this relation between formulae and degrees (whatever they are) is as follows:

$i \geqslant A.$

Could the degrees be *ordered* in some way so that some A's are *more* in error than others? Let us try to suppose so. But then what does 'truth' mean? No error? Well, why not? Let us suppose that there is a *minimal* degree of error, called '0'. Thus the degrees will be ordered by a relationship written '$i \geqslant j$', and we suppose that for all degrees i we have $i \geqslant 0$.

The plan is to be a bit more abstract than Łukasiewicz in using ordered sets rather than fractions. In the first place fractions like $\frac{5}{6}$ are too mysterious at the start (we may want to use them later), because they are too much used for other purposes. Ordered sets being more abstract can enjoy a variety of interpretations. Of course, many ordered sets can be isomorphically represented by sets of fractions (or, even better, real numbers), but this may not be significant. In introducing this abstraction and in using the terminology of error note that we have turned things around: the *minimal* degree of error (which we call '0') corresponds to the *maximal* truth value (what Łukasiewicz calls '1'). It will be seen below exactly why this change makes certain properties easier to describe. For the moment we can remark that the change makes the table for → less curious:

→	0	1	2	3	4	5	6
0	0	1	2	3	4	5	6
1	0	0	1	2	3	4	5
2	0	0	0	1	2	3	4
3	0	0	0	0	1	2	3
4	0	0	0	0	0	1	2
5	0	0	0	0	0	0	1
6	0	0	0	0	0	0	0

Here the *integers* have been used for *counting* the degrees. Fractions are more properly used when a question of *proportion* is to be asked. At the moment we do not know whether there will be more to the idea beyond a simple counting and ordering. In the table we write numerals merely as a convention for conveying this amount of structure. At least we can agree that by placing truth at the 0-end of the scale we make it easy to leave the false-end open. Let us not ask just now why these degrees are *linearly* ordered.

The mystery of the table for $\to$ is far from being removed, however, by these inconsequential notational changes. We still have to provide a story to explain the pattern and symmetry of the table. We then have to try to sell the story. Note that there must be more than a mere ordering of degrees involved in view of the very regular *shift* from row to row. Before we get to that, the question is: why all those 0's? That is the easy part of the table and does depend only on the ordering. Let us define

$A \geqslant B$ iff whenever $i \geqslant A$, then $i \geqslant B$.

(We can be a little vague about the range of the variable i here since the same definition will apply to any system of degrees.) We read '$A \geqslant B$' both as 'A implies B' and as 'A is more in error than B'. This is a metalinguistic relationship and *not* a statement *within* the language. But from the table we see that there is a connection:

$A \geqslant B$ iff $0 \geqslant A \to B$.

That is to say, $A \to B$ is true iff A implies B. Certainly this is a necessary condition on any *connective* in the language that is going to function as an implication operator. What needs agreement here is the definition of '$A \geqslant B$'; but if degrees were to be reasonable at all, this seems pretty obvious.

To explain the table is to explain '$i \geqslant A \to B$' which we could read as 'A implies B (not outright but) to within degree of error i'. Can we indeed explain an inexact notion of implication? From the table with the Łukasiewicz pattern, we can observe that the answer depends on the 'distance' between A and B. If

A is more false than B, the degree of implication *is* exact, as we have noted. If B is just a 'little' more false than A, then (by the table at least) we want $A \to B$ to be 'almost' true. If B is very much more in error than A, we want $A \to B$ to measure this discrepancy on a sliding scale. The assumption here is this: the *distances* between degrees must again be expressible as degrees. Take two degrees j and k. We need to be able to determine this relationship:

$$k \geq i + j$$

in order to be able to say (when $k \geq j$) that the distance between them is at least up to degree i. (I have written ' $+$ ', but take this as a ternary relationship for now.) Granting this, we can define:

$$i \geq A \to B \text{ iff whenever } k \geq i + j \text{ and } j \geq A, \text{ then } k \geq B$$

If we agree that $k \geq j$ iff $k \geq 0 + j$, then this definition does indeed reduce to that for "$A \geq B$". In other words, when $A \geq B$; then $i \geq A \to B$ shows the *shift* needed to move A up to B. We could even make this more ideographic if we wrote:

$$i \geq A \to B \quad \textit{iff} \quad i + A \geq B,$$

but this is only meant to be suggestive. In any case, if we assume the *numerical* meaning for "$k \geq i + j$" as the variables range over the integers (say, in the interval between 0 and 6), then we have a perfect correspondence with the table for $\to$ handed down to us by Łukasiewicz.[3]

This is hardly as exciting as getting the Ten Commandments, but it seems to make a small amount of sense. Truths (or should I say 'Falsehoods'?) are classified by degrees. The classification is taken to be 'numerical' in the respect of being able to check distances (by subtraction really) against other degrees. Thus we suppose not only a linear ordering but a little *linear algebra* of degrees. Is it completely nutty? I suppose so, but then again why not? Instead of unanalysed atomic propositions (p, q,

$r, \ldots$) could we not have atomic predicate symbols (R, S, $T, \ldots$) and individual constants ($a, b, c, \ldots$) for which an error estimate like:

$i \geqslant Rab$

was somehow 'natural'? This means that if we are 'careful' up to i (say, in adjusting our tools), then the test for truth will be positive. If we are more careful or more accurate, then the test may *not* be positive. What is rather too idealized for this story is the assumption that the test will always turn out the same if done with the same accuracy. But if we could live with that assumption, it would seem that there is some chance that this logic is of some use. But it would take very much more development of a kind *not* to be found in the literature at the present time. And why just Łukasiewicz connectives? In this spirit there might be others that were just as interesting.

Since we have no convincing evidence of a use for the Łukasiewicz system to present here as a logic of error, we shall not detail the formal system. However, it should be mentioned that the multiple entailment relation

$A_0, A_1, \ldots, A_{n-1} \vdash B_0, B, \ldots, B_{m-1}$

has a simple interpretation by degrees:

whenever $i \geqslant A_t$ for all $t < n$, then $i \geqslant B_u$ for some $u < m$.

The axiomatic treatment of the logic with rules expressed in terms of $\vdash$ seems quite satisfactory, though some problems yet remain.[4]

2 A LOGIC OF RISK?

The second idea for a use for many-valued logic is due to Robin Giles.[5] He would no doubt prefer to talk of a logic of *commitment*, but being less optimistic (as in the case of error) I shall use the word 'risk'. The approach is game-theoretic in nature.[6] A player *risks* something in asserting a proposition, and we make this risk *cumulative* in the sense that multiple assertion of a proposition carries a corresponding multiplication of the risk. Instead of the material entailment relation we had in the degree interpretation, we shall have a cumulative entailment which we write as:

$$A_0, A_1, \ldots, A_{n-1} \Vdash B_0, B_1, \ldots, B_{m-1}$$

Intuitively speaking this means that a certain position of the game is *safe* for *me*. (*You* are the other player, by the way.) I will let you go first, if you wish. You go ahead and assert *all* the A's, in the meantime I will assert *all* the B's. We will have each risked something, and we will have had to pay each other what we lost by making these assertions. The position was *safe* for me because the loss incurred by me was *less than* your loss, so I have a *net gain* (or at least no loss in case we came out equal).

One might well ask what this has to do with logic and with many-valued logic in particular. The first answer is that there are simple rules about how to *deduce* that a position is safe given that certain others are safe. The table of inference rules illustrates this. The notation is to be read as follows. The Greek letters stand for *sequences* of formulae. The *tilde* (as in '$\tilde{\Gamma}$') means a *permutation* of the sequence. The *comma* (as in "Γ, A") means the *adjunction* of the indicated formulae. The *multiple* (as in '$n.\Gamma$') means the *repetition* of all the formulae the indicated number of times. The symbol '$\varnothing$' is the name of the *empty* sequence.

INFERENCE RULES FOR $\Vdash$

(Z) $\quad \varnothing \Vdash \varnothing$

(A) $\quad \dfrac{\Gamma \Vdash \Delta}{\Gamma, A \Vdash \Delta, A}$

(M) $\quad \dfrac{\Gamma \Vdash \Delta}{\Gamma, A \Vdash \Delta}$

(P) $\quad \dfrac{\Gamma \Vdash \Delta}{\Gamma \Vdash \tilde{\Delta}}$

72   *Does Many-Valued Logic Have Any Use?*

(T) $\dfrac{\Gamma \Vdash \Delta \quad \Delta \Vdash \Theta}{\Gamma \Vdash \Theta}$

(S) $\dfrac{\Gamma, A \Vdash \Delta, A}{\Gamma \Vdash \Delta}$

(D) $\dfrac{n.\Gamma \Vdash n.\Delta}{\Gamma \Vdash \Delta}$ (where $n>0$)

It can be shown[7] that in the case of a set of unstructured atomic formulae, a relationship:

$$A_0, A_1, \ldots, A_{n-1} \Vdash B_0, B_1, \ldots, B_{m-1}$$

follows from the stated rules if and only if *for all* numerical evaluation functions $\#$ that map (atomic) formulae to *non-negative* real numbers it is the case that:

$$\# A_0 + \# A_1 + \ldots + \# A_{n-1} \geq \# B_0 + \# B_1 + \ldots + \# B_{m-1}$$

Thus the rules, in this simple case, generate exactly the positions safe for *all* games. The same would hold if we took certain given entailments as *axioms*. We would then make deductions from them, and we would use only those $\#$ that made them safe.

So far this is not especially interesting. What Giles noticed is that the *connective* of implication can be given a game-theoretic characterization based on this very natural rule:

> He who asserts A→B *agrees to assert* B *if his opponent will assert* A.

The table expresses this idea with entailments.

RULES FOR →

(→) $\dfrac{\Gamma \Vdash \Delta \quad \Gamma, A \Vdash B, \Delta}{\Gamma \Vdash A \to B, \Delta}$ $\dfrac{\Gamma, B \Vdash A, \Delta}{\Gamma, A \to B \Vdash \Delta}$

With hindsight it is not surprising that such rules characterize

Łukasiewicz implication because the operation in any case is just numerical *subtraction*, in the sense that:

$$\#(A \to B) = \#B - \#A$$

provided:

$$\#B \geq \#A,$$

otherwise we have:

$$\#(A \to B) = 0.$$

(The two cases here, by the way, technically correspond to the two premisses needed in the first rule for →.) The real point is that *all* the rules are very simple when phrased in the game-theoretic language, and so Giles will argue that on *intuitive grounds* we are led to the Łukasiewicz system. The argument will be even better if Giles can convince us that such entailments are natural for, say, physical theories (his original motivation), *and* if we can find ways of using the formalism to give 'neat' axiomatic theories. This latter will require much more investigation of quantifier calculus, but at least now we have some reason to try. Further, I feel that we can also see definite hope for the usefulness of this kind of logic which was not clear from the original presentation.

NOTES

1. An extensive bibliography can be found in N. Rescher, *Many-valued Logic*, McGraw-Hill, 1969.
2. See 'Background to formalization' in *Truth, Syntax and Modality* (H. Leblanc, ed.), North Holland, 1972.
3. The *form* of this semantical interpretation, which is very much like possible-worlds semantics for modal logic is due independently to the author and A. Urquhart. See for a fuller discussion and for references D. Scott, 'Completeness and axiomatizability in many-valued logic' in *Tarski*

Symposium (L. Henkin, et al., eds.), *Amer. Math. Soc.*, 1974 (in press).
4. More discussion and details are to be found in the papers cited in notes 2 and 3.
5. The papers by Giles are not yet published. The author learned about the approach from two preprints: 'A non-classical logic for physics' (1972) and 'Physics and logic' (1973).
6. The method is very close to that advocated by J. Hintikka, *Logic, Language Games and Information*, Oxford, 1973.
7. The method of proof is that in D. Scott, 'Measurement structures and linear inequalities', *J. Math. Psychology*, vol. 1 (1964), pp. 233-47.

Comment

BY T. J. SMILEY

I agree with Professor Scott in thinking that there may be a use for many-valued logic, even though my own candidate—a use for 3-valued logic in connection with the theory of descriptions—would be different from his. Of his two candidates, he gives more space (if not more support) to the idea of a many-valued logic of error, in which the truth-values of Łukasiewicz's system would stand for different degrees of error. By a degree of error Scott does not mean a probability, and he rightly emphasizes that the logic of probability is not many-valued. I shall argue in reply that Scott's logic of error is not many-valued either, and that he is wrong about errors for the same sort of reason as he is right about probabilities. This leads me to scrutinize his choice of a scale of degrees of error, to see if we could derive a many-valued logic by postulating a different scale.

In §2 I shall say something about logical consequence, starting from the observation that two systems of many-valued logic may have identical truth-values and truth-tables and theorems and still differ over the inferences they count as valid. The systems Scott presents differ in this way from each other and from any system based on the conventional idea of 'designating' some of the truth-values; and I want in particular to compare the conventional idea with Scott's approach to many-valued logic in terms of 'valuations'.

1. A MANY-VALUED LOGIC OF ERROR?

Scott remarks that it only takes a moment's thought to see that the probability of 'if A, B' is not a function of the probabilities of A and B. But the same moment's thought shows that the degree of error of 'if A, B' is not a function of the degrees of error of A and B, for the point is the same in each case: we want to accept 'if A, A' without being forced to accept 'if A, B' for every B that happens to have the same probability or degree of error as A. And if this failure of 'if' to be probability-functional is an objection to a many-valued logic of probability, its failure to be error-functional must surely be an equal objection to a many-valued logic of error.

This objection is not insuperable. After all, isn't it the stock objection to the classical 2-valued logic that 'if' is not truth-functional? And isn't the stock rejoinder that even if the classical system cannot represent 'if', it can represent 'and' and 'not', and with these we can define a truth-functional substitute for 'if', viz. material implication. If this sort of rejoinder is unacceptable then its inability to represent 'if' will indeed be fatal to the claims of a many-valued logic of error (together with, let it be said, every other formal system in existence). So let us accept the rejoinder, and limit the question to the system's ability to represent conjunction and negation.

As a candidate for a many-valued logic of probability we

might think of Łukasiewicz's system whose truth-values are the the real numbers from 0 to 1, the designated value being 1 and the relevant truth-tables being $\#(\sim A) = 1 - \#A$ and $\#(A\&B) = \min(\#A, \#B)$. There is no doubt that Łukasiewicz's '$\sim$' correctly represents negation, nor that in terms of his system '&' satisfies the conditions commonly put forward as defining conjunction, viz. $A\&B \vdash A$ and $A\&B \vdash B$ and $A,B \vdash A\&B$. The temptation to accept '&' as representing conjunction must nonetheless be resisted, for the brute fact is that the probability of 'A and B' is nowhere near being a function of the probabilities of A and B (e.g. let the probability of A be $\frac{1}{2}$ and compare the probability of 'A and A' with 'A and not-A'). By this test, then, neither Łukasiewicz's nor any other many-valued system can be the logic of probability.

To answer the corresponding question about Scott's logic of error, it is necessary to understand how its truth-values are defined. Although Scott only glances at this in his present paper, he has explained it very fully elsewhere (see his list of references). We are asked to envisage a set of *valuations* or assessments of a set of propositions as true or false. This has the effect of dividing the propositions into a number of *types* according to their pattern of assessment, two propositions being of the same type if every valuation that counts one as true counts the other as true and vice versa; and the truth-values are introduced as labels for these types. A set of m valuations may thus give rise to as many as 2^m truth-values, but in practice the number may be much less than this, as we shall see. This is Scott's approach to many-valued logic in general: for the logic of error he makes the particular assumption that the valuations form a series of increasing generosity of assessment, i.e. that each valuation counts as true all the propositions that its predecessors count as true (as well as some that they count as false). A set of m such valuations will divide the propositions into not more than $m+1$ types, and Scott gives these numerical labels from 0 to m. Since on this reckoning each truth-value equals the number of valuations that assess propositions of that type as false, they may appropriately be called 'degrees of error'. The idea is illustrated in Figure 1, where the v_i are assumed to be a series of increasingly generous valuations and the rows of ts and fs express the different patterns of assessment which are compatible with this assumption. The rows thus characterize the possible types of proposition, and the number to the left of each row is the corresponding numerical degree of error.

	v_0	v_1	v_2	v_3	v_4	v_5		A	$\sim A$
0	t	t	t	t	t	t		0	6
1	f	t	t	t	t	t		1	5
2	f	f	t	t	t	t		2	4
3	f	f	f	t	t	t		3	3
4	f	f	f	f	t	t		4	2
5	f	f	f	f	f	t		5	1
6	f	f	f	f	f	f		6	0

Figure 1   *Figure 2*

This defines the truth-values in terms of valuations: where are we to find the valuations? Scott suggests that they arise from *inexact* methods of measurement, and I shall address myself to this case; but I also want to consider how a logic of error can be derived from exact measurements, and I think the comparison of the two cases will help explain why neither produces a many-valued logic

An observer's apparatus may only enable him to record (say) distances to within $\pm i$ units: his measurements are inexact, though not therefore incorrect. Another observer's 'personal equation' may cause him to systematically overestimate distances by i: his measurements are exact, though incorrect. An observer of either kind can produce a valuation in Scott's sense by assessing the relevant propositions in the light of his own measurements; but whereas the exact observer can assess them literally (whether rightly or wrongly is beside the point) as true or false, the inexact observer cannot do this. For example, suppose his own measurement only records that a distance $d = 100 \pm 5$. If on the strength of this he assesses the proposition '$d=200$' as false the word needs no gloss, but if he assesses '$d=100$' as 'true' he can only mean 'true for all I know to the contrary'. Whatever his choice of words, his criterion for assessing propositions can only be whether they are *consistent* or *inconsistent* with his own incomplete data. The difference for logic is that the classical 2-valued truth-tables for 'and' and 'not' apply to a true/false dichotomy but not to a consistent/inconsistent one. Let us look at the two cases with this in mind.

If the degrees of error are defined in terms of the valuations produced by a number of exact observers, we can use the classical table to compute the truth or falsity of 'A and B' on any valuation from the truth or falsity of A and B on that valuation, and thereby we can compute the total degree of error of 'A and B' from the degrees of error of A and B. This has the gratifying effect of making 'and' error-functional, with the truth-table of Łukasiewicz's '&'. But we run into trouble when we try to apply the same method to 'not'. Suppose, for example, that A has degree of error 1, i.e. it is assessed $f\,t\,t\,t\,t\,t$ in Figure 1; then not-A demands to be assessed $t\,f\,f\,f\,f\,f$, but there is no such row in the figure. It would be an understatement to say that 'not' is not error-functional, as if it were merely a matter of the degree of error of 'not-A' failing to be uniquely determined by the degree of A. The fact is that there may not even exist such a thing as the degree of error of not-A: the bare admission of negative propositions is incompatible with the particular ordering of the valuations that was presupposed when the degrees of error were defined. This comes out very clearly in a more concrete example. Let each v_i in Figure 1 be an observer who overestimates distances by i; then to secure the required ordering of their valuations we must confine ourselves initially to a restricted class of propositions, viz. those of the form '$d>n$' or '$d \geqslant n$'. It is not surprising that conjunctions should also be admissible, since the conjunction of any two such propositions is necessarily equivalent to one or other of them. But negations are not admissible without destroying the ordering of the v_i, since the observers who are *more* generous in their assessment of '$d \leq n$' or '$d < n$' as true will be *less* generous in their assessment of '$d \geq n$' or '$d > n$'. Note in this connection how deceptive is the appeal of Łukasiewicz's '$\sim$'. It appeals at first sight as a symbol for negation because its truth-table inverts the order of the degrees of error (cf. Figure 2), whereas what negation really calls for is an inversion of the order of the valuations that lie behind them.

This trouble over negation does not arise when the degrees of error are defined by the valuations of inexact observers. We can go surprisingly far towards constructing a truth-table for 'not', at least if we assume with Scott that there exists a zero degree of error, i.e. that some propositions are actually assessed as 'true' in every valuation, as in row 0 of Figure 1. This amounts to assuming that each observer's measurements are internally consistent (since otherwise every proposition would be formally inconsistent with them), and it follows that A and not-A will never both be inconsistent with an observer's data. Taking Figure 1 as an example again, this enables us to write down a t for not-A wherever the row of A has an f; and the order we have assumed for the valuations dictates that we should write ts to the right of every t so obtained. In this way we get Figure 3, which in turn is summarized by Figure 4. The plausibility of Figure 4 can be tested in a more concrete example by taking each v_i in Figure 1 to be an observer who can only measure distances d to within the limits $d \pm i$. Let d actually be 100 and so consider '$d \neq 100$' as an example of a proposition of degree of error 1 (since it is excluded by v_0's measurements but is compatible with everyone else's), and '$d = 200$' as an example of a proposition of degree of error 6 (since it is excluded by every v_i's measurements). The negations of both propositions, '$d = 100$' and '$d \neq 200$', are obviously compatible with every v_i's measurements and so have degree of error 0, as predicted.

Does Many-Valued Logic Have Any Use?

v_0	v_1	v_2	v_3	v_4	v_5
?	?	?	?	?	?
t	t	t	t	t	t
t	t	t	t	t	t
t	t	t	t	t	t
t	t	t	t	t	t
t	t	t	t	t	t
t	t	t	t	t	t

Figure 3

A	not-A
0	?
1	0
2	0
3	0
4	0
5	0
6	0

Figure 4

A comparison of Figure 4 and Figure 2 shows that Łukasiewicz's '$\sim$' is again no answer to the problem of representing negation; but Figure 4 is not the answer either, since it is incomplete. To complete it we need to be able to ascribe a fixed degree of error to the negations of propositions of degree 0, and this turns out to be impossible. Thus in the example just given we have seen that '$d=100$' and '$d \neq 200$' both have degree of error 0, but the negation of one has degree of error 1 while the other has degree of error 6.

I have argued that negation is not error-functional whether the degrees of error are defined with reference to exact or inexact measurements. Conjunction is error-functional in the exact case but not in the inexact one, for data which are consistent with each of A and B may or may not be consistent with 'A and B', depending on the connection (or lack of connection) between A and B. The question now is whether these arguments apply to Scott's system alone or to other logics of error as well. Scott's adoption of a numerical scale of truth-values reflects two assumptions: that propositions can be ranked in simple order of greater or lesser degree of error, and that the difference between two degrees of error is another degree of error. Measurement theory calls this an *interval scale*, but other scales are possible: e.g. an *ordinal scale* reflecting the assumption of simple order alone, or a purely *nominal scale* reflecting the absence of any special assumptions. Might conjunction and negation be error-functional on an ordinal or nominal or some other scale of error?*

The argument used in the case of inexact measurement rests only on the fact that conjunction and negation are not truth-functional in the individual valuations, and does not seem to involve any assumption about the order, etc., of the valuations. Of course, my picture of inexact measurement is a simplified one which takes no account of statistical inexactitude, but the introduction of statistics will merely make the connectives even less truth-functional. It would thus seem that we cannot hope to base a many-valued logic of error upon inexact measurement. In the exact case the moral of the argument is that if we are to represent conjunction and negation then, since every 2-valued truth-function is definable from them, we must postulate the existence of degrees of error answering to the result of applying any 2-valued truth-function to the component ts and fs of any existing degrees of error. Nominal and ordinal scales do not meet this requirement, and there is just one scale which does: I do not know whether it has been given a name in measurement theory but I shall call it a *subset scale*. By a subset scale I mean one appropriate to the case in which each of a set of features may be present or absent independently, so that there needs to

* Apart from any intrinsic plausibility it may have, the attraction of an interval scale is that it permits Scott's ingenious interpretation of Łukasiewicz's truth-table for '→'. Without an interval scale he would need to devise an alternative table for '→', and the validity of the deduction theorem suggests itself as a possible formal guiding principle. It is not difficult to show that the deduction theorem holds in a logic based on an ordinal scale if and only if there exists a zero degree and '→' has the truth-table: $\#(A \rightarrow B) = 0$ when $\#A \geqslant \#B$, otherwise $\#(A \rightarrow B) = \#B$. On a nominal scale the corresponding table required is: $\#(A \rightarrow B) = 0$ when $\#A = \#B$, otherwise $\#(A \rightarrow B) = \#B$. Interestingly enough, both these truth-tables have previously been devised in quite different contexts: the first by Dummett (see the *Journal of Symbolic Logic*, vol. 24, p. 97) and the second by Shoesmith (who showed that it characterizes material implication, since it contains the classical truth-table while being contained in a Boolean-style one). On a subset scale the only connective to satisfy the deduction theorem is material implication.

be a degree on the scale corresponding to every subset of the given set. A subset scale preserves Scott's assumption that the difference between two degrees is a degree, but replaces his simple ordering by a partial ordering that mirrors the way the subsets of a set are ordered by inclusion. In the logical context, a set of m independent valuations will define a subset scale of 2^m degrees of error, corresponding to all the possible patterns of ts and fs arising from the individual valuations. For example, suppose we assess geometrical propositions as true or false in Euclidean geometry, hyberbolic geometry and elliptic geometry respectively; we thereby define an 8-valued logic of error whose degrees range on a subset scale from 'true in all three geometries' to 'true in none' (cf. Rose, 'Eight-valued geometry', *Proc. Lond. Math. Soc.*, ser. 3, vol. 2, especially pp. 42f.).

With a subset scale we seem to have the possibility of a many-valued logic of error; but though its truth-values and Boolean-style truth-tables for conjunction and negation are different from the classical ones, they determine the same theorems and valid inferences (indeed, unless this were so we would not have successfully represented conjunction and negation). As long, therefore, as the system is limited to conjunction and negation it will be a many-valued interpretation of classical logic rather than a many-valued logic in any distinctive sense. To obtain a distinct logic we shall have to include some connective which is truth-functional in terms of a subset scale without being classically truth-functional. Nothing could be easier than to do this as a purely abstract exercise: to make sense of it is another matter.

2 LOGICAL CONSEQUENCE

To define a many-valued logic it is not enough to describe its truth-values and truth-tables: one must also explain how the assignment of the various truth-values determines whether a proposition is a theorem and, more generally, whether a proposition follows from others. As one would expect, Scott carefully supplies the necessary information, but still his paper bears out the point in a particularly striking way. For it turns out that the same truth-values and truth-tables of Łukasiewicz can be used to define no fewer than three quite different systems—systems whose theorems are the same but which differ over such fundamental matters as the validity of *modus ponens* or the equivalence of a conjunction to the joint force of its components. (One might even say there are three and a half systems, for it would appear that Łukasiewicz himself did not take logical consequence seriously, and so his own many-valued 'logic' is a system of theoremhood alone.) The rival methods of defining logical consequence used by these systems each have their own interest and their own generality, and I shall outline them before venturing some brief critical comments.

1. The *designation method* is the conventional method of defining a many-valued logic. Certain truth-values are 'designated', and a proposition is said to follow from others if it takes a designated value whenever they all do. (Theoremhood can be treated as the limiting case of consequence from no premisses; e.g. on this method the theorems are the propositions that always take designated values.)

2. The *valuation method* is used by Scott for his logic of error and is presupposed by my own discussion of alternatives to it. A set of valuations is postulated, and each truth-value is associated with a particular pattern of truth and falsity with respect to the various valuations. A proposition is said to follow from others if it is true in every valuation in which they are all true, and then this definition is worked out in terms of the associated truth-values. Scott applies the method to a generalized idea of consequence, involving a variable number of conclusions as well as premisses, but it is sufficient for my purpose to keep to the more familiar context of a single proposition as conclusion. Within this context the valuation method is formally equivalent to what might be called the *closure method* of defining a many-valued logic (*J.S.L.*, vol. 27,

pp. 432ff. and 378). On this method, which is motivated by Tarski's idea of the deductive closure of a set of propositions, a closure operation is defined on the truth-values and a proposition is said to follow from others if its truth-value always falls inside the closure of theirs. The equivalence is clear once it is realized that both methods boil down to ways of designating a number of subsets of the truth-values, whether via the closed subsets of the closure method or the subsets true under the individual valuations on the valuation method. In the same spirit the designation method can be regarded as a special case of the other two, in which exactly one subset of truth-values is designated.

3. The *game-theoretic* method is well described by Scott in presenting his version of the logic of risk, and I need only refer to his summary of the game in question as a debate in which a participant risks something by each act of assertion. Each truth-value is associated with a potential quantum of loss, and a proposition is said to follow from others if the loss risked by its assertion never exceeds the total risked by theirs. (Scott applies this method too to a generalized idea of consequence, but again I have kept to the case of a single conclusion.) This definition assumes that losses can be added and compared, and so imposes an arithmetical structure on the truth-values in a way the other two methods do not.

To see how the different methods work out in practice, consider Łukasiewicz's truth-values and truth-tables. If we follow Łukasiewicz in designating the value 0 (assuming Scott's numbering of the values), we get the conventional Łukasiewiczian logic, in which the definition of logical consequence is: $A_1, \ldots, A_n \vdash B$ if and only if $\#B = 0$ whenever $\#A_1 = \ldots = \#A_n = 0$. If we follow Scott's choice of valuations we obtain his logic of error, in which $A_1, \ldots, A_n \vdash B$ if and only if $\max(\#A_1, \ldots, \#A_n) \geq \#B$. And if we adopt the game-theoretic method we get the logic of risk, in which $A_1, \ldots, A_n \vdash B$ if and only if $\#A_1 + \ldots + \#A_n \geq \#B$.

Consider now the *modus ponens* principle $A, A \to B \vdash B$.

This holds good in the conventional system (for the truth-table for $\rightarrow$ shows that $\#B=0$ whenever $\#A=\#(A\rightarrow B)=0$), and in the logic of risk (for $\#(A\rightarrow B) \geqslant \#B - \#A$, whence $\#A + \#(A\rightarrow B) \geqslant \#B$). But, as Scott is aware, *modus ponens* is not valid in the logic of error, for when $\#A=1$ and $\#B=2$, say, max $(\#A, \#(A\rightarrow B))=1$. Again, consider the principle that a conjunction is equivalent to the joint force of its components, i.e. that $A\&B \vdash C$ if and only if $A, B \vdash C$. This holds good in the conventional system (since $\#(A\&B)=0$ if and only if $\#A = \#B=0$), and in the logic of error (for by definition $\#(A\&B)=\max(\#A, \#B)$). But the principle is not valid in the logic of risk, for though $A, A\rightarrow B \vdash B$ we do not have $A\&(A\rightarrow B) \vdash B$, as can be seen by taking $\#A=1$ and $\#B=2$.

A list of premises in the logic of risk cannot be treated as a set: their multiplicity of occurrence needs to be taken into account too. This is why the conjunction principle fails, for though $A\&B \vdash C$ implies $A, B \vdash C$ and $A, B \vdash C$ implies $A\&B, A\&B \vdash C$, we cannot equate $A\&B, A\&B \vdash C$ with $A\&B \vdash C$ and so cannot make either implication reciprocal. The idea of counting the multiplicity of occurrence of propositions can be traced back to Aristotle: what is new is the particular way it affects the logic of risk, via the rule that a cumulative risk attaches to reiterations of the same proposition. For this reason 'game-theoretic' may not be the most apt term, for what distinguishes the logic of risk is not just that it is based on a game of assertion but that the game is played according to a particular rule about reiteration; and physicists might have preferred Lewis Carroll's rule 'what I tell you three times is true', though doubtless libel lawyers prefer Giles's 'what I tell you three times is expensive'.

Scott's work on the formalism of the logic of risk is likely to inspire as much interest as Giles's work on its foundations, and I shall limit myself to a simple query. Scott raises the question of using his formalism to give neat axiomatic theories, and warns that this will require much more investigation of the calculus of quantifiers. But even at the level of propositional calculus, the system envisaged by the logic of risk is

Łukasiewicz's infinite-valued one; and at least on the designation method this has a non-compact relation of logical consequence. I wonder whether the same is true on the game-theoretic method, for if so it would surely rule out an axiomatic treatment from the start?

When giving his conference paper Scott voiced a criticism of the conventional approach to many-valued logic, which I can best convey by quoting from another of his papers: 'One quirk of many-valued logic that always puzzled me was the distribution of *designated elements*. They were somehow "truer" than the others; their invariable assumption was required of a formula to count as a *tautology*. Care was always needed in awarding designation lest rules such as *modus ponens* fail. On the one hand we were denying bivalence by contemplating multivalued systems; but on the other, a return to bivalence was provided by the scheme of designation. But not quite: there was always something fiendish in the way that the connectives jumbled up the designated and undesignated values. The Łukasiewicz three-valued system ... is a good example. The trick of designation works—almost by accident. It just strikes me as being a half thought-out idea, a happy (but unmotivated) compromise.' (*Background to Formalization*, p. 266.)

I have a great deal of sympathy with this as an historical observation, but I think the method of designation can be defended for the future if not the past. The way to defend it is to read 'true' for 'designated'. The method of defining logical consequence then needs no justification, for it now reads as saying that a proposition follows from others if and only if it is true whenever they are all true. What does need explaining is how there can be more than two truth-values. The answer is that propositions can be classified in other ways than as true or untrue, and by combining such a classification with the true/untrue one we in effect subdivide the true and untrue propositions into a larger number of types. For example, given any property Φ of propositions, there are prima facie four possible types of proposition: true and Φ, true and not Φ, untrue and Φ, untrue and not Φ. If Φ is unrelated to truth, like 'obscene' or 'having something to do with geometry', all four types can exist and we get four truth-values, two being designated and two undesignated. If Φ has any bearing on truth some of the types may be ruled out; e.g. if Φ is (perhaps) 'about the future' or 'meaningless', the type 'true and Φ' will be empty, leaving three truth-values of which just one is designated. One cannot foretell how the connectives will behave with respect to this or that classification of propositions, but to the extent that the types of compound propositions turn out to be functions of the types of their constituents, so we shall get a many-valued logic.

I shall not try to argue in favour of any particular system of many-valued logic based on the designation method, but the mere possibility of such a system presents a difficulty for Scott. I remarked earlier that, for a given set of truth-values, the designation method of defining logical consequence is in effect a special case of the valuation method, viz. that in which only a single valuation is postulated. Scott, however, wants to use valuations to do more than define logical consequence in terms of pre-existing truth-values: he wants to use them to define the truth-values themselves, by identifying the different truth-values with the different patterns of assessment produced by a set of valuations. As we noted in §1, a set of m valuations cannot produce more than 2^m valuations in this way, and in particular a single valuation cannot produce more than two truth-values. The difficulty for Scott is that this makes it impossible to reproduce a conventional system in his terms if it has more than two truth-values. (To put the point another way: in a conventional system all the designated values, and all the undesignated ones, are equivalent as far as logical consequence is concerned; but this is impossible if the values are defined in Scott's way, since a difference in truth-value means a difference in assessment in some valuation or other, and every such difference is reflected in the relation of logical consequence. In the conventional version of Łukasiewicz's system, for example, the fact that we can assign the value 1 to the premises and 2 to the conclusion does not affect the validity of *modus ponens*, since 1 and 2 are both undesignated values; but it does affect it in Scott's 'logic of error' version, since it means that there is a valuation in which the premises are true and the conclusion is false; and I am arguing that some discrepancy of this sort is inevitable.) Since I do not think Scott intends his approach to rule out the conventional one, the solution of the difficulty would seem to be for him to accept that truth-values are not always definable in terms of valuations alone. Once this is agreed we are free to regard the valuation approach to many-valued logic as embracing the conventional one as a special case; and though questions can still be asked about the meaning of 'logical consequence' if more than one valuation is used to define it, I prefer to end on what I hope is a note of agreement.

Comment

BY J. P. CLEAVE

Professor Scott, together with other philosophers and mathematicians, questions the utility of many-valued logics. E. Beth [1] (p. 231) remarked that 'at present the various languages of modal logic and of many-valued logic are merely studied, they are hardly ever used'. Łukasiewicz justified his own systems of many-valued logic by appeal to future contingent events. This justification is not regarded very seriously; L. Chwistek [3] (p. 132) wrote that 'the philosophical arguments which Łukasiewicz employs and in particular the Aristotelian classification of events into contingent and necessary are quite naïve and antagonize the reader'. In view of this and his own introductory remarks, it is not clear why the Łukasiewicz systems should be rescued after remaining for fifty years a mere cerebral bauble.

Not all non-classical logics lack justification. Intuitionism is a way of mathematical life based upon a constructive notion of 'existence'. The logic of intuitionism was isolated by Heyting in 1930. The problem, mentioned by Professor Scott, of finding a down-to-earth justification for intuitionist logic is not merely one of replacing the heady wine of 'basal intuition', 'free becoming', etc., by warm English beer, because the essential features of this logic are present in E. Bishop's work on constructive mathematics [2], which is devoid of Brouwerian mysticism. The principal problem is one of understanding the constructive notion of existence.

Most working mathematicians assume that their subject concerns something called the 'universe' which consists of definite 'objects' clearly labelled with properties all sitting 'out there' waiting to be discovered. From such a point of view the classical logic is quite natural and a *formal* understanding of intuitionism can be achieved by various devices such as replacing the term 'constructive' with the classical term 'recursive'. Constructivists, however, see this as a misrepresentation of their ideas (Bishop[2], Heyting[6]; see also the papers by A. Heyting and R. Péter in reference 7, etc). Personally, I believe that a sound philosophical basis for constructive reasoning can be provided by the sort of theory of language, logic and social action expounded by Kamlah and Lorenzen [8].

Intuitionists, too, can achieve a formal understanding of classical mathematics, as remarked by Heyting [6]. But are they not also justified in demanding a sound philosophical basis for classical mathematics, which is, after all, founded on ancient Greek dogmas such as the 'law of the excluded middle'?

Neither is every many-valued logic without use, though none are alternative modes of mathematical reasoning. The many-valued logic I am most familiar with is the logic based

on the so-called 'strong tables' of Kleene. This logic arises naturally from three sources:
 (i) the logic of partial recursive predicates. Here the truth-values are so defined that the connectives produce partial recursive predicates when applied to partial recursive predicates (Kleene) [9].
 (ii) Körner's theory of inexact classes, where the definition of a class takes the form of conditions for 'membership' together with conditions for 'non-membership'. It can happen here that the definition of a class might, for some individuals, determine neither membership nor non-membership (Körner) [10].
 (iii) Hájek's study of automated research [5]. The problem here is to determine automatically (that is, by computer programme) hypotheses which are verifiable on the basis of some (finite) experimental material: one must allow that for some object a and property P no information has been provided experimentally on whether a has or has not P—and in this case the formula for $P(a)$ is assigned a third 'truth-value'—neutral.

Unlike the Łukasiewicz systems, this three-valued logic cannot be axiomatized by *designating* some of the truth-values. For there are no sentences which are *true* under all evaluations and those sentences which are *non-false* (i.e. *true* or *neutral*) under all evaluations are precisely the classical tautologies. The relation of the three-valued logic to the classical two-valued logic is found by studying the relation of (semantic) *logical consequence* which shall be denoted by '$\rightarrow$'. The following results can be obtained:

 (i) Let $P, Q, \ldots$ be the predicate letters occurring in the formula A. Then $P, Q \ldots (x)(P(x) \lor \neg P(x)) \rightarrow A$ if, and only if, A is a classical tautology.
 (ii) The logical consequence relation can be completely axiomatized, that is, a Gentzen type of formal system

can be constructed in which a sequent (A, B) is derivable if, and only if, $A \to B$.
(Further details can be found in [4].

I conclude that this three-valued logic is both mathematically and philosophically justified and has a clear and simple relation to classical logic.

REFERENCES

1. E. W. Beth. *The Foundations of Mathematics*, North-Holland, Amsterdam, 1959.
2. E. Bishop. *Foundations of Constructive Analysis*, McGraw-Hill, U.S.A. 1967.
3. L. Chwistek. *The Limits of Science*, Kegan Paul, London, 1948.
4. J. P. Cleave. 'The notion of logical consequence in the logic of inexact predicates', *Zeitschrift fur Math. Logik u. Grundlagen d. Math*, 20 (4), 1974, 307–324.
5. P. Hájek, K. Bendova, Z. Renc. 'The GUHA method and the three-valued logic', *Kybernetica*, 7 (6), 1971, 421–35.
6. A. Heyting. 'Infinitistic methods from a finitist point of view', pp. 185–92 of *Infinitistic Methods*, Pergamon, 1961.
7. A. Heyting (ed.) *Constructivity in Mathematics*, North-Holland, Amsterdam, 1959.
8. W. Kamlah, P. Lorenzen. *Logische Propädeutik*, Bibliographisches Institut, Mannheim, 1967.
9. S. C. Kleene. *Introduction to Metamathematics*, Van Nostrand, 1952.
10. S. Körner. *Experience and Theory*, Routledge & Kegan Paul, 1966.

Comment

BY R. GILES

Since the work Professor Scott has referred to is not yet in print [1-3] a brief description of the dialogue interpretation of $Ł_\infty$ seems to be called for. Before I can give the rules of the dialogue some preliminary matters must be made clear.

First, the notion of a prime proposition used here differs somewhat from the classical notion: in one respect it is narrower, in another more general. Classical propositions may be divided into two types: those, such as 'the bar is open' for which a definite testing-procedure is available and those, for instance "the divine is perfect", which admit no such procedure. For the present purposes propositions of the second type are not admitted. We require that there corresponds to each prime proposition an *elementary experiment*: i.e. an experimental procedure that culminates in a definite *outcome*, 'yes' or 'no'. In the case of a classical prime proposition this outcome is taken to determine the truth-value of the proposition. Thus the elementary experiment is implicitly assumed to be *dispersion-free* in that if the procedure is repeated (under the same conditions) the same outcome is obtained. Now, it is natural to adopt the concept of an elementary experiment as a foundation stone in the formulation of a physical theory, for such a theory is concerned with the making of predictions and the most basic sort of prediction relates to the outcome of such an experiment. However, elementary experiments in physics generally show *dispersion*: when a trial is repeated, even under precisely controlled conditions, the outcome is not necessarily always the same; not only errors but also thermal, statistical, or quantum effects can be responsible for this. Dispersive experiments also arise in everyday life: for instance, 'Spin a coin. If "heads" the outcome is "yes".' It is clear that if this elementary experiment is repeated (in the spirit which is intended) the outcome is not always the same. Accordingly, both for the formalization of physical theories and for practical applications, we are led to broaden the notion of a prime proposition by allowing it to refer to *any* (possibly dispersive) elementary experiment: i.e. to define a prime proposition as *an expression to which there corresponds a definite elementary experiment*. (Here 'definite' means that all observers agree as to (a) whether the experiment has been correctly carried out and if so (b) what the outcome is.)

If (the elementary experiment corresponding to) a prime proposition is dispersion-free a truth-value can be assigned to it and classical logic can be applied. However, in the dispersive case this is not possible. In particular, we can no longer take the classical view that the meaning of a prime proposition is determined by laying down the conditions under which it is true. To obtain an alternative let us recognize that the *function* of a proposition is to be asserted and, taking a view that might be employed in legal circles, let us adopt the following basic principle:

(A) *The meaning of any proposition is to be given by laying down a definite commitment that is assumed by him who asserts it.*

A sentence is thus a proposition if and only if such a commitment has been laid down. A simple way to make each prime proposition (as defined above) a proposition in this sense is to introduce the principle:

(B) *He who asserts a prime proposition undertakes to pay $1 should a trial of the corresponding elementary experiment yield the outcome 'no'.*

This assigns a 'meaning' even in the case of a dispersive prime proposition, when the classical procedure breaks down. Note that repetition of an assertion increases the commitment.

To build a logic on this basis we may apply the classical procedure of assigning a meaning to a compound proposition in terms of the meanings previously assigned to its components. It is convenient to adopt the following rules (P and Q denote arbitrary propositions):

Proposition	Obligation
$P \lor Q$	To assert P or Q at one's own choice.
$P \land Q$	To assert P or Q at opponent's choice.
$P \to Q$	To offer to assert Q if opponent will assert P.
F	To pay \$1.
$\neg P$	To offer to pay \$1 if opponent will assert P (i.e. same as $P \to F$).
$\exists x P(x)$	To assert $P(n)$ for some n (own choice).
$\forall x P(x)$	To assert $P(n)$ for some n (opponent's choice).

If any proposition is asserted by one player (say 'me') these rules govern an ensuing dialogue (with 'you', say) which ends in a *final position* in which we are each committed to a number of propositions, all prime. These propositions are then tried, and the debts incurred under (B) paid.

Because of the last clause, although the rules resemble those of Lorenzen's dialogue interpretation of intuitionistic logic they determine an 'outdoor game' in Hintikka's sense, whereas Lorenzen's rules are concerned with establishing logical identities—an 'indoor game'. In this respect the game is more like Hintikka's game-theoretic interpretation of classical logic (see §3 of his paper), but (a) $A \to B$ is not here equivalent to $B \lor \neg A$ and (b) we are not assuming that the prime propositions are dispersion-free.

Who wins? With dispersive prime propositions the same final position will result in a different financial outcomes on different occasions. However, there will be certain final positions (depending on my beliefs) which seem 'acceptable' to me, in that I expect on average a non-negative gain. To reach one of these is, as far as I am concerned, a 'win'. Thus if (and only if) for a given initial assertion P I have a strategy that ensures an acceptable final position then I will be willing to assert P, and we may say *P is true (for me)*. In this way truth re-enters the theory, albeit only in a subjective form.

Certain plausible axioms can be laid down governing the form of the set of all acceptable final positions. From these the existence of a 'risk function' (denoted "#" in Scott's paper) can be established, and it turns out, as Professor Scott has indicated, that this risk function satisfies the truth tables of Łukasiewicz logic.

REFERENCES

1. 'A non-classicall ogic for physics', *Studia Logica*, vol. 33, pp. 397–415 (1974).
2. 'A logic for subjective belief', in *Proceedings of an International Research Colloquium on Foundations of Probability and Statistics and Statistical Theories of Science*, University of Western Ontario, London, Ontario, 10–13 May 1973, vol. 1, Reidel, forthcoming.
3. 'A pragmatic approach to the formalization of empirical theories', in *Proceedings of the Conference for Formal Methods in Methodology of Empirical Sciences*, Warsaw, 17–21 June 1974, Reidel, forthcoming.

III/Identity, Necessity and Physicalism*

David Wiggins

I

When metaphysical importance is plausibly ascribed to a result in formal logic this is an exciting, not to say stirring, event. In part, this is because visible progress is something not unknown in formal logic, whereas in philosophy—well, some people wonder how much progress there is. My own view is both that there is progress in philosophy, and that formal logic has had at least a little to do with the progress, but it is not always a straightforward matter to read the right philosophical significance into formal results. They serve as nothing else can to destroy nonsense but, beyond that, even theorems may in application provoke controversy. All the same, *pace* one school of thought, it seems to me that such controversy is almost always metaphysically fruitful and philosophically innovative.

* An earlier and in certain important respects substantially different version of this contribution was published in *Philosophia* for January 1975 under the title 'Identity, Designation, Essentialism and Physicalism'. There is also some overlap at some points with 'Continuity, Identity and Essentialism' in *Synthese* for 1974–5. For the formal development presupposed here of 'necessarily' as a predicate-operator see my 'The *De Re* "Must": a note on the logical form of essentialist claims' forthcoming, with an *Appendix* by C. A. B. Peacocke, in *Semantics* edited by Gareth Evans and John McDowell (Oxford University Press, 1975).

This paper is to consider one claim of this kind, namely Saul Kripke's contention that the modal theorem $(a=b) \supset \Box (a=b)$ excludes philosophical materialism.[1] It would be ungracious for me to begin a paper which is at least at two points quite critical of Kripke without saying that I believe Kripke is right to hold that the theorem bears upon the mind-body problem (even if it is no help to Kripke's Cartesianism): and that I yield to none in my admiration of the wit, invention and integrity of philosophical purpose which shine through Kripke's writings on these subjects.

At risk of repeating what may be very familiar I shall start with a summary of Kripke's position in "Identity and Necessity". He begins by remarking that some have been disturbed by the following derivation.[2] Consider Leibniz' Law

1   $(x)(y)(x=y \supset (Fx \equiv Fy))$.

As one instance of (1), provided that the letter F may stand proxy for such modal properties of objects as *is necessarily identical with x*, we get

2   $(x)(y)(x=y) \supset (\Box(x=x) \equiv \Box(y=x))$.

But by the truth of $(x)\Box(x=x)$—reading $\ulcorner \Box \phi a \urcorner$ as saying that $\ulcorner \phi a \urcorner$ is true of any world containing a[3]—and by the consequent superfluity of the third clause, viz.,

3   $\Box(x=x)$,

(2) must entail

4   $(x)(y) [(x=y) \supset \Box(y=x)]$.

But how, it has been asked, can this be accepted? If we must normally discover identities empirically, they cannot be true necessarily.

Kripke's reply may be seen as falling under three heads: (A) he shows how to find a way to accept (4); (B) he shows why one should want to accept (4); and (C) he draws out the supposed consequences of accepting (4).

(A). Sentence (4) generalizes upon the case where we have a particular identity statement made by the use of names or demonstratives. Where identities are stated by means of definite descriptions, and where a sentential operator such as 'not' or 'necessarily' is present, we must according to Kripke pay careful heed to matters of scope. Consider

5   The first Postmaster General of the United States is identical with the inventor of bifocals.

Kripke insists that it is a contingent matter that (5) is true—and that this does not count against (4).[4] All (5) with (4) should lead us to expect if we follow Russell's theory of descriptions, is

5′ $(\exists x)(\exists y)[(w)(FPMGw \equiv w=x)$ & $(z)(IBFz \equiv z=y)$ & (necessarily $(x=y))$]

The necessity attaching to the third clause of this expansion of (5) results from intersubstituting what (4) demonstrates to be equivalents.

Most of the residual resistance to the idea of (4)'s holding will rest, according to Kripke, on a confusion of the categories of *necessity* and *a priority*. If x is necessarily y then x *must be y, cannot not be y*. But to say this, which is a metaphysical claim, is not the same as to say that x's identity with y is *a priori*. By *a priori* is or should be meant that this can be told independently of all experience. That is an epistemological claim and irrelevant to (4). The supposed coextensiveness of the two claims would 'require some philosphical argument to establish it' (p. 50).

(B). When these obstacles are cleared away what is there positively to recommend (4)? Well, there are still (1) and (3), which on Kripke's view do no less than entail (4). Any sentence (1)′ or (3)′ which instantiates either (1) or (3) with regard to entities a, b is manifestly *about a* and *b* themselves, not the senses of their names, or their associated concepts, or their 'counterparts' in other worlds, or about anything at all other than a and b. To someone who doubted this I think Kripke might reply that (3)′ says that a can't but be a; the fact that this is the outcome of logical or conceptual rather than causal constraints hardly constitutes grounds to deny that it has in all relevant respects the same logical form as "a can't throw further than a". And this last must surely be like 'a can't throw further than b' in being about a. So surely there is no easy escape from (4). But, in the absence of more positive support for (4), perhaps this exacerbates what some already see as a situation of paradox. Here Kripke's strategy seems to be to provide an informal argument for (4), *in addition to* the formal argument.

Kripke is not the first to have wished to champion (4). Ramsey supposed that true statements of the form '$a=b$' would have to be necessary truths.[5] Ruth Barcan Marcus, who appears to have been the first to present a formal derivation of (4), has long accepted this conclusion and defended it on lines strongly reminiscent of *Tractatus Logico Philosophicus* 4.243.[6] That passage depends on a special view of proper names, however. In Kripke's informal argument, the proper names which are in question are common or garden ones, naturalistically viewed. His position depends not at all on the distinction between logical and other proper names: according to him it depends on the distinction between rigid designators, such as proper names or functors like '$\sqrt{25}$' (p. 144), and non-rigid designators. A designator is rigid (p. 145) iff it designates the same object in all possible worlds. Hence a designator such as 'the inventor of bifocals' is non-rigid.

Equipped so, Kripke argues as follows (p. 154):

If names are rigid designators then there can be no question about identities being necessary, because 'a' and 'b' will both refer to this same object x, and to no other, and so there will be no situation in which a might not have been b. That would be a situation in which the object which we are now also calling 'x' would not have been identical with itself.... One could not possibly have a situation in which ... Hesperus would not have been Phosphorus.

Those who resist this conclusion, and claim that they can imagine the circumstance of Hesperus not being Phosphorus, are confusing the hypothetical circumstance of our not *calling* Hesperus 'Hesperus' and the (putative but impossible) circumstance of Hesperus not *being* Phosphorus. The world in which things are differently *called* is irrelevant to the problem. The problem is what is to be said by us about a possible world in which Venus has a different position in the evening from its position in ours. 'That would not be a situation in which Phosphorus would not have been Hesperus ... A difference in position in the same world is not grounds for thinking that such identity statements are contingent. ... To take them so is to miscontrue the relation between *a name* and a description *used* [in and of our world] *to fix its reference*, to take them to be synonyms.'[7]

(C). What follows from this, according to Kripke, is a complete transformation of the status to be accorded to that philosopher's standby

6   'Heat is molecular agitation.'

This is a true identity, but not a contingent one.

Naturally, (6) is *a posteriori*. But how could it be contingent? It is true that there is a certain external phenomenon which we sense by touch, which produces a sensation which we call 'the sensation of heat', and which we discover to be a high degree of molecular agitation in the object touched. But 'heat', like 'molecular agitation', is a rigid designator of that external phenomenon. It is neither synonymous nor necessarily co-extensive with the description by which we pick it out—'cause of the sensation human beings call "the sensation of heat"'. To imagine a situation in which the latter happens to be satisfied by some different phenomenon shows nothing about heat itself.

Now consider

7   Being in pain at time *t* is being in neural state *n* at time *t*.

This is supposed by those who champion it to hold contingently. But if it is contingent at best, then it is false. And, the reason it is contingent at best is that we *can*, according to Kripke, coherently imagine neural state n not being what affects us with the sensation of pain. 'What affects us painfully, or with the sensation of pain', unlike 'cause of the sensation of heat', is a rigid designator. Coherently to imagine state n *not* being what affects us painfully is to imagine n's not being *pain*. It is to conceive the possibility of (7) being false. 'Although we can say that we pick out heat contingently by the contingent property that it affects us in such and such a way, we cannot similarly say that we pick out pain contingently by the fact that it affects us in such and such a way.... The experience itself has to be *this* experience, and I cannot say that it is [a] contingent property of the pain I now have that it is a pain ...'. Of n, on the other hand, we can say this. So (7) does not withstand the threat posed to it by the conceivability of n's not being what affects us with the sensation of pain.

This is a summary of Kripke's argument for (4) and not-(7), bare but not innocent of a fair measure of interpretation and reorganization. An assessment would seem to involve the following points:

1. Kripke's presentation of the theorem and his informal arguments in its behalf (which may appear to depend crucially upon possible worlds and rigid designation). [= Section II ensuing.]
2. The proof of the theorem itself. [= Section III, below.]
3. The implications of the theorem for materialism. [= Section IV below.]

Unfortunately, (1) and (2) must delay the progression to (3).

2 KRIPKE'S INFORMAL PRESENTATION OF THE THEOREM

I shall lead into this with what may be a minor matter. It appears to me to be minor given my preferred understanding of the modal theorem. But lovers of the distinction of rigid and non-rigid designation may differ with me over its importance. It is this: at some points in his exposition Kripke's whole argument is made to seem to depend on the idea that true identity statements of a certain class are necessarily true statements if and only if *rigid designators* flank the '=' sign. We have already seen this at p. 154. In the same way Kripke writes at p. 160.

> We use both 'heat' and 'the motion of molecules' as rigid designators for a certain external phenomenon. Since heat is in fact the motion of molecules, and the designators are both rigid, ... it is going to be necessary that heat is the motion of molecules.

But some may object that theorem (4)—if that is meant to be the formal counterpart of this informal argument—is not a claim about rigid designators at all. It says that whatever x may be and whatever y may be if x is y then necessarily x is y. Maybe there is something metalinguistic latent in the 'necessarily'. We shall touch upon that in due course: and if there is something metalinguistic in the 'necessarily' then this will occasion certain difficulties for the derivation. But there is nothing about rigid designation in theorem (4). So why does it figure in the informal argument?

One way of proceeding here is by the observation that, on the Russell–Smullyan treatment of definite descriptions favoured by Kripke, descriptions are not direct substituends for 'x' and 'y' in (4). One must write out the identity (6) in primitive notation without using a description operator, at the same time fortifying the rigidly designative clauses with a $\Box$, thus:

$$[(\exists x)(\exists y)(\Box((z)(z \text{ is heat } \equiv z \text{ is } x)) \ \& \ \Box((w)(w \text{ is high molecular agitation} \equiv w = y)) \ \& \ (x = y)]$$

The utility of theorem (4), then, is to license the prefixing of a box $\Box$ to the last clause above too, $\Box x = y$. We may then use the modal theorems:

$$[\Box p \ \& \ \Box q \ \& \ \Box r] \supset [\Box (p \ \& \ q \ \& \ r)]$$
$$[(\exists x)(\Box(\phi) \ \& \ \Box(\psi) \ \& \ \Box(\chi)] \supset [(\exists x)\Box(\phi \ \& \ \psi \ \& \ \chi)]$$

to derive

$(\exists x)(\exists y)[\Box[(z)(z \text{ is heat} \equiv z \text{ is } x)$ & $(w)(w \text{ is high molecular agitation} \equiv (w=y))$ & $(x=y)]]$

On this view, Kripke's point must be that a proposition like the one here with three occurrences of $\Box$—and entailing a proposition of the latter kind—will be available when and only when both terms in an identity statement are rigid designators. The asymmetry between (6) and (7) then comes down to this. The $(\exists x)(\exists y)\Box$ [...] statement corresponding to (6) is true, but a certain conceiving is supposed to show that any $(\exists x)(\exists y)\Box$[....] statement corresponding to (7) is false. And, if this statement is false then (7), which implies it, is false too.

This will do very well (and I shall read Kripke so) for the time being. But on this view the 'necessarily' of theorem (4) is still apparently to be explained in terms of some invariance in the truth of the statement $\ulcorner \phi \urcorner$ (e.g. in terms of ϕ's holding true[8] in respect of all worlds w such that w is a so and so world, where the 'so and so' condition may require to be specified in various different ways into which there is no need yet to enter). The approach to the 'necessarily' still seems to derive from the *de dicto* and may be infected with all the problems of quantifying into opaque contexts which Quine has made infamous. So we may be led to wonder whether Kripke's attack on (7) can be phrased in such a way as to be free of these problems, to make 'necessarily' more purely *de re*, and to be independent of rigid designation. In due course I shall try to do precisely this, and to motivate a different view from Kripke's of the 'necessarily' involved in (4). I shall try to see (4) as simply saying of anything x and anything y, however described, that if x is y then x necessarily is y, however x and y are described.[9] But at this particular point I am only concerned with the extent to which the distinction of rigid and non-rigid designation is essential to the proper deployment and/or defence of (4).

It seems to me that, though the distinction figures in this interpretation of one method of *application* of (4)—not the only method (see III below (*ad finem*, (A))—the distinction is actually inessential to the *defence* of (4). For we can recast Kripke's argument as follows: if individuals x and y in this world are identical, then anything in any other possible world which is identical with x will be identical with y. For if x is y there is no being identical with x without being identical with y.

This exceedingly simple argument is patently dependent upon cross-world identification of individuals. But Kripke's own version, wrapped up as it is in terms of rigid designation—designating one thing in all possible worlds—is no less dependent upon that. It may be objected that my material mode version of the argument is open to the objection that it comes without provision against the supposedly parallel argument (which Leibniz, and in our own time David Lewis, have found compelling, but it is surely unconvincing on a postulational view of possible worlds) that, if Caesar crosses the Rubicon in this world, then no individual in another possible world which fails to cross the Rubicon in that world is Caesar. Herein it may be said lies the advantage of Kripke's version in the formal mode. His version does not invite this parallel and builds it into the very definition of a rigid designator that it designates one and the same thing, if anything, in *every* possible world. But the advantage is illusory. For Kripke then faces the same question which I face. Only he faces it in the form: *are* there any rigid designators? Whether one faces this question or the material mode question which my version faces, the eventual answer to it will surely be found with the canons of possible world postulation. This is to say that it will reside in the answer to the question whether the correct rules for cross-identification of individuals debar the provision in another world of twins for what is one individual in this world.

The answer to that question is, I take it, this. I may frame the counterfactual supposition of individual x being F and G, and I may also frame the supposition of x's being F and *not* G. But there is no coherent way to turn these two suppositions into any *single* supposition about x which is their logical product. But that is what is involved for some value of G in providing x with twins in another world.

Mutatis mutandis this possible-worlds answer is available both for Kripke's argument and for my variant on his argument. The general problem of cross identification they have in common. But Kripke has done much to defuse that issue. Possible worlds are not things we discover or observe with a telescope. They are constructions which *we*, who entertain and explore the suppositions to which they correspond, *make for ourselves*. There is no more problem about identifying the individuals about which we are making suppositions than there is about identifying the properties and relations which enter into the supposition. Admittedly we are not free to construct *any* world we wish, and we cannot insert any individual we wish into any arbitrary role in any possible world we please. It is not open to us to construct the possible world in which Julius Caesar is a clay pipe or a paddle steamer or the number fifty-seven. But about this too Kripke has had plenty of illuminating things to say. The principal criticism I should myself urge against his stipulations is that they are actually too stringent (and that he exploits their stringency to derive improbably strong conclusions about how individuals must be). Or rather this is the criticism to which I should accord pre-eminence amongst criticisms *internal* to the possible world approach. About the possible world approach as a whole I feel so sceptical that I want in this and the next section to inquire to what extent theorem (4) can be rendered independent of that whole style of explication of modality. Although this must impede our progress to the mind-body problem, there is no substitute for a good understanding of (4) if it is to be *applied* anywhere.

I hope I am not in a minority of one in taking modality itself, and the question to which theorem (4) was meant to be the answer, markedly more seriously than possible worlds. Possible worlds are an algebraic device, I should claim, or nothing. But if a device is *all* they are then there should always be a way to dispense with them on any disputed point. Even if within the possible world system of thought Kripke's argument for (4) is unassailable, the real question is what argument one can find for (4) if he denies himself a conceptual apparatus with the expressive power of possible world talk. This is desirable anyway. But in debate with those who have found the formal argument for (4) flawed by opacity problems, it is nothing less than a precondition of not begging the question.

First I shall review an instructive failure at providing a more economical argument. In rejecting the rigid/non-rigid designator distinction as superfluous (and in rejecting as pernicious a use of the distinction which Kripke has not licensed, and which has become widespread in spite of Kripke's explicit caution against it) it[10] was never my intention to cast doubt upon the old and well established distinction between a proper name and a definite description, or upon Kripke's and others' condemnations of the favoured description theory of the sense of proper names. The view which he and I and many others have held of these it is for me most congenial to put as follows: The sense of a proper name simply consists in its having been assigned whatever reference it has been assigned.[11] To know the sense of n is to know to which entity n has been assigned, a single piece of knowledge which may be given in countless different ways by countless different descriptions. Any competent speaker who properly grasps a description or ostension given in such a context grasps it as leading him to the thing itself identified by the name of the thing. But then if we attach the name n_i to bearer b_i and the name n_j to bearer b_j (if the 'onus of match' here is on the sense not the reference) and if $b_i = b_j$ then, whether we wish it or not, the sense of n_i will be the same as the sense of n_j.

Now, the argument continues, consider the two propositions

10   Hesperus = Phosphorus
11   Hesperus = Hesperus

The sentences which express (10) and (11) are composed in

exactly the same way from expressions which have not only the same reference but also the same sense.[12] Given the established theoretical relation of sense and truth-grounds, it may be said that nothing which constituted the truth (or falsity) of (10), no fact, situation or state of affairs, could fall short of constituting the truth (or falsity) of (11). So whatever necessity (11) has, (10) must apparently have too. Perhaps it was something of this sort, a relatively austere argument and apparently innocent of possible worlds, which was really driving Kripke's argument through to its conclusion. But if so then that is sad. For there seems to be a real difficulty in the contention that 'nothing which constituted the truth (or falsity) of (11) could fall short of constituting the truth (or falsity) of (10)'. For everything hangs in this far from straightforward claim on a strict and special reading of 'constitute'. It should put one on one's guard, for instance, that it makes an important and quite puzzling difference if we switch from 'constitute the truth of' to 'probabilify'. What in any case justifies the idea that one can substitute even words with the same sense inside the square brackets within the context 'It is necessary that [Hesperus = Hesperus]'? Surely the paradox of analysis (like Benson Mates' observation that 'Nobody doubts that everybody believes that every Greek is a Hellene', need not have the same truth-value as 'Nobody doubts that everybody believes that every Greek is a Greek') must be sufficient discouragement of any easy acceptance of the idea that the intersubstituends' identity of sense guarantees intersubstitutibility of designations of the same thing within contexts not demonstrably extensional.

The suspicion is started that the argument for (4) does after all depend on some expressive power peculiar to possible world talk: that we cannot yet honestly claim that such talk is being used as a mere calculating device. It is time then to look again at the formal derivation of $(x=y) \supset (necessarily\ x=y)$.

I shall submit that there is only one clear way of interpreting (4)'s proof as sound; that this frees the question which (4) purports to answer from all designative or referential issues; and that, interpreting (4) as I shall suggest, anyone who accepts the genuinely *de re* modalities (to which speaking ordinary English already in my opinion commits us) must accept (4). The discussion will leave open the question whether *de re* modality itself can be explained otherwise than in terms of possible worlds (though I feel sure that it can and must be susceptible of an alternative style of clarification).

3 THE BARCAN–KRIPKE DERIVATION RE-EXAMINED

It is natural to begin a scrutiny of this with a look at the transition from (1) to (2). What kind of property is being *necessarily identical with x* (e.g. with Cicero)? In an earlier account of some of these matters[13] Kripke defined $\ulcorner \Box \phi a \urcorner$ to be true in the real world iff $\ulcorner \phi a \urcorner$ holds in every world which is possible relative to the real world. But this is not quite the same definition as he offers in 'Identity and Necessity', where he writes 'we can count statements as necessary if whenever the objects mentioned therein exist, the statement would be true'. I am not sure, but the change may have been made in order to distinguish clearly the *de re* from the *de dicto* occurrence of 'necessarily' and help defeat the problem of opacity. It may also be connected with a possible difficulty at step (3). I start with this difficulty.

It is not enough for the argument to appeal at (3) to a premiss $\Box (x)(x=x)$ which says: take whatever world w you will and take what individual x you will in that world, it holds in w that $x=x$. This is surely true, but scarcely the premiss the argument needs. What is needed is this: take any individual x you will then, whatever world w you pick, it holds that $x=x$ in world w. But the difficulty with that premiss is that many worlds lack many individuals which other worlds have. Kripke's response to this problem (p. 137) is as we have seen to make a ruling whose consequence for, e.g., $\Box (y=x)$ is that it shall mean that *wherever x and y exist, the statement that $y=x$ is true*. This secures (3) for him, but it only raises another problem about stops (1) and (2) of the Barcan argument. Is there any reason to think that, if it be explained so in terms of *statements*, '$\Box(\ldots = x)$' (or '*is necessarily identical with x*') stands for a genuine property?

Why for the purposes of the soundness of the argument should this matter, it may be asked? Richard Cartwright has shown why it matters in 'Identity and Substitutivity' (in the same volume as Kripke's 'Identity and Necessity'). It is not true that designations of the same thing are *everywhere* intersubstitutable. If steps (1) and (2) of the Barcan proof represented this idea then the proof would not be sound. What really is true is that *if $x = y$ then every property of x is a property of y*. Why, it may be asked, is even this true? Well, suppose there were terms t_1 and t_2 designating z, and there was a context of t_1, $\phi(t_1)$, and a context of t_2, $\phi(t_2)$ such that the first was true and the second false. Suppose, for the sake of the argument we are interested in, that the purported property—call it Q-is e.g. that property which the open sentence '... is necessarily identical with Cicero' stands for. Then Cartwright's way with scholars like E. J. Lemmon[14] who have wished, unlike Kripke, to allow this as a real attribute to Cicero and deny it to Tully, is to ask: How can there be some one thing (the thing identical with Cicero and with Tully) which both has and lacks Q? The question is unanswerable. That is why (1), or Leibniz' Law, properly understood, *must* be true. But now what about the credentials of Q itself and all like properties, considered as candidates in the context of the Barcan argument to be properties but *explained* à la Kripke? So explained, will they count as properties at all? The Kripkean explanation of '$Q(a)$' will be 'wherever a exists, the statement that a is Cicero is true'. Cartwright would press against such an attribute as Q, defined thus à la Kripke, the question 'Are we sure that Q is a well defined property?' For surely if there is no such thing as *the* statement that z is Cicero, Q is illegitimately defined by Kripke's method. And once this question is raised one sees immediately that there isn't any such thing as *the* statement to that effect.

Let us see what can be done to refurbish *being necessarily identical with Cicero* as a genuine property. This will make it possible to interpret (1) as relating to properties and restore the soundness and validity of the argument for (4). A device suggested by W. V. Quine for dealing with some apparent quantifications into opaque contexts[15] may prompt an elucidation of □ (z = Cicero) along these lines: the statement *about* z which says *of* z that it is identical with Cicero is true with respect to any world w containing z. The Cartwright point now reads: However clear and definite you make your choice of z, there is still no such thing as *the* statement to that effect. For there will be at least as many statements of the form '... = Cicero' as there are ways of referring to z. Someone might try saying that □ (z = Cicero) means that whatever world you pick, if z exists in that world, then *any* statement about z to the effect that z is Cicero is true with respect to that world. The trouble is, that isn't true. Consider the statement that the author of the line 'O fortunatam natam me consule Romam' is Cicero. This statement is not true with respect to the world in which Cicero is neither consul nor a self-congratulatory denouncer of Catiline. Here of course is where rigid designation may come in. Perhaps the best explanation of □ (z = Cicero) is then: whatever world you choose, if z is in that world, then *any statement made about z by means of rigid designators* and saying of z that it is identical with Cicero will be true with respect to that world.

This amendment appears to be reasonably faithful to Kripke's general style of explanation of *de re* necessity. Rigid designation has its uses after all. But, if this is what 'necessarily' is meant to mean as it figures at step (2), then what would have happened, if we had taken as a value for z something without any proper name (say the first silicon particle touched by me after alighting from a train at Temple Meads, Bristol, England, on July 5th, 1974)? Then since there *is* in fact no rigid designator for the thing, we reach the result that any statement about it saying of it by means of a rigid designator that this nameless thing is Cicero is true. For there is no such statement. Hence this or anything nameless is necessarily Cicero! Such difficulties are not always allowed to matter, but one may find them symptomatic of a blurring of the distinction between the *de re* and the *de dicto*.

Bear it in mind, throughout this argument about the Barcan derivation, that all I am trying to do is to defeat a certain kind of *explanation* of what 'necessarily' means as it figures in the explanation of the predicates standing for such properties as Q. *If* the explanation were accepted, then Q and its ilk wouldn't after all be well-defined properties.

If we look again at the amended definition of Q we shall see that all the troubles just rehearsed are gratuituous. They are gratuitous rather if only we may be allowed to abandon the enterprise of reducing the *de re* 'necessarily' to the *de dicto* 'necessarily'. The definition we have arrived at forces us to read the phrase 'about z' and 'saying of z', as Quine would say, transparently. Intersubstitution of identicals and existential generalization must be already guaranteed at this place. What then does all the other metalinguistic material, 'statement', 'rigid designator', etc., accomplish? Why not say 'a is necessarily Cicero' simply means 'a cannot help but be Cicero' or 'nothing can be a unless it is Cicero'? What could be more *de re* than that? These analyses do not eliminate modality in favour of something else. They are at best *elucidations* of what ordinary people already understand. They are that or nothing. But they do suffice to dispel the illusion that the relevant necessity is linguistic. (And in the same spirit, for the benefit of those who are lost without possible world talk, we may say: *nothing in any possible world is a unless it is Cicero*. We may speculate for a moment why Kripke did not say this. I have wondered whether it was because it makes the project of eliminating the possible-world theorists' quantifications over *all possible objects* seem even more difficult.)

If we say of a in this style that a must be Cicero what does the 'must' govern? It does not say that the sentence 'a is

Cicero' is true in every world possible relative to our world. No sentence of this form has the slightest chance of being true in every such world. It does not operate upon a sentence at all. I once suggested that what this sort of 'must' governed was not the sentence but its predicate.[16] If this were granted, then the transparency of the predicate *necessarily identical with* would follow immediately, together with the intersubstitutability of identicals and the accessibility of subject place(s) to the variables of quantification.

Freed of problems of opacity and of special pleading about rigid designation the argument for any substitution instance of (4) will then go as simply as this:

$a = b \supset (Fa \equiv Fb)$
a nec-is a
b nec-is a

And we shall be able to prove quite generally that if x and y have the relation *identical* then they have the relation *necessarily identical*.

(1) $(x)(y)((x=y) \supset (Fx \equiv Fy))$
(2λ) $(x)(y)((x=y) \supset ((x \text{ has } (\lambda z)[[\text{Nec}[\lambda r \lambda s[s=r]]], [x,z]])$
    $\equiv (y \text{ has}(\lambda z)[[\text{Nec } [\lambda r \lambda s[s=r]]], [x,z]]))$
(3λ) $(x) (x \text{ has } (\lambda z)[[\text{Nec}[\lambda r \lambda s\ [s=r]]], [x,z]])$
(4λ) $(x)(y)(x=y) \supset (y \text{ has } (\lambda z)[[\text{Nec}[\lambda r \lambda s[s=r]]], [x,z]])$

The importance of this derivation is that it is independent of problems either of opacity or of possible worlds. A defender of the latter might even use it, I suppose, to justify setting up an apparatus of possible worlds like Kripke's. Without it, however, he is begging the question against most people who doubt (4)—especially if he uses possible worlds in the usual manner to define 'necessarily $\phi(a)$'.

At this point we may perhaps venture a step further and conclude from the fact that a must be b that it is inconceivable (*de dicto*) that a should not be b. But in ascribing to the sentence 'a is b' (or to some conditionalized version of it) the property of having an inconceivable negation—if we take this step—we are not ascribing logical or strict analytical necessity to it. Nor is this inconceivability of the thought that $a \neq b$ what (4) itself claims. The *de dicto* inconceivability is a new and additional claim of a different sort *based*, securely or insecurely, upon (4). (Insecurely, I think, but this is not the place to enter upon that.)

There is hardly time or space to pursue here the questions which this point of view will force upon anybody who adopts it, but I shall briefly note several of the more obvious points.

(A) If the 'necessarily' in (4) modifies the '=' and only that, we may see our way to say quite bluntly (though quite ambiguously) that the first Postmaster General necessarily is the inventor of bifocals. To counter conflation with other readings of the sentence, or to deprecate the misunderstanding 'Do you mean that he couldn't help but invent bifocals?' we shall still need a scope distinction. But it relates only to the 'necessarily'. The scope of 'necessarily' is in fact even smaller now than that of □ on the Russell–Smullyan approach.

(B) An essentialist will assert not only that Hesperus is necessarily Phosphorus but also that Hesperus is necessarily a heavenly body; similarly, that Caesar is necessarily a man. The necessity the essentialist is concerned with is of a piece with that which occurred in (4). What is said here is:

16 $[\text{nec}(\lambda x)(\text{heavenly body } x)]$, [Hesperus]
17 $[\text{nec}(\lambda x)(\text{man } x)]$, [Cicero]

Anything that is Hesperus must be a heavenly body, and anything that is Cicero cannot help but be a man. I have explored the consequences and rationale of the resulting essentialism elsewhere.[17] It models the 'necessarily' of essentialist claims upon the transparent *de re* necessities of ordinary English. Byron could not help but limp, was able to swim the Hellespont, and at various times owed (had the obligation to repay) much money. Whatever necessities and capacities inhered in him inhered in him under any name or description of him—'the man who published in 1813 the *Bridge of Abydos*', 'the author of *Beppo*' or what you will. The chances of giving a plausible *de dicto* analysis of these things seem to me to be negligible. Let us see the *de re* necessity of essence then as the limiting case of of the other *de re* necessities which we are already stuck with. Suppose that all the various necessities and grades of necessity which we account as *de re*, nec-ϕ, nec-ψ ... are ordered in respect of their notional separability from their bearer, having regard to how easy or difficult it is to conceive of removing ϕ, ψ ... from the owner of the attribute. Then essentialist necessity arises at that limit where the removal of the feature in question is incompatible with the persistence of the bearer itself. Here, at this point, a feature is fixed to its bearer by virtue of being inherent in the very individuation of it. Within the province of *de re* modality the causally inflexible passes over at a certain threshold into a different inflexibility which is conceptual. If it is Cicero we are concerned to single out, then what we single out, if it is indeed Cicero, *must* be a man. *Being a man* is an individuative prerequiste, however things change, of any candidate for identity with Cicero actually *being* Cicero. It is a prerequisite in a way that being an orator—however great the upheaval in thinking of Cicero not as an orator—or bald, or vain, or a friend of Maecenas, or having any other merely qualitative characteristic is not. Similarly, once it is Tully we individuate and Cicero (who is the same as Tully) we individuate the things we individuate must on pain of eventual incoherence be the same.

(C) The view I have sketched of (4) will not, I am aware, be complete without the construction of a truth-predicate and definition of satisfaction for a language containing not only names, predicates and quantifiers, but also modifiers of one and two place predicates and open sentences of arbitrary truth functional and quantificational complexity. I have attempted to discharge this obligation in another place.[18]

4 THE PHILOSOPHICAL IMPLICATIONS OF THE MODAL THEOREM

Let us return now to the philosophical significance Kripke imputes to theorem (4). I believe that Kripke has thrown new light from an unexpected quarter upon an old dispute.[19] But I do not believe (4) has any Cartesian import.

The most important question perhaps about Kripke's argument relates to the contrast he makes between (6) and (7). But if there really is the radical difference Kripke finds between (6) and (7) then the grounds for thinking (6) true should be both better than, and importantly different from, those for thinking (7) true. The grounds for (6) get us all the way to (6), and having reached there we are then somehow borne forward to the conclusion that heat is necessarily molecular agitation. How, one wonders, do the grounds for (7) fall short of this standard? Why don't the grounds themselves, if they really are grounds for believing (7), carry us *the whole way* to the necessity? Kripke's statement of the difference between (6) and (7) invites the question in this form. But if my re-interpretation of (4) is correct then the question can be put another way. If we can find any grounds at all for '*n* is pain', then why can't we use these, with (4), to show that, contrary to what might have been supposed, *n necessarily-is* pain?

Here, evidently, and on either view, we must ask: What are the grounds for thinking (6) true? For our certainty that (6) is true may not be matched by any certainty about *why* it is true.

One argument which I piece together from Kripke himself for (6) is this:

8   Heat is the cause of the sensation of heat
9   Molecular agitation is the cause of the sensation of heat
∴   (6)

An argument like this may certainly supplement the scientific reductions of thermo-dynamics to statistical mechanics. (Cp. the argument—: Increase in heat is what causes metals to melt, increase in molecular agitation (mean kinetic energy) is what causes metals to melt, therefore (6).) The trouble is that here seems to be a parallel argument for materialism

10   pain is what affects us painfully
11   neural state n is what affects us painfully
∴   (7).

If this really is the situation, however, then any comment must begin by noting what Kripke does not point out, that on any description-theory both arguments are deductively valid. If they are sound as well, then theorem (4) already assures us that n necessarily-is pain.

Kripke finds an asymmetry between the rigidity of 'what affects us painfully' and the alleged non-rigidity of 'cause of the sensation of heat'. To imagine (11) failing is to imagine (7) failing because 'pain' and 'what affects us painfully' are both rigid and codesignative. They cannot come apart. Whereas, 'cause of the sensation of heat' being non-rigid, to imagine (9) failing is not in itself to imagine (6) failing. Very well. But the whole impact which the distinction between rigid and non-rigid designation can have on an argument is already registered completely in its translation by means of the theory of descriptions and so far as validity is concerned the arguments are on a level. So it seems that Kripke ought to find the conceivability of not-(7) reason to fault either the *truth* of (10) or the *truth* of (11) or the *univocality* of 'affect'. His argument and his method are seriously incomplete on this point, I feel. Matters are if anything even worse on the predicate-modifier view of *necessarily*. But rather than pursue this question further, I take up a prior point.

Kripke argues that, contrary to the argument (10) (11) ⊢ (7), we can readily imagine neural state n not being what affects us painfully. He writes 'The materialist has to show that these things we think we can see to be possible are in fact not possible ... that requires some very different philosophical argument from the sort which has been given in the case of heat and molecular notion. And it would have to be a deeper and subtler argument than has appeared in any materialist literature that I have read.' But perhaps we should not be intimidated by this dread challenge. Maybe a man is the final authority on what he can imagine. But the sincere claim to have imagined can scarcely demonstrate real conceivability. Maybe a man's imagining p holding at least shows that it is conceivable that it is conceivable that p. I don't know. But again the conceivability of the real conceivability of something is not the same as real conceivability (Indeed it is one of the achievments of Kripke's other work to have discouraged such conflations.)

So we must ask: Is it conceivable in the philosophically serious sense that n should fail to be what affects us painfully? Let us concede it to Kripke, at least for argument's sake, that if n need not affect us painfully than (7) is false—because pain *must* affect us painfully. This is not quite beyond argument because, as Ronald de Sousa has pointed out,[20] it is not excluded by Kripke's scheme, after his admirable distinction of necessity and a priority, that a proposition be contingent and yet *a priori*. But having mentioned it, let us leave on one side this other way to physicalism. Reverting to our question, let us note that the point of asking 'Could n fail to be what affects us so painfully?' is even clearer on the predicate-operator view of 'necessarily'. Consider the property of being what [i.e. the one thing which] necessarily affects us (in some specific way s) painfully. According to Kripke, this property applies to pain and not to n. So it may seem (7) must be false. But the difficulty is: are we really sure the property *doesn't* apply to n? (Note by the way that, on this approach, we can appeal to Leibniz' Law directly, instead of proceeding via (4).)

Here I think we need to know better what n is. If we are serious about what (10) and (11) mean then, because of the uniqueness implied by 'what affects us painfully', it is no trivial matter to identify even a candidate for n. Is it the state some man was in at a particular place and time—a universal presumably capable of having other instantiations? Or is it a particular event or process dated and logically tied to a particular time, place, agent and circumstance?

Take the second interpretation first. The event n recorded by (11), when, where and as it occurred, would then have to be the very event which affected the patient painfully, when and where and as that occurred. Might that event n, the neurophysiological event specified in terms of time, place, agent, causes and effects, *not* have been what affected the patient painfully? (An interpretation of this question which we presumably have to try to consider is: 'Does n affect him so in every possible world in which n exists?') Certainly, if this or that had been different (if the patient had been anaesthetized, say) then a blow similar to that which actually struck him might not have resulted in pain. But that would scarcely be the event n at all. Event n befell a man who was not anaesthetized: and whatever else may be essential or inessential to n, such causal features as this seem scarcely separable from anything with a claim to be n.[21] Or consider the event of the man's being hurt or affected painfully by pain. Would that very event really have happened without n's happening? There are interesting questions here into which I should have liked to enter of the symmetry or asymmetry of thing-individuation and event-individuation, but there is reason to think that Kripke's real concern is with the state interpretation.

The state interpretation of (7) leads to questions of equal difficulty. We are *only in business at all* with (7) if (11) is true. And (11) must if it is true serve to identify some single state n which is what affects us with the relevant specific painful sensation. For (11) actually to be true however, the neural state n will have to be something identified in terms which transcend such variations in circuitry, brain chemistry, or whatever as exist between all the creatures which are capable of experiencing the particular kind of pain in question. Suppose we so specify the state (very roughly) as *that functional state* n *of the central nervous system which accounts for the patient's tendency, while such and such state persists in consciousness, to avoid objects he*

believes to be responsible for initiating or aggravating the state.
What this specifies must, if (11) is to be true, and 'affect' be univocal, be something generic (rather than a determinate physiological state or specific brain-state peculiar to one class of patients). It must be what Putnam would call a *functional* state—not anyway a specific purely physicochemically characterized state.[22] In other words, n will be a state with a role specified in terms of the organisation of a whole system. Now Kripke says we can imagine (a) the state n existing even though there is no pain at all, and (b) the 'creature being in pain, but not being in any specified brain state at all . . . we can imagine definite circumstances under which this relationship would have been false. Now, if these circumstances are circumstances, we cannot deal with them simply by saying that this is just an illusion, something we can apparently imagine, but in fact cannot, in the way we erroneously thought that we could imagine a situation in which heat was not the motion of molecules.' But now that n is more accurately specified in terms of the whole nervous system and we know better what we are talking about, I ask the question again. Can we? It is not obvious that we really can.

What is the status of the specification I have given above for n. It is not intended as a synonym for 'pain', no more than 'the animal which I showed your child yesterday, by the entrance of the Zoo' is intended as a synonym of 'giraffe'. The specification is simply intended to enlarge upon what pain appears actually to be, and to home upon that state which, in the world as we have it, we ascribe to ourselves, to others, and to at least some animals. Rightly or wrongly we believe there is such a state. The issue between Kripke and myself is whether I have the right to use this kind of 'fix' upon pain and whether the state I try to pin down in this way, namely pain, is a physical state and a state of the central nervous system. I claim that it is and that, once we have picked it out for what it is, we shall find it hard to deny that it necessarily is. In a moment we shall inquire into what is implied by these claims, and into the concept of the 'physical'. Once this last is accomplished, we shall have transcended the curious situation which threatens—that I have to beg the question against Kripke and Kripke has to beg the question against me for us to debate the issue of pain at all.

I have pointed n in the direction of pain. Let us now point pain in the direction of n, and see if they will touch. Well, they will only touch if pain is essentially a state of the body, indeed of the central nervous system. Is it conceivable that pain should not be this? At least one historical philosopher has had a motive to attempt to describe pain without any reference to the body:[23]

> Again I had some reason for holding that the body I called 'my body' by a special title really did belong to me more than any other body did. I could never separate myself entirely from it, as I could from other bodies. All the appetites and emotions I had felt in the body and on its account. I felt pain, and the titillations of pleasure, in parts of this body, not of other, external bodies. Why should a sadness of the mind follow upon a sensation of pain, and a kind of happiness upon the titillation of sense? Why should that twitching of the stomach which I call hunger tell me that I must eat; and a dryness of the throat that I must drink; and so on? I could give no account of this except that nature taught me so, for there is no likeness at all, so far as I can see, between the twitching in the stomach and the volition to take food; or between the sensation of an object that gives me pain and the experience (cogitationem) of sadness that arises from the sensation.

Perhaps it is no accident that this comes from the *Meditation* which Kripke actually quotes. But what an extraordinary description this is of pain as a sadness of the mind. The translation is not at fault, however. This is what Descartes has to say to be consistent with his own view of the relation of body and mind. But how can one help but misdescribe pain if one leaves out the body?

It might be said on Kripke's behalf that I have pulled pain and state *n* together by redescribing *n* in terms which were not strictly neurophysiological or physicalistic at all. It was the materialists' mission to account completely for the world in terms of physics and chemistry;[24] and in the strict sense of 'physical' which is consonant with that programme *n* no longer resembles a physical state of an organism at all. Now this is an important contention and there is much I should want to concede to it, but it is scarcely a Cartesian or dualistic argument. I do not deny the desirability of defining a narrow sense of 'physical' and leaving the future of fundamental physical science to determine its exact extension. It seems right to doubt that in this sense *n* is physical. But there is an equally important sense in which *x is physical if an account of what x is necessarily involves matter*. And in this sense *n* is certainly physical. So, I think, is pain, like almost any mental attribute of feeling or perception. What is left after one subtracts these faculties is not enough to constitute any mind we have experience of.

This distinction of two senses of 'physical' is indispensable to anyone who wishes (as I do) to maintain that mental properties enjoy the relation of *supervenience* to the strictly (i.e. fundamental science) physical properties, even though in the other sense of 'physical' they are just one kind of matter-involving physical property.[25] The distinction of the two senses is equally fundamental to the formulation of a question which all supervenience-theorists must face in due course if they are to make themselves fully clear. Having dissociated himself from all attempts (as implausible in theory as comical in practice) to reduce mental attributes to (fundamental science) physical attributes, any supervenience theorist characteristically maintains that if A completely matches B in all of its physical properties then A must have any mental property that B has. Does this mean that if A matches B in all at least of its matter-involving properties *apart* from mental properties, then A will match B in all its mental properties too? Or does it mean something stronger—that if *A* matches *B* in all its fundamental science physical properties then *A* will match *B* in all its mental properties. A consistently motivated physicalist will maintain this too. But the claim provokes three questions. First, does the thesis need to be qualified to exempt the intentional aspect of certain mental properties? Second, is it consistent with the rationale of physicalism to enter such qualifications? Third, can the claim be defended as arising from any sort of conceptual necessity? I think the outcome under each head will be favourable to physicalism, but here I will only remark, about the third, that membership of a property in the class of physical in the sense of scientifically fundamental physical properties depends on the property's claim to be a member of the smallest set of properties needed to give a causal account of all the physical (matter-involving) phenomena to be encountered in reality. Note the distinctness and interdependence of the two ideas of the physical: and note that in this light we see that physics and chemistry (and neuro-physiology?) earn their preeminence by satisfying a requirement whose origin is nothing less than conceptual.

5 CONCLUSION

The main force of Kripke's attack was directed at the central state materialists, who have insisted on defending their thesis as a contingent one. They have insisted that *n need* not be pain or painful. Against them I think he brilliantly succeeds. But the outcome is not, I believe, to justify a position like Kripke's own, which seems sometimes to be even more Cartesian than the central state theorists', but to revive for consideration and refinement the claims of a much older thesis, which one might call conceptual materialism, namely the position of Thomas Hobbes. For Hobbes would appear to have held that all mutation *must* be motion[26], that any true subject of discourse must be a material object,[27] and that spiritual phenomena or divine apparitions, if real at all, must as a matter of conceptual necessity be 'subtile Bodies' or 'thin substances' and 'not Ghosts incorporeall, that is to say Ghosts that are in *no place*; that is to say are *no where*; that is to say, that seeming to be somewhat, are nothing.'[28]

NOTES

1. See 'Identity and Necessity' in Milton K. Munitz (ed.) *Identity and Individuation* (NYU, 1971) which I have supplemented at some points from 'Naming and Necessity' in *Semantics of Natural Languages* (eds. Harman and Davidson) Dordrecht, 1971. The latter (see especially footnote 77, presumably written some time after 'Identity and Necessity') suggests the need for caution, greater than perhaps I have exercised, in ascribing any positively Cartesian position to Kripke.
2. Including long ago the present writer. Since Kripke has fixed on him as hostage, I yield to the temptation to declare that before the article Kripke cites ('Identity Statements' in *Analytical Philosophy, Second Series* ed. R. J. Butler, Oxford, Blackwell, 1965) emerged from the press in 1965 the acts of writing down and defending the view disenchanted the writer with almost every aspect of it. Explicitly it was recanted in *Identity and Spatio-Temporal Continuity* footnote 7. An alternative view was sketched in "Sentence-Sense, Word-Sense, and Difference of Word-Sense' in Jacobovits and Steinberg (edd.) *Semantics* (C.U.P., 1971), note (b) p. 16—a view of the matter partly formed by reflection on Geach's remarks at the end of the chapter on Frege in P. T. Geach and G. E. M. Anscombe, *Three*

124 *Identity, Necessity and Physicalism*

    Philosophers (Blackwell, Oxford, 1969); see also *Reference and Generality*. Cornell, 1962, pp. 133ff.
3. Cp. Kripke, op. cit., p. 137, 'Let us interpret necessity here weakly. We can count statements as necessary if whenever the objects mentioned therein exist, the statement would be true.'
4. 'If we substitute these descriptions for the universal quantifiers in (4) the only consequences we will draw [from (4)] is that there is an object x such that x invented bifocals, and (as a matter of contingent fact) an object y such that y is first Postmaster General of the U.S., and, finally, it is necessary that x is y. What are x and y here? Here x and y are both Benjamin Franklin and it can certainly be necessary that Benjamin Franklin is identical with himself. So there is no problem if we accept Russell's notion of scope.... That Russell's distinction of scope eliminates modal paradoxes has been pointed out by many logicians, especially Smullyan.' Kripke refers here to A. Smullyan in *J.S.L.*, 1947, reprinted at p. 35 in *Reference and Modality* (ed. L. Linsky, O.U.P., 1971). In this connection note also Cartwright's 'Remarks on Essentialism' in *J. Phil.*, 1968.
5. *Foundations of Mathematics*, pp. 59–60.
6. See *Boston Studies in the Philosophy of Science* (N.Y., 1963) pp. 71ff. and *J.S.L.* vol. XII (1947), p. 15.
7. Page 155 foll.
8. Or conceivably some conditionalized variant upon ⌜ϕ⌝ holding true. But this is not manifestly the same idea as the one quoted at footnote (3). Let me stress that, in the absence of Kripkean formal semantics for contexts containing both □ and proper names, I am forced to put more emphasis on this p. 137 quotation than would otherwise be fair. But in the circumstances there is no alternative recourse.
9. This is how Kripke himself wants to see (4). See op. cit., page 138. But he adds 'But from statement (4) one may apparently be able to deduce [that] various *particular*

statements of identity must be necessary' (my italics). On the account of 'necessarily' to be presented here it is dubious that the necessity of any *statements* will be strictly logically deducible.

10. Namely the still mysterious idea that a given definite description may occur sometimes rigidly, sometimes non-rigidly. See 'Identity and Necessity' page 149, footnote 10. Nobody has ever provided satisfactory distinct sets of *truth* conditions for the 'two uses of definite descriptions'. My own erstwhile attempt in 'Identity Statements', op. cit., is pragmatical not semantical in character. Donnellan's subsequent attempt to differentiate the truth-conditions (in 'Reference and Definite Descriptions', *Phil. Review* 75 (1966), pp. 281–304) depends on the surely incredible idea that if I say 'the man drinking champagne is F' and the man I mean, although drinking water, is F, then *what I say is true*. (To say that the idea is not credible is not to say that F is not *true of* the man I mean.) When modalities combine with definite description ambiguity is normal, but can be completely accounted for by scope distinctions. The rigid/non rigid, referential/attributive distinctions are superfluous.

11. Cp. my 'Identity Statements', p. 58, op. cit. and G. E. M. Anscombe, *Introduction to Wittgenstein's Tractatus* (Ch. on Theory of Descriptions), London, 1959. See also Frege's *Nachgelassene Schriften*, p. 133 (Felix Meinter, Hamburg 1969), and his explanation of how '$\mu\omega\lambda\upsilon$' and 'Nausicaa', in the absence of any reference for them, have their sense. 'Nausicaa' gets a sense for itself by behaving *as if* it named some girl. Applying this to the case where there is reference as well as sense we arrive at something akin to the contention about proper names in the text. 'Tully' gets its sense by naming Tully.

Kripke himself claims that genuine proper names have *no* sense; but if the sense of an expression is what Frege claimed it to be, viz, the contribution the expression makes to the truth-grounds of sentences in which it occurs (Cp. Frege *Grundgesetze*, I. 32 quoted and commented upon at p. 17 of my 'Sentence-Sense, Word-Sense, and Difference of Word-Sense', op. cit.) then this must be an unfortunate way of putting his point—just as unfortunate as his tendency to equate Millian connotation with Fregean sense. Mill's and Frege's respective explanations of these are different and the applications coincide extremely poorly. Consider the case of predicates for instance. The denotation of 'white' is for Mill the class of white things. This is neither the Fregean sense nor the Fregean reference of 'white'. The reference of 'white' is for Frege the concept of *white* or *what it is to be white*. Since the only thing in Mill's scheme which is remotely like this is whiteness and since whiteness is what Mill counted *the connotation* of 'white', the only possible correlation one could find between Frege's doctrine and Mill's would be an equivalence of connotation and reference, not denotation and reference.

12. We need not quantify over senses, still less propositions, here. We may say (10) and (11) and their constituent expressions match arbitrarily closely in sense, where sense is conceived simply as a property with which language users invest expressions. The same remark applies *mutatis mutandis* to all uses of the word 'sense' in the present article.

13. 'Semantical Considerations on Modal Logic', *Acta Philosophica Fennica* (1963) reprinted in Linsky, *Reference and Modality*, O.U.P.

14. 'A Theory of Attributes Based on Modal Logic', *Acta Philosophica Fennica* (1963). Cp. Richard Montague and Donald Kalish, 'That', *Philosophical Studies*, 10 (1959).

15. 'Quantifiers and Propositional Attitudes' in Linsky, op. cit.

16. Cp. My *Identity* (1967), op. cit. Part III, 3.2 (ii) (old edition) 'although my conclusions (e.g. Dvii) reinstate some *de re* modalities of the form $\Box fa$ where f is a substance

sortal, they do nothing to suggest that the correct way of generalizing such is the mysterious $\Box[(\exists x)(f(x))]$—which would presumably have the mysterious consequence that this was ontologically the poorest of all possible worlds— rather than $(\exists x)(\Box f(x))$'. What may have been wrong with this was to have used $\Box$ instead of a distinct predicate-modifier *nec*. The relation of the two signs, and the possibility of defining $\Box$ in terms of *nec*, is a matter for independent investigation.

For related contentions see P. T. Geach *Logic Matters*, p. 174, the reprint of an article originally published in Polish in *Ksiega Pamiatkowa ku czi Kota-rbinskiego*. (Państwowe Wydawnictwo Naukowe, Warsaw, 1967.) Cartwright also gestured in this general direction in another article in 1968 when he remarked that Smullyan's method of treating modality with definite descriptions could not be expected to distinguish every ambiguity in the scope of 'necessarily'. (See 'Some Remarks on Essentialism', *J. Phil.*, 1968.) See also R. Stalnaker and R. Thomason "Abstraction in First Order Modal Logic", *Theoria*, 3, 1968.

17. Cp. 'Continuity, Identity and Essentialism', op. cit.
18. Cp. 'The *De Re* "Must"': a note', op. cit.
19. On which see David K. Lewis, 'An argument for the identity theory', *J. Phil*, LXIII (1965), and Donald Davidson in 'Mental Events' in *Experience and Theory*, ed. Foster and Swanson (U. Mass., 1971).
20. *Canadian Journal of Philosophy*, 1973-4, reviewing Kripke's 'Naming and Necessity'.
21. See Donald Davidson 'The Individuation of Events' in Rescher (ed.) *Essays in Honour of C. G. Hempel* (Reidel, Dordrecht 1969), 'Casual Relations' in *J. Phil.*, November 1967, pp. 692-3. I think the way that these leave the situation is that the only plausible criterion of identity for events capable of doing what a criterion of identity must do, is a criterion which makes their identity

part and parcel of their proximate causes and effects. So much does not commit one who uses the argument in the text above to the stronger conclusion that every fact about an event, its exact spatio-temporal position, the clothing worn by the participants etc., is essential to it.

22. Hilary Putnam 'Psychological Predicates' in *Art Mind and Religion* (Capitan and Merrill, eds.) Pittsburgh 1967; 'Minds and Machines', in *Dimensions of Mind*, S. Hook (New York, 1960); 'Brains and Behavior', in *Analytical Philosophy* Second Series ed. R. Butler (Oxford, 1965); 'The Mental Life of Some Machines', in *Intentionality, Minds, and Perceptions*, ed. H. N. Castañeda (Detroit, 1966); 'Robots: Machines or Artificially Created Life?', *Journal of Philosophy*, LXI, 21 (12 Dec. 1964), pp. 668–91. See also the review by David K. Lewis in *J. Phil.*, LXVI, 1969, p. 23. I side here with Putnam against Lewis on the issue whether pain can be both a neurophysiologically specified brain state and also a functionally specified physical state. *If* different particular brain states $B_i \ldots B_k$ realize pain in different creatures, and *if* pain is some state in which all these creatures share, then (by transitivity) '$B_i \neq B_j$' precludes 'B_i = pain and B_j = pain'. It cannot help to say in reaction to this that then B_i = human-pain, and B_j = dolphin-pain. If we really believe that there is a pain humans and dolphins share—something generic or universal that both species can have—then human pain is the *same* pain as dolphin pain. But then if human pain were a neurophysiologically determinate state B_i, human pain would have to be the same neurophysiologically determinate brain state as B_j. (See my *Identity*, op. cit., pp. 3.4.) But *ex hypothesi* $B_i \neq B_j$. If pain is as universal as we suppose then its realization by B_i and B_j must not be confused with its instantiation by B_i and B_j. In the use I have made of Putnam's ideas here, more hangs on what the functional thesis denies than on what it asserts about the strength of the analogy between men and machines. The principal

force of using it for purposes of my argument is to flesh out the *generic* versus *specific* distinction.

After the Bristol conference William G. Lycan's useful 'Mental States and Putnam's functionalist hypothesis', *Australasian Journal of Philosophy*, vol. 52, No. 1 1974) came to notice. The author ably distinguishes the functionalist theory from Armstrong's and others' identity theories, and usefully clarifies Putnam's doctrine as (in effect) the doctrine that pain is a particular logical (functional) state of a physical object O, where O realizes an *abstract* machine. By the last Lycan means that O realizes a *kind* of machine, where kinds of machine are specified by something analogous to a Turing machine table. The logical (functional) state in question is the physical correlate in O of the relevant logical state Pain of the abstract machine which O realizes (belongs to). He concludes that nothing precludes the identification (equation) of the particular functional state pain of the physical object with that physical state of O which *realizes* Pain. He maintains that *realizing* and *identity* no longer need to be distinguished so far as concerns the relation between the neurophysiologically specific brain state of the particular person O and the state of pain in person O. This contention has two aspects: (i) that pain is something physical, (ii) that the physical thing that pain is in any particular case is the brain state which realizes Pain.

(i) is surely true and this is brought out very clearly and quite independently by the analysis of 'physical' which I have attempted in the text. For pain is matter- or body-involving, even if it cannot be characterized in full generality in purely science of matter (neurophysiological) terms. Nothing prevents a state being both functional in Putnam's sense and physical in the matter involving sense.

(ii) I still reject. Lycan writes (p. 56), 'A logical state of a PTM (physical Turing machine) is a physical state, and the adding machine [which has had one component replaced with another component which does the same job] is now in a numerically and qualitatively different physical state, even though the new state has at least one crucial thing in common with the old one (viz. realizing the same logical state of the same abstract Turing machine), and even though the adding machine continues to obey the same machine table. Here is a parallel case: consider the state of my having on a red hat. I take off my fireman's hat and put on a bell-hop's hat. I am no longer in the state of having on a fireman's hat, but I am still in a state of having on a red hat. *It does not follow, however, that my state of having on a red hat was not the same state as that of my having on a fireman's hat, unless this last means just that the two states are not necessarily or logically the same*, which is true; my earlier state of having on a red hat was not numerically identical with my present state of having on a bell-hop's hat.' (My italics.)

There is no reason to reject the analogy; but there is some reason to doubt what Lycan says about the analogue itself (and not only for reasons having to do with the dubious point about necessity at the end of the italicized portion.) If slipping on the bell hop's red hat even as the fireman's hat comes off maintains or simply renews the state of being *red-hatted* (wearing a red hat of any shade) then there is some one state, viz., being red hatted, which survives the change of headgear. Lycan writes 'a state of having on a red hat' but it is *the* state of being red hatted. Since wearing the fireman's red hat (and being *vermilion red*-hatted say) did not survive the change of headgear we can only conclude that this state of wearing a fireman's hat is not numerically the same state as that of being simply red-hatted. For this last state *was* sustained. Lycan begs off the task of exploring the ontology of states (p. 50), but if we take them seriously there will inevitably be a lot of them. For it seems that (whether states are particulars, whether states are universals, whether some states are particular and some states are universal, or whether states subtly undercut all such distinctions—nobody knows) the state of being simply red hatted and the state of wearing a fireman's hat are, even with respect to a man who is actually wearing a fireman's hat, to be distinguished. Both are physical states in my second sense of physical—but one is extremely unspecific. (Similarly a man or woman could be addicted to the state of being continuously married without necessarily being against divorce. In a few years' time reform may carry us to the point where he or she may be able to complete a divorce and marry at the stroke of a pen. With the help of carbon paper between relevant documents he or she will be able to change spouses without for one moment jeopardizing continuity of marriedness. It seems we must distinguish, as states in one person, between *being married to someone* and the less indeterminate state of *being married to Y*.)

23. Descartes, *Meditations*, VI, pp. 112 and 113 in P. T. Geach and G. E. M. Anscombe (translators) *Descartes: Philosophical Writings* (Nelson, London and New York, 1954).
24. Cp. B. A. W. Russell, Introduction to Lange's *History of Materialism* (Routledge & Kegan Paul, 1925) 'The two dogmas which constitute materialism are: First the sole reality of matter; secondly the reign of law.'
25. On supervenience and mental properties see (1) Donald Davidson 'Mental Events' in Foster and Swanson (eds.) *Experience and Theory* Amherst, MA, University of Amherst Press, 1970; (2) Paul Ziff, 'The Simplicity of Other Minds' in *J. Phil.*, vol. LXII, No. 20 (21 October 1965) especially page 576 (=page 169 of the reprinted version in Ziff's *Philosophic Turnings*, Ithaca, N.Y., Cornell University Press, 1956).
26. A kind of transcendental demonstration that all mutation is motion is offered at *De Corpore*, 9.9, depending only upon the causal cum representative theory of perception.
27. The preeminence of body is built into Hobbes' fourfold

distinction of *bodies, accidents, phantasms* and *names,* and his reductivist approach to the abstract. His whole philosophy of logic requires that the subject of Descartes' verb 'cogito' belong to the category of body. Cp. *Second Objection* to Descartes *Meditations* '... from this [the cogito] it seems to follow that a conscious being is something corporeal; for the subject of all acts seems to be conceived only in terms of body or matter.'

28. *Leviathan*, Part 3, Chapter 34, 'Of the significance of SPIRIT, ANGEL and INSPIRATION in the books of Holy Scripture'. Cp. Fifth and Fourteenth *Objections* (op. cit.) ad init., and Fourth *Objection* ad fin.

Comment

BY RUTH BARCAN MARCUS

In his paper Professor Wiggins discusses the principle that identicals are necessarily identical and some of the uses to which that principle has been put by Saul Kripke. That principle seems intuitively obvious to me for if the notion of necessity makes any sense, what could be more obvious than that necessarily a thing is the same as itself, *de dicto, de re,* or any way you choose. That it fell out as a theorem

$$\text{(NI)} \quad (x)(y)((x=y) \supset \Box(x=y))$$

in my axiomatic treatment of quantified modal logic with identity introduced in a Russellian way was not a reason for taking it as true.[1] Some found it a reason for rejecting that formalization or indeed any formalization of quantified modal logic. There are of course formal systems of quantified modal logic in which the principle fails in its unconstrained version.[2]

That it fell out as a theorem, along with metatheorems which constrain intersubstitutions within the scope of modal operators suggested that such formalizations would be useful in clarifying our notions of necessity. There remained at that time, other more controversial modal principles, such as: If possibly necessary *P* then necessary *P* and subsequent work in modal logic and semantics gave us a way of rationally debating such questions.[3]

But the thesis about identity and necessity was not obvious to others and there seemed to be a surfeit of counterexamples. We all know that discussing those counterexamples is like being caught in a revolving door. It engenders that feeling of helplessness which must have been Euthyphro's when he complained that the arguments seemed to turn round and walk away.

Before proceeding to some of the questions about the principle raised by Professor Wiggins it will be useful to present Kripke's account by way of the familiar counterexamples, or to be cautious, my interpretation of that account. Sort the counterexamples into two kinds: (1) Clearly contingent statements that *seem* also to be categorical statements of an identity such as 'The evening star is the morning star.' (2) Categorical identity statements that seem also to be contingent like 'Hesperus is Phosphorus.' With respect to cases of the first kind, contingencies that appear to be categorical identities, analysis shows them not to be categorical identity statements. There are at the outset ambiguities to be resolved. Am I saying about a specific thing, Hesperus, that it is both a first star of the morning and a first star of the evening or am I saying that there is a unique something which is both evening star and morning star and so on. The two mentioned alternatives do not exhaust the ambiguities, but what counts is that for each of the alternatives into which it can be disambiguated and still preserve its obvious contingency, we will no longer have a categorical identity statement. Whether the choice is the theory of descriptions or analyzing the descriptive phrase using abstraction, the identity sign will be flanked by variables or proper names and a component of the form '$(x=y)$' may be replaced by '$\Box\,(x=y)$' without going from truths to falsehoods. The analysis may contain weaker equivalences but since they are not identities the theorem doesn't apply. A source of the difficulty in such cases of the first sort, contingencies that look like fully analyzed identities, is that we often, in indicating which object it is we want to say something about, use expressions (as Kripke puts it) to fix the reference which at the same time describe the object mentioned and sometimes even incorrectly describe it. We need a way in language of sorting a thing from its properties so that we may entertain the possibility of its not having this or that property. Proper names serve this purpose. Nor need we know of any set of properties other than trivial ones which uniquely characterize the object in order to correctly use a proper name. Proper names are a way of mentioning an object without a commitment to any of its properties excluding trivial ones. The baffling question of how in the absence of direct encounter a speaker can so use a proper name has been illuminated by causal or historical accounts.[4] Quoting Professor Geach, 'For the use of a word as a proper name there must in the first instance be someone acquainted with the object named. . . . But language is an institution. . . ; and the use of a name for a given object . . . like other features of the language can be handed on from one generation to another; . . . Plato knew Socrates, and Aristotle knew Plato, and Theophrastus knew Aristotle, and so on in apostolic succession to our own times.' It appears therefore that for the analysis of counterexamples the distinction between proper names and other modes of fixing reference is central. Kripke will later enlarge the substitution class of individual variables to include those definite descriptions which, like proper names, are indifferent to scope even in modal contexts. He will also include higher order designators which share such properties under the more general classification of rigid designator.

It remains to say of the first kind of counterexample like

'The evening star is the morning star,' that of the several alternatives for disambiguation, one of them is where the descriptions are being used *as* proper names. One imagines someone saying, "Yes, I know it's not a star but let's call it 'The Evening Star' anyway." Capitalization is a practice for marking such use. But in that case, the example would be a counterexample of the second kind. A categorical identity statement which *seems* to be contingent.

Turning to counterexamples of the second kind, consider 'Hesperus = Phosphorus'. It is an unambiguous identity statement requiring no further analysis yet its truth was empirically determined. We have come to believe that where the determination of the truth of a proposition is empirical it is *a posteriori* and hence contingent, so it cannot be necessary. Here Kripke proposes that we distinguish the way in which a truth is determined from the kind of truth it is. Keeping in mind the distinction, he argues as follows: If 'Hesperus is Phosphorus' is contingent, its denial must be possible, and possible relative to this world with its linguistic and scientific practice. It is true that before the determination of that identity it was *conceivable* that two objects were named but conceivability is also an epistemological characterization to be classified with knowable, believable and the like. Once the identity is discovered, the statement that Hesperus is Phosphorus says no more or less than that Hesperus is Hesperus and if we do not balk at the necessity of the latter we shouldn't balk at the necessity of the former. To persist with an argument like the following: granted that in this world Hesperus is Phosphorus; but there might be another world, perhaps like ours and even containing Hesperus but it has another object, the morning star which is Phosphorus, so it is possible that Hesperus isn't Phosphorus, is to be confused about possibility. Kripke reminds us that possibility is relative to our world including the totality of its linguistic and scientific practice. For an object to be Phosphorus, the Phosphorus of our world, it has to be that very thing in any other world. Otherwise it would be a case of calling something else by the same name. So, if it is a true identity in this world it will be true for that very same object in all worlds in which it exists. Hence it is necessary.

I find the analysis illuminating and productive. I'll cite an example. It suggests a straightforward and plausible analysis of the notion of conceivable. What is conceivable is relative to what is known and what is known, both individually and collectively, may vary with time. We might say for some proposition P, that P is conceivable at a given time if it is consistent with known necessary truths at that time. Relative to individual or collective knowledge, this defines a notion of individual or collective conceivability that seems to fit our philosophic usage. Only after the discovery that Hesperus was Phosphorus did its denial contradict a known necessary truth. Similarly, the truth or falsity of a mathematical conjecture are both conceivable for so far as we know neither contradicts a known necessary truth yet neither it nor its denial is contingent. What is possible is conceivable, but not conversely.

It does seem to me that Kripke has got us through the revolving door at least so long as we stay with concrete well defined objects like planets which can be properly named in familiar ways. When he extends his claims to abstract individuals like numbers which somehow also acquire proper names, and to higher order objects and identities like 'Heat is the motion of molecules', 'Water is H_2O', 'Being in pain at time t is being in neural state n at time t'', where there is only an analogue of naming, in *those* cases the arguments are not quite as clear or persuasive—or at the least, need elucidating.

1. In his first section Wiggins raises the following question about the extended application of the principle (NI). He says that Kripke's whole argument about identities being necessary is made to seem to depend on the idea that true identity statements of a certain class are necessarily true *if and only if* rigid designators flank the '=' sign. But Wiggins asks, is the principle a claim about rigid designators at all? It just

says that whatever x may be and whatever y may be if x is y then necessarily x is y. The distinction Wiggins claims, is actually inessential to the principle.

I do not believe that the theory of rigid designators is being used to defend the principle. In the putative counterexamples we have been discussing it does turn out that rigid designators flank the identity sign. But when we are dealing with higher order objects like Water and Heat and Man and Pain there is no excluding '=' signs even after analysis which are not flanked by rigid designators as in the case of 'Husband=married male'. The importance of the role of rigid designators is in explaining how what appear to be contingent identities turn out to be necessary. Kripke is very sketchy and often obscure on the issue and I'd like to flesh out the background theory as I see it. There are says Kripke nouns like 'Water', 'Heat', 'H_2O' which share important features with proper names. They don't pick out the very same individual in all worlds in which that individual exists but they pick out either the same set or, where the sets are not coextensive, the absent objects are those that don't exist in that world. In the case of Hesperus we started with that object in this world and the name picked out that individual in all circumstances in which it existed at all. In the case of water, it isn't just our water that gets picked out, for that may not even exist in other worlds. It is whatever we would call water if it existed in ours. With Hesperus we have the very thing before us as the paradigm. In the case of water our paradigm is a *sample* of the stuff. We name that stuff water although at the time of naming we may be ignorant of many of its properties, even its essential ones. There might as in Putnam's twin earth examples[5] be another world which was just like ours which had a transparent fluid wherever we had water and everything they knew or believed about it we knew or believed about water. They may even speak our language and call it 'water' but it wouldn't be water unless it was that very same stuff. The apparent contingency of Hesperus having the property of being identical with Phosphorus comes from confusing contingency with empirical determination. Similarly the apparent contingency of a *sample* of stuff being water is that I must first determine empirically that it is water. There remains nevertheless an important difference between the two cases. When I discover empirically that Hesperus is Phosphorus what I have discovered is already an identity. What the criteria were for that determination is a separate question. No further move is required for us to identify Hesperus and Phosphorus. But suppose I discover in this world that anything is water just in case it is H_2O. We have a generalization over a material equivalence

1   $(x)\,(\text{Water}(x) \equiv H_2O(x))$.

As it stands it does not justify identifying water with H_2O any more than a material equivalence would justify identifying man with featherless biped. What is supposed to justify going from (1) to

2   $W = H_2O$

is that 'W' and 'H_2O' are rigid designators. Behind that claim lies a modal argument. But first we have to characterize a rigid designator. What it seems to designate is an essential property; a property which if something has it, it has it necessarily, whatever the world it is in. Suppose we characterize the rigidity of 'H' as follows:

3   $\Box(x)(Hx \supset \Box(y)((y=x) \supset Hy))$.

If we take the 'H' in (3) as naming H_2O and say the same for water

4   $\Box(x)(Wx \supset \Box(y))((y=x) \supset Wy))$.

Then in conjunction with the scientific discovery that samples of water are H_2O and conversely, it's going to follow (but only in a system at least as strong as S_5, which tells us something about these metaphysical necessities) that

5   $\Box(x)\Box(Hx \equiv Wx)$.

Consequently it is going to be the case that

6   $(x)(Hx \equiv Wx) \supset \Box(x)\Box(Hx \equiv Wx)$.

Now (6) looks very much like the principle about identities being necessary with the same perplexities. A seeming contingency appears after all to be necessary. Still it isn't an identity. But we might adopt

7   $\Box(x)\Box(Hx \equiv Wx)$

as a *criterion* for identity of higher order objects like H and W. It is a reasonable criterion and some have proposed it. So part of Wiggins' claim is justified. The rigid designators are required not to establish the principle but to establish the identity. Having done that, as we did more directly with Hesperus and Phosphorus, the principle (NI) will apply without riders about rigid designators. But Wiggins says something more. He says that Kripke claims the identity statements seem to be true *if and* only if rigid designators flank the identity sign. Kripke is obscure on this point which presents a special problem for designators of higher order objects. If it is to be allowed that 'husband = married male' is a true identity statement it would appear that rigid designators need not flank an identity sign unless of course the domains of possible worlds includes not only such individuals as are or might be husbands but abstract objects like husbandhood. Such a presumption is clearly not in the letter, or even the spirit, of possible world semantics. An identity like 'husband = married male' is conventionally established. It is if you like *a priori*, necessary, and satisfies (7). But it is with respect to the identities we *discover*, like water being H_2O, that the rigidity of the designators is crucial.

Let us elaborate against the background of Kripke's modal semantics. What are those objects associated with propositional functions, those higher order things we call attributes or universals? Well, the semantics is very extensional and quite impoverished. Those abstract entities, the universals, may be seen as sets of world indexed sets of individuals. There are some, corresponding to essential properties, i.e. kinds, species, substances, which may be characterized as follows: the world indexed sets are coextensive, modified by the rider about existence. More specifically P is such a property just in case Pw_i and Pw_j fail to be coextensive only if members of Pw_i which are not members of Pw_j are not in the domain of w_j. When we discover non-trivial essential properties we may, given the facts, discover identities which go beyond clearly *a priori* ones established by convention. Furthermore, given that they are identities, they are so necessarily. And that is how we go from such mundane truths of this world like something (some sample) being water just in case it is H_2O to necessarily water and H_2O are identical. In any case that is my version of the Kripke story.

One of my difficulties with the analysis (nor is it the only one) is deciding when some sign is in fact a rigid designator. We are supposed to perform a thought experiment. Someone named a certain sample of a certain substance 'Water'. That sample is the paradigm of that stuff. If something is water then it is so necessarily for otherwise it wouldn't be the same stuff as the original sample. Furthermore anything in any other world, if it is water, is also the same stuff and necessarily water. Otherwise it would be something that was just called 'Water'. So 'Water' is a rigid designator. But what of abstract objects like numbers. Where is the paradigm, or the object. I also find the thought experiment difficult when we move from *substances* like gold and water to *states* like heat and motion of molecules and pain. But a discussion of that would not be commentary on Mr. Wiggins' paper.

2. In his second section Professor Wiggins raises questions about the legitimacy of the proof of the necessity of identity statements (NI). The proof, as I originally stated it, did use abstraction and he wants to question the legitimacy of taking

the abstract as denoting a genuine property. Now Cartwright is correct when he says you can't take any old sentence in English and replace any old singular term with a variable and place a capped variable or lambda operator in front and get yourself a predicate which denotes the very property that was being ascribed to the object. Try it for example with 'Giorgione was so called because of his size.' If you want to use abstraction you've got to get the property out of the subject before it will work for you. And the same is true not just for abstraction, but the principle of substitutivity of identicals and just about any other logical principle. That's the sort of thing we do when we put sentences into logical form, or if they are ambiguous sentences, we put each of the disambiguating alternatives into logical form. But I see no reason why the abstract formed from '$\Box(\text{Cicero} = \text{Tully})$'

8 $\quad \hat{x} \Box (x = \text{Tully})$

isn't the most straightforward of properties. It is the property of being necessarily identical with Tully. And furthermore whatever the circumstance, it is only Tully who has that property.

Against the background of modal semantics, where a property is a function which takes an individual as argument and a proposition as value, or what comes to the same thing, a possible world as argument and a set of individuals as value, the property represented by (8) will take a unit set as value in each world where Tully exists, and (this is where the necessity comes in) the member of each set will be Tully himself, or, identically, Cicero. The same cannot be said for the property of being the author of the line 'O fortunatam . . .'; it is simply a different property, for its extension may vary from world to world even in worlds where Tully exists. No theory of rigid designators is needed to legitimize either property. But we do give an account of why, if two designators are rigid and pick out the same object in this world, then they are intersubstitutible up to and including what Kripke calls metaphysical contexts.

Now it is true that the strong extensionality of modal semantics generates a lot of funny properties. Pick any old set of individuals in each world and taken together they constitute a property. But those are not the properties Wiggins is regarding with suspicion.

It does seem to me that Wiggins has misunderstood the whole notion of rigid designators for he then goes on to say that if we do not have a rigid designator for an object any statement that that very thing is identical with Cicero will be true or alternatively, that it will be necessarily true that anything nameless will be identical with Cicero. Not so. Cicero and only he is necessarily identical with Cicero even if he had remained nameless. As it turns out, conveniently for philosophers, he has two names.

Incidentally, and as an aside, if Wiggins did in fact encounter a first silicon particle after alighting from the train at Temple Meads, he could name it that and mark the use with capitals. He could then say of that thing, using its name, that it might not have been in the vicinity of Temple Meads. If by encountering it he really meant that he picked out some very well defined particular particle which he is describing in that way, then using the name he could even say without contradiction that 'The First Silicon Particle Encountered By Wiggins Alighting From Temple Meads Station in July 1974 isn't made of silicon.' He could certainly say that it wasn't identical to Cicero.

3. I'll now turn to some comments on the third part of Wiggins' paper with which I largely agree. It does not seem that Kripke's arguments are any great boost for Cartesianism. At best, they are arguments against certain versions of contingent identity theory. It is in fact possible to concoct some strongly anti-Cartesian arguments in the Kripke style. Here are two examples:*

There was a time when it was conceivable that souls or

* Adapted from an example of F. Feldman in an unpublished paper.

minds were things which entered and left living bodies. Animals it was also believed had living bodies and presumably no minds. Suppose Descartes named his mind 'Descartes' and his living body 'the Descartes Machine.' Subsequently scientists showed that Descartes is identical to the Descartes machine. Scientists can do that sort of thing. They showed Hesperus to be identical with Phosphorus, and a particular flash of light to be a particular stream of photons, and that an instance of heat was just an instance motion. To suppose now that there is a possible world which contains the Descartes Machine without Descartes, or Descartes without the Descartes Machine is only to suppose that there are worlds with objects which may be similar to Descartes' living body, or similar to his bodiless mind, but neither of those objects would be that very same thing, i.e. Descartes.

The previous argument may be no great comfort to Descartes but it does leave open the possibility of dualism in some *other* world in which there might be objects very much like our minds and others very much like our living bodies, although of course none of them would be the very same thing as any earthly creature. It also seems to leave room for the contingent identity theorist. Our bodies and minds may be necessarily identical but there might be counterfactual circumstances in which other minds and other living bodies are contingently connected. But let's do the rigid designator test on Mind and Living Human Body. No matter if being living human body is a state and mind is a state. So are heat and the motion of molecules. If something is a living human body it is so necessarily for if it weren't that it would cease to exist altogether. A corpse is not a living human body. And furthermore, that has to be the case in all possible worlds even where that world's living human bodies don't exist in ours for if that weren't the case they wouldn't be the same species. *We* are after all the paradigms. Run through the test again for minds which I will spare you. Now (paralleling the argument for water and H_2O given above) since it is also the case that having a mind and having a living human body are coextensive in *this* world, we have established an identity between living human body and mind. That is even less comfort to the Cartesian but given that identities are necessarily identical, it is no comfort to the contingent identity theorist either.

As for Kripke's particular example, he has made much of the fact that to be affected by a sensation of pain is to be in pain but to be affected by a sensation of heat is not to be in heat. Still the choice of the example is useful for it can be pressed, since heat and pain are both states rather than stuff. There was a time when it was believed that it was heat stuff entering or leaving a body which caused its temperature to vary just as some American plains Indians believed it was mysterious objects which entered a body which were pains and which the shamen was supposed to extract. Now as it turns out, heat is not stuff composed of physical parts; it is rather a state of physical parts. No particular collection of physical parts are required to yield up a given amount of heat. Any old molecules will do. Also it doesn't require that each of the molecules be moving in some specific way. So all kinds of different stuff the molecular parts of which may move in different ways can give us the same heat. Also, the heat of a given contained system cannot be identified with the heat of any of its parts. Furthermore, there are all kinds of ways of producing the same heat in a contained system of molecules. So the conditions for producing the heat state are very general and there are, it would seem, theoretically many models for the production of the same heat states. Now you can say the same sort of thing about pain. The important difference is supposed to be that although heat is a state and not itself stuff, it is a state of physical stuff, a kinetic state. Pain, Kripke wants to argue, can never be a physical state. The identity between heat and molecular motion is a state to state identity and he wants to say that it is impossible to have state to state identities between physical and mental states. The mental state he argues will always have some property necessarily which the physical state can have at best only contingently. But his argument is based on a particular example, the identification of some particular neural state, c-fiber stimulation, with pain. But even the heat state of a system cannot be identified with the state of any of its parts or even with any particular chemical make up of those parts. As Wiggins has pointed out, there is no reason to suppose that any particular hardware or chemistry need be required to produce a pain state. It does not seem to me at all obvious that there can't be some very general physical state (which may have many physical models) which won't also be necessarily pain just as mean kinetic energy or motion of molecules is necessarily heat.

Now I think that what makes the Kripke argument so appealing is that we can't conceive at this time what it would be like even to speak were such an identity to be discovered. But the Kripke theory is also a theory of meaning change and, as Putnam reminds us, labours in the linguistic and scientific community are divided. It may take a while before discovered identities work their way into the language. So the theory is not a theory about what would or wouldn't be odd to say on this or that occasion. There was a time when saying 'Speed up the molecules of some H_2O' would have had no meaning at all. And then a time when it would be very odd to say *that* instead of 'Heat up some water.' It is still a bit odd, but not all that much.

Kripke at the end of *Naming and Necessity* says that the argument about the impossibility of psycho-physical identity can be made more vivid by the following. We are supposed to imagine God creating the world. Then Kripke asks,

> What does [God] need to make the identity of heat and molecular motion obtain? Here it would seem that all he need to do is create the heat, that is, the molecular motion itself.... How does it appear to us that the mere creation of molecular motion still leaves God with the additional task of making molecular motion into heat? This feeling is indeed

illusory, but what is a substantive task for the deity is the task of making molecular motion *felt* as heat.... What about the case of the stimulation of C-fibers? To create this it would seem that God need only to create beings with C-fibers capable of the appropriate type of physical stimulation; it would seem though that to make the C-fiber stimulation correspond to pain God must do something in addition to the creation of C-fiber stimulation. If these things are in fact within His powers, the relation between the pain God creates and the stimulation of C-fibers cannot be identity.

Now that is surely true. But the only moral to be drawn from that parable is that God couldn't have made pain wholly and only out of C-fibre stimulation any more than He could have made Eve out of the rib of Adam.

NOTES

1. *Journal of Symbolic Logic*, vol. 12 (1947), pp. 12–15.
2. S. Kanger, *Theoria*, vol. 23 (1957), pp. 1–11; J. Hintikka, *Acta Philosophica Fennica* (1963), pp. 65–81.
3. Papers of S. Kripke, pp. 83–94 and J. Hintikka, op. cit., in *Acta Philosophica Fennica* (1963). Also S. Kanger, *Provability in Logic*, Stockholm, 1957.
4. S. Kripke, 'Identity and Necessity', in M. Munitz (ed.) *Identity and Individuation*, New York, 1971. S. Kripke, 'Naming and Necessity', in *Semantics of Natural Languages*, G. Harmon and D. Davidson (eds.), Dordrecht, 1971. K. Donnellan, 'Names and Identifying Descriptions', in *Semantics and Natural Languages*, G. Harmon and D. Davidson (eds.), Dordrecht, 1971. The passage quoted is from P. Geach, *Logic Matters*, California (1972), p. 155.
5. H. Putnam, *Journal of Philosophy*, vol. LXX (1973), pp. 699–710.

Comment

BY IAN HACKING

I cannot comment on the subtle matter of mind and body. My reasons for doubting the inapplicability of modal logic to such issues are even more reactionary than those of Professor Wiggins. These comments are restricted to questions of modal logic and identity that arise without the aid of philosophical psychology.*

Like Wiggins I am concerned with the proposition

4 $(x)(y)((x=y) \supset \Box(y=x))$

and its derivation from

1 $(x)(y)((x=y) \supset Fx = Fy)$.

Unlike him I think (4) is false and the derivation invalid even when the box of necessity is given a *de re* interpretation. In (I) below I give a counterexample which I hope falls somewhat outside Professor Marcus' apt classification. (II) offers an explanation of why the derivation of (4) from (1) does not go through. My argument has little to do with necessity. I believe that, like most questions in modal logic, the difficulties discussed by Wiggins arise before modality has been introduced, and are a result of mistakes that are prior to modality. In the present instance, what we must understand is identity, not necessary identity. Finally in (III) I shall draw a few specific consequences for Wiggins' own proposals.

1   WHO IS DONCASTER?

I start from a suggestive phrase of Wiggins: the only true sense in which Tully is necessarily Cicero is that in which, in common

---

* I have incorporated into these comments a number of remarks which other members of the conference made after the papers had been read. Thus a parenthesis of the form '(as X said)' indicates a suggestion that came up in discussion. The responsibility for any misreporting in these passages is entirely my own.

speech, we are able to say that Tully can not help but be Cicero, or that Tully could not but have been Cicero (p. 111). Using only proper names I shall try to describe a case in which $a=b$, but such that a could help being b, or could have been other than b.

A crystal ball employing physics, not magic, has been perfected. It projects a moving picture on the screen, accompanied by living stereo. Like the time machine in the old comic strip *Alley Oop* we cannot control what it picks up. We have to be content with what we are given, which will always be a scene just twenty years in the future. We are watching what looks like the saloon of a cruise liner peopled by, among others, a lounge lizard called Doncaster, a deplorable man in his fifties who appears to make a living as a card sharper and by extracting insurance money from lonely widows. As we sit and watch he comes to seem increasingly familiar. There are too many turns of phrase, mannerisms when walking and talking, and vestiges of character to deny it outright: although we recognize no one else on the boat, this man looks like me, twenty years on.

It is possible, we conjecture, that Hacking is Doncaster. That is an epistemic possibility. Moreover, someone now living, at present in his early thirties, is Doncaster. We discount the possibility that Doncaster is, in 1994, an adolescent in disguise, or that in that future era, middle aged men are being created *de novo* without any past. Finally the word 'Doncaster' as used both by the people on the screen and by us as we sit and discuss him, is undoubtedly a proper name. It is a name that we learn and use in almost exactly the same way as we master and use a host of everyday proper names.

I do not care for this smooth, cultivated, hollow Doncaster. I grudgingly grant that if I carry on in my present life style I could well end up as Doncaster. So I decide to follow the advice that Pascal gives in his celebrated wager in the *Pensées*, *infini-rien*. I adopt a life of holy water and sacraments, and mingle only with the pious. By living this sort of life I become the sort of person that cannot be Doncaster. I act in such a way as practically to preclude my being Doncaster. No course of action is guaranteed to succeed, but as Pascal knew well, faith and life-styles are catching. If in this position you doubt such a view of human nature, you should shoot yourself. That will virtually guarantee that you are not Doncaster, although there remains a logical and perhaps physical possibility of resurrection &c. Note that by adopting Pascal's wager and succeeding in moulding my character away from Doncaster, I have not made anything on the screen false. I have only ensured that someone other than me is Doncaster.

Thus far, as I tell this story, Hacking, as it turns out, is not Doncaster. But suppose I do not follow Pascal's way? Twenty years on I find myself in the saloon, wryly reflecting as I play my fifth Ace that I watched this very scene twenty years before. It is true that Hacking is Doncaster. But is it necessarily true that H is D, or is H, as Wiggins puts it, necessarily D? Surely not, for I could have done something to prevent my being Doncaster. I could have adopted Pascal's wager, or shot myself dead. Having had the grim warning in Bristol in 1974 it is positively my fault that I am Doncaster.

Those who dislike the argument will toy with the obvious philosophical fantasies. One can deny that future contingents are true now, and claim that 'Doncaster' is not yet a proper name, although it will be in 1994. Or one can embrace fatalism: contrary to what I believe, if I am Doncaster, no ruse of suicide or virtue that I try will work; the surgeons will restore my blasted heart, or vice will insinuate my Pascalian soul. Whatever I try to do, my fate is sealed, so the fatalist rejects my belief that I could be different. But I am sure that Professor Marcus' 1947 proof of the proposition (4) was not intended to prove the disjunction of fatalism or the denial of present truth of future contingents. I hope we can put those issues to one side.

I assert, then, that in this story 'Doncaster' and 'Hacking' are being used as proper names, that $H=D$, but H could have helped being D, could have been other than D. Hence there is no good sense in which Hacking is necessarily Doncaster.

Have I committed some modal error, such as confusing epistemic and metaphysical necessity? It is part of standard fatalism that if it is true that 'I could do x,' but I do not do x, then the 'could' is epistemic, for it denotes mere ignorance of a predetermined future. I have invited everyone to forget that boring move. I contend that I am free to act so as to preclude being Doncaster, and that there is no kind of metaphysical necessity of my being Doncaster compatible with such freedom.

Note that my explanation of this freedom is conducted entirely in terms of names for individuals in this world. Professor Körner reminds us of a similar fantasy found at the end of Leibniz's *Theodicy*. Minerva shows to Sextus at Dodona three possible future evolutions of his life. Here there are three possible worlds, only one of which is the actual world. Although the referring expression 'Sextus' can be used of each individual in the three worlds, it refers to the actual Sextus in at most one of those portrayals. In my story, written after the advent of rigid designators, it is important that the 'Doncaster' names an individual in this world, actually alive today.

It will be asked if I am not using 'Doncaster' merely as a concealed description, 'the man who, in 1994, does the things we notice on this screen.' Surely not. Even if it were we who first used the label 'Doncaster,' and did not hear it uttered in the projection room, it would not follow that D was merely a concealed description. When Special Branch notice a shadowy figure always on the fringe of riots, union meetings, and peace demonstrations, they start calling him 'Charlie.' The very name 'Charlie' becomes, in due course, a proper name, Of course if there is no such man—MI6 have faked the films and planted them on their sister service—'Charlie' is no name. But if there is a man who is recognized in this way, then I think that the word 'Charlie', in the mouths of Special Branch when they say, 'There's Charlie again, let's get the b . . . . .,' is just as much a name when they next utter that sentence as when they finally spot Charlie in the flesh. So even if it were we who coined the name 'Doncaster,' it would still be a name. But (as Professor Kneale has noticed) my story makes the name 'Doncaster' and its usage almost exactly parallel more familiar names. We witness the use of the name and use it ourselves.

Finally it will be asked if 'Doncaster' is a rigid designator. If in the end it be granted that $H = D$, but that H could have been other than D, then, for all its namelike qualities, we may conclude that D is not a rigid designator. As Professor Scott proposed in conversation, we could then amicably conclude that (4), and also (1) hold only when the identity sign is flanked by rigid designators (aside from the cases of which Professor Marcus reminds us, when it is flanked by names of concepts in *a priori* identities). Hence the tale of Doncaster provides no counterexample to (4). In my opinion such a move would be degenerate. The doctrine that names and some other expressions are rigid is an important one, intended among other things to explain many a facet of naming and necessity. If we are to engage in what the late Imre Lakatos called monster-barring, and practise the analytification of important propositions, we almost strip them of their interest. I want to keep (4) importantly false rather than emptily true. But of couse Doncaster alone does not suffice to establish the falsehood. We need to understand why (4) is false and its proof from (1) unsound.

2 WHAT IS IDENTITY?

Kanger, Hintikka and others have constructed systems of modality, possible world semantics, and cross world identification in which (4) is false. Hintikka has implied in discussion that this is enough: there are several ways of solving the problems about modality and quantification into opaque contexts. One involves Kripke's devices, another Hintikka's. We ought not, he implies, to argue vainly about alternative solutions. But those of us who are, like Wiggins and myself, of a more reactionary temper, like to have ultra-mundane solutions explained in terms of this world, and we retain the suspicion that in this world, the number of solutions may be smaller than Hintikka urges. So although what Carnap called the principle of tolerance is better than stubborn insistence that only one solution is right, I wish to see what we think of identity in this world.

There are two traditional concepts of the identity of individuals. One is that of Leibniz, who held that individuals are identical if and only if they share their properties. It is convenient to regard this as a definition of *Leibnizian identity*. Kant maintained that two spatio-temporal individuals may share all their properties but still be numerically different, and so I shall speak of *Kantian identity*, which is perhaps a primitive. At any rate I have no idea how to define it. Perhaps Kantian identity embraces several distinguishable primitive notions. In 1963 Professor Marcus wrote of strong and weak concepts of identity, which, to remind us of our predecessors, I call Kantian and Leibnizian. Since I aim at some semblance of historical accuracy I shall not use that non-denoting phrase, 'Leibniz's law', for although many people, not including Leibniz, use the expression they seem to use it in different ways.

In both the Leibnizian and the Kantian concept, proposition (1) is agreed: if two individuals are identical, then they share all their properties. Then (4) is proved by asserting that necessary identity is a property. Those who have denied (4) have usually rejected the substitution as an abuse of modality. But there is, to my mind, a much more natural objection. I shall express it in vigorous words: *Identity is not a relation between individuals. Being identical to Cicero is not a property of Cicero*. Hence being necessarily identical to Cicero is not a property.

Seventeenth-century philosophers thought that they had a fairly clear idea of what counted as a kind of property, and neither Leibniz nor Kant would ever have thought for a moment that identity is a relation or being-identical-to-Cicero is a property. I should be glad to defend that assertion on another occasion. I am not of course here concerned with the Leibnizian conjecture that spatial and temporal relations are not 'real' relations but only phenomenal. That is an issue about which Leibniz disagreed with his contemporaries. But there would never have been any controversy as to whether identity is a relation between things. How are we to make plain to the twentieth century this evident truth of the seventeenth? We should perhaps also answer the question that Professor Anscombe asked, exactly what is to count as an individual about whose identity we are discussing? Both questions require an immense amount of philosophy. It might be a consequence of doing that philosophy that we became dubious of the very distinction between individuals and properties. I think, however, that I can bypass this issue, and present an argument about Leibnizian identity that holds whatever we think individuals and properties are.

As a preliminary to what I take to be the fundamental theory, recall the definition of identity in *Principia Mathematica*. It employs a notion of Leibnizian identity. But since *PM* is a ramified theory of types, the definition of identity for individuals must be in terms of predicates of type 1 and level 1. (Following Church I use the word 'level' where *PM* uses 'order,' to avoid confusion with our other usage, as in 'first-order logic'.) The definition, on page 57 of the second edition, is accompanied by an interesting discussion about the application of the axiom of reducibility to identity. We observe that without an axiom of reducibility that applies to modal as well as nonmodal notions—an axiom stronger than any Russell would have countenanced—the proposition (4) is not provable, because identity to Cicero, and hence necessary identity to Cicero, are of type 1 and level 2. Proposition (1) follows from the *PM* definition of identity only for F of type and level 1.

This is a formal observation. I would urge that a ramified theory of types is just the theory which we require for the description of nature, rather than of mathematics, but that is another topic. For the present, note only that if we did have a concept of individuals and of real properties represented by predicates of type 1 and level 1, then we should, in that theory, have blocked the derivation of (4) by expedients that have nothing to do with modality.

These observations about the type and level of identity are only an introduction to a deeper argument that can be traced back to Wittgenstein. In surveying the literature, I have found many references to him and to Ramsey, but their lessons seem not to have been learned. In the *Investigations* Wittgenstein mocks the thought that 'being identical to itself' is a property of his table lamp. In the *Tractatus* he thinks that true statements of identity are a byproduct of our language: a fortuitous consequence of the fact that we have two names for the same thing. If we were to have a better notation there would be no identity statements at all. This doctrine about identity is connected with his theory of tautology. Tautologies are also a by-product of the notation. We have various logical operators, including the sentential connectives and the quantifiers. From these it is possible to derive what we call logical truths. Such truths are consequences of the rules of language but are different in kind from true identity statements. I assert, however, that they are the same kind as laws of identity such as transitivity (as opposed to particular identity statements about individuals). Thanks to his notorious theory about objects Wittgenstein favoured Kantian rather than Leibnizian identity, and so there is no discussion of this small point in the *Tractatus*. My proposal is essentially an injection, into certain parts of the *Tractatus*, of a Leibnizian concept of identity.

What is it for a logical truth to be a byproduct of the notation? Gentzen taught us that the familiar connectives and quantifiers can be defined by rules of a sequence calculus, regarded as a metatheory of deduction. We may generalize on this idea. Let there be given a categorical grammar including a category of names, of sentences, and of predicates (i.e. of operators forming sentences from names) and pretty well as much else as we can now formalize. Then we can consider the class of sentence-forming operators that can be defined on top of this language by means of Gentzen-type rules for which cut-elimination is provable and for which the subformula principle holds. In an unpublished study called *What is logic?* which a number of you have heard or read, I argue that this exactly characterizes what a logical constant is. The subformula principle is one which tells us that the meaning of the compound sentences is given by the meanings of the components (in a sort of Do-It-Yourself semantics kit), and cut-elimination means that we are preserving the transitivity of deductibility. Now whether or not my theory about logic is correct, it is fairly clear that any constant defined in this way deserves to be called a logical constant. Any truth which is simply a result of adding Gentzen rules to a given categorical language has the right to be called a logical truth, and, to explicate Wittgenstein, a by-product of the notation.

Let us then purify our initial categorial language by deleting from it any operators that can be defined in the manner of Gentzen. Thus we now think of ourselves with a language which includes names of individuals, whatever they are, and predicates expressing properties and relations, whatever they are. It will also include what Professor Prawitz calls name and predicate parameters. But it does not include Leibnizian identity, which is defined by the following pair of rules:

$$\frac{\Gamma \vdash Fa, Fb, \Theta \quad \Gamma, Fb, Fa \vdash \Theta}{\Gamma, a=b \vdash \Theta} \quad (=L)$$

$$\frac{\Gamma, Fa \vdash Fb, \Theta \quad \Gamma, Fb \vdash Fa, \Theta}{\Gamma \vdash a=b, \Theta} \quad (=R)$$

In $=R$ the F are predicate parameters only, and in $=R$, F does not occur in Γ, Θ. We also add rules for whatever usual logical constants we desire, and also for '$\square$'. This is easily done for S4, but some subterfuges enable us to do it for S5 as well. In such a system, cut-elimination is provable, and also $(=L)$ holds as a derived rule for any F built up out of the usual constants and indeed '=' also. But it does not hold in general for F built up out of '=' and '□'. Hence although we can deduce that (4) holds for any F built up out of the usual logical constants, it does not hold for necessary-identity.

I believe that this little first-order system is a good neutral explication of Leibnizian identity. In our initial categorial language we included names and predicates for whatever we think the real objects and properties are; then our logic allows us to construct numerous complex sentences. (4) does hold for all real properties including whatever we put into our initial language but it demonstrably fails to hold for necessary-identity. Such a system will indeed have a possible world semantics not unlike that developed by Professor Hintikka, but I would claim for it the virtue of having been explained entirely in terms of a this-worldly concept of identity and by a familiar this-worldly syntax. Also, for those of us who believe that a ramified theory of types is a good language for describing nature, it is readily extended to theories of unbounded type and level.

3 WHAT IS NECESSARY IDENTITY?

Wiggins urges that *de re* modalities attach to predicates, not sentences. Thus to say that God is necessarily omnipotent is not to say that a sentence, 'God is omnipotent', is necessarily true, but that God has a property, necessary-omnipotence. After today's discussion, chiefly between Wiggins and Kripke, I think I understand one of the things that is at issue. Suppose that for parsimony we seek only one explanation of necessity, through which all others are to be defined, just as we have an explanation of negation for sentences and thereby explain negation for predicates. A majority of logicians supposes that the best starting point is like that for negation: first characterize necessity for sentences, and treat necessity of properties as a paraphrase of this notion. Wiggins insists that *de re* modalities must be taken as primitive, perhaps with *de dicto* ones following in train. Let me call these two approaches *de re* and *de dicto*. I wish to remain neutral between them, but to point out that my own theory on identity yields different results in the different approaches.

In Wiggins' *de re* theory we do not automatically form predicates for properties by abstraction from arbitrary open sentences. That is, we do not look at the open sentence, □ (*Fx*), and use that to characterize the property of being necessarily-*F*. Rather we have to treat being necessarily-*F* as a property that is logically prior to or at least independent of the open sentence with its *de dicto* modality. I like this idea. In the case of the *ordinary de re* abilities and capabilities of people, as described by Wiggins on p. 113, it appears that properties, not sentences are in question. As for the *extraordinary*, I think that necessary-omnipotence is perhaps a primitive property, not to be explained in terms of the necessity of the proposition that God is omnipotent.

The *de dicto* philosopher has a ready argument to show that identity and necessary identity are properties: he constructs the open sentences. Wiggins has a harder task. Since he cannot start from open sentences he must first show that his nec-identity is a property. Wiggins does give a form of argument to this effect. But he takes for granted that identity is a property. I think that Wiggins intended part of his paper to deal with sceptics of (4) such as myself, yet far from being in a better position than the *de dicto* philosopher, Wiggins' case seems weaker. How on earth can one argue, except from the paraphernalia of open sentences, that 'being identical to oneself' is a property at all? Wiggins urges on p. 111 that nec-identity is a sort of limiting case of the ordinary *de re* modalities but he gives no reason for believing in this alleged convergence. It certainly cannot follow from the observation that Dr. Lewy has repeated with peculiar vigour, that *one and the same thing* cannot possibly both have and not have *one and the same property*, with the consequence that we cannot *possibly* deny what Lewy calls Leibniz's law. It is no part of my theory given in (II) above that one thing can both have and not have one property. If a and b are names of the same thing, the sentence, $\Box\,(a=a)$ is demonstrable, whereas the sentence $\Box\,(a=b)$ is not. This is no counterexample to 'Leibniz's law', for my argument is based on the fact that neither of these sentences is ascribing a property to anything. Incidentally, it is not a consequence of my analysis that $\Box\,(a=b)$ has to be false when the names differ, I assert only that it is not a demonstrable truth.

The *de dicto* philosopher who infers properties from open sentences is on much firmer ground than Wiggins. He can, I think, protest that even if I have a coherent and correctly formalized and interpreted notion of identity, there is still a stronger concept of identity of the sort envisaged by Kant. The tale of Doncaster makes me a little sceptical of this claim. If H is identical to D, but could have helped being D, there seems nothing worth calling 'necessity' or 'necessary identity' such that of necessity H is D, or H is necessarily identical to D. Discussion of Kantian versus Leibnizian identity would, however, take us too far afield, and, among other things, we should have to embark on the philosophy of space and time. Let me grant that there may be two notions of identity, one Leibnizian, and one Kantian. And let me even pretend that to be Kantian-identical, whatever that is, is to be necessarily-Kantian-identical, whatever *that* is! What of mind and body?

Professor Marcus points out on p. 140 that the rigid designator interpretation of (4) is much less satisfying for abstract objects, such as numbers, and for natural kinds, minds, and other higher order entities. She does not, I think, isolate the cause of the trouble. The distinction between Leibnizian and Kantian identity promises the following diagnosis.

Philosophers as diverse as Kant, Strawson and Carnap have urged a notion of non-Leibnizian identity for spatio-temporal individuals, but all have agreed that the identity of indiscernibles holds for concepts, abstract objects, and higher order entities in general. Consider, let us say, the Putnam twin-earth example cited by Marcus on p. 137. There is no absurdity in aliens (a) having exactly the same beliefs about some of their stuff, which they call 'water,' as we have about our water, and yet (b) their stuff being different from our stuff. That is, we imagine that unbeknownst to them or us, our water has powers and properties different from that of their stuff. But if their stuff had exactly the same properties and powers as our water then their stuff simply is water. I have never heard an argument that Kantian identity applied to anything other than spatio-temporal individual things. So I believe that the only concept of identity pertaining to the abstract and the higher order is Leibnizian. This may explain Professor Marcus' misgivings. (4) does not hold for the relation of Leibnizian identity of type 1, and there is no reason to think it will for identity relations of higher type. Hence I cannot comment on the disagreements between Kripke and Wiggins about mind and body, because the concept of identity which they use does not appear to be in any way relevant.

Reply to Comments

BY DAVID WIGGINS

I

1.1 In the relatively confined space of a *Postscript*, and hemmed in between two commentators of such opposite persuasions, I cannot answer all of the challenging points raised by Ruth Barcan Marcus, Ian Hacking and the other participants. But I will take on as many of them as I can.

1.2 Hacking says that in questions of modality and identity he is even more of a reactionary than I am. In terms of this ordering of positions (my sense of what counts as reaction whether about the housing problem, worker participation, or the subjunctive conditional is too weak for me to protest), my procedure will be to work from right to left. This means, roughly, from Hacking to Marcus.

II

2.1 Hacking thinks that it is false that

4    $(a=b) \supset \Box(a=b)$

and equally false that (in my preferred mode of stating Miss Barcan's 1947 result)

4λ $(a=b) \supset (\text{Nec } [\lambda x \lambda y[x=y]]), [a][b]$

He offers a counter-example to both, in the shape of the Hacking-Doncaster story. He faults the proof of (4) for accounting even identity as a property, let alone necessary identity. He then proposes a formal system in which he hopes (4) will be not forthcoming. I have not tried to pursue the misgivings which Hacking's formal proposal aroused in me, because these pall into insignificance when compared with my objections against Hacking's even wanting his formal system to do what he says it does do. For I maintain that his counter-example to (4) and (4λ) is no counter-example, and that his objections to identity and necessary identity as relations are inconclusive.

2.2. *Doncaster is Hacking $\supset$ Hacking is necessarily Doncaster*

Suppose Hacking can foresee the future infallibly with the apparatus he describes. Suppose he had foreseen it that very July 1974 afternoon in Wills Hall in the University of Bristol. And suppose what he had seen was, as he describes it, a seedy middle-aged card sharper twenty years thence. What I want to know is this. Where, at that very moment of precognizing by Hacking, *is* that card sharper Hacking precognizes? Well, either at Wills Hall in Bristol, or not there. Either he coincides with Hacking as he precognizes or he doesn't coincide. But either way there is nothing Hacking can do about his identity or non-identity with Doncaster. If he is Doncaster, he can't help but be. What the example illustrates is the actual plausibility of (4) or (4λ). Not that the disproof of a purported counter-example demonstrates that the contingency theorist is mistaken: and I strongly sympathize with Hacking in thinking that the contingency theorist's position has been underestimated in recent times. The question has been positively begged against him. But when I wrote my paper for the conference at Bristol I thought that my version of Miss Barcan's proof would at least give a contingency theorist some legitimate cause for worry. I thought that, since neither rigid designation nor possible worlds were involved in my version of the proof, he could not escape by making objection to these features. The one thing I did not anticipate, having made something of a fool of myself, I fear, by offering for this very contention a fallacious proof (which convinced me from 1961 to 1964 and surfaced in the article Kripke was attacking), was that the contingency theorist would assert that identity was not a property or relation.

2.3 Hacking cites Wittgenstein's *Tractatus* with approval on identity. At one point he even describes his own project as the injection of Leibnizian identity into the *Tractatus*. Presumably he would simply cross out 5.5302, or treat it as an irrelevant remark about Kantian identity. But I am as dubious about Hacking's two concepts of identity, the Leibnizian and Kantian, as I have always been about Professor Marcus' stronger and weaker concepts of identity. Neither he nor she have talked me out of the perhaps excessively plain man's description of the situation. "We use this concept of identity every day; but unfortunately there is some disagreement and even confusion among philosophers about it. It is evident in particular from their arguments about the Identity of Indiscernibles that different philosophers have different conceptions of identity." Different conceptions are not different concepts. There can be dispute between different conceptions about which is more correct, or nearer the truth. There is no general reason to think that these disputes are rationally or in principle irresoluble. As remarked, the key issue between the two conceptions of identity is the Identity of Indiscernibles. Of course that is an old, even hackneyed, question. But, philosophy being what it is, this scarcely shows that we've run out of steam. I shall digress for a moment to show there's still something fresh to be done about the Identity of Indiscernibles, and to say what I can to discredit the notion that we have more than one *concept* of identity, before I attempt to tackle head-on the argument that identity is not a property or relation.

2.4 The Identity of Indiscernibles or $[((F)(Fa \equiv Fb)) \supset (a=b)]$[1]

Wittgenstein remarked in the *Tractatus* that this principle denies the logical possibility of a universe consisting only of two qualitatively distinguishable spheres. The objection has impressed insufficiently where it needed to impress, but that is not the end of the matter. Let us pursue one of the other objections. Does the F in this principle range over all genuine or extensional properties? Let us call this the *promiscuous* view. Or is some restriction meant to operate to disqualify properties whose definitions involve identity itself, and all the other properties whose exclusion is demanded by parity of reason (e.g. such monadic and polyadic properties as require definitions already presupposing place-, time-, and thing-individuation)?[2] Call the latter the *sober* or *Leibnizian* view of the principle. The difficulty is this. On the promiscuous view the principle of Identity of Indiscernibles is vacuously true because *identity with a* will count as a property of *a*. But on the sober view (which would obviously be Hacking's own view) the principle actually seems to exclude a much homelier situation than the one Wittgenstein envisaged: the possible existence in this world (in my pocket, say, or the top drawer of Hacking's writing desk) of a perfectly symmetrical object. Its top half (say) would be identical with its bottom half: and the left side of the bottom half would be identical with the right side of the bottom half, and any residual eighth of the object will be identical with some (other?) eighth of it.... We are left in the end with nothing. Surely this must raise the price of maintaining the principle. I say only that the principle *seems* to exclude symmetrical objects because of some doubt about how exactly the sober view marks out the relevant subset of the totality of extensional predicates over which the variable F ranges in $(Fa \equiv Fb)$.[3] But my point is that we shall not have finished the argument, nor run out of steam, until Hacking or some other Leibnizian actually tries to do this. And it is a necessary (though not sufficient) condition of finding two notions of identity, a Kantian and a Leibnizian notion, as Hacking does, that the question of the identity of indiscernibles should seem irresoluble by philosophical argument.

2.5 Identity as a relation: Hacking's strategy

Hacking's procedure for demonstrating that identity is not a relation is somewhat confusing. His first argument relates to the proper definition of identity in the ramified type theory which inspires the formal system he himself favours. His second argument is an allusion to a 'deeper argument that can be traced back to Wittgenstein'. He says 'In surveying the literature, I have found many references to him and to Ramsey, but their lessons seem not to have been learned. In the *Investigations* Wittgenstein mocks the thought that "being identical with itself" is a property of his table lamp ... in the *Tractatus* he thinks that true statements of identity are a by-product of our language: a fortuitous consequence of the fact that we have two names for the same thing. If we were to have a better notation there would be no identity statements at all.' Then, with the idea that 'tautologies are a by-product of the notation', he presents his own formal system; and as I have already said, I am unpersuaded by the motivation for it. Faced with all this, let us begin with the argument Hacking says can be traced back to Wittgenstein. Presumably the relevant passage is *Tractatus* 5.5303.[4] That passage reads:

'Roughly speaking, to say of two things that they are identical is nonsense, and to say of one thing that it is identical with itself is to say nothing at all.'

I do not think one can take such stuff seriously after Geach's discussion of relative pronouns in *Reference and Generality*. Pending a positive account of property or relation, and a full justification of its title to define the one thing we ought to mean by a property; and pending, what would also be required, an explanation why Leibniz's principle must be restricted to just those predicates which stand for such properties; it is difficult to find anything but rhetoric or confusion or both in this argument.

2.6 Identity as a relation, continued: Wittgenstein and others on self-identity etc.

I allege there is confusion in the argument. Still Wittgenstein is not apparently alone in supposing that if a man says truly that Hesperus is Phosphorus then he says that Hesperus is identical with itself, notorious though it is that substitution in 'saying' contexts is dangerous. The same idea surfaces in a highly dialectical passage of Frege at the beginning of *On Sense and Reference*: 'it would seem that "$a=b$" could not differ from "$a=a$", provided that "$a=b$" is true. A relation would thereby be expressed of a thing to itself, and indeed one in which everything stands to itself but no other thing.' (Note by the way that the idea—if Frege really embraced it and I think it is not obvious he did—that '$a=b$' is, *if true*, tantamount to '$a=a$', and that '$a=a$' is tantamount to 'a is itself', did not prevent Frege from counting '$=$' as a relation word in the *Grundgesetze*.) The thought has taken on a life of its own. It emerges again in Kripke's 'Naming & Necessity' (again without the denial of relationhood): 'it is for example [wrongly] thought that: if you have two names like "Cicero" and "Tully" and say that Cicero is Tully you can't really be saying of the object which is both Cicero and Tully that *it is identical with itself.*'[5] It is a confusion, surely, on both sides to suggest we might be saying *that*. But Professor Marcus too, if I may look forward to her, uses exactly the same sort of language. 'That principle, [the principle that $a=b \supset \Box(a=b)$] seems intuitively obvious to me. For if the notion of identity makes any sense, what could be more obvious than that necessarily a thing is the same as itself, *de dicto*, *de re* or any way you choose.' I think this is a scandalous account of the matter when it is directed against the contingency theorist. His belief is not that it is contingent that *a is itself* but only that it is contingent that *a is b*. The contingency theorist of all people can scarcely be supposed to allow that these claims coincide. Indeed what argument has been offered by anybody for their coincidence? Inasmuch as there has been any argument on the subject at all, it all goes the other way. I mean Geach's argument in *Reference and Generality* about reflexive pronouns in general. Applied to the case in point it shows that he who says that $a=a$ predicates of a what only a can have, the one place property $\lambda x(x=a)$. Or, if you will, he predicates of the couple $[a,a]$ the two-place relation $(\lambda x\, \lambda y\, (x=y))$. But, whichever of these we take, to ascribe it to its subject or subjects is not the same as to ascribe to a the one-place property which is ascribed by a man who says that a is identical with itself or $\lambda x(x=x)$, $[a]$. (That $\lambda x(x=a)$ and $\lambda x(x=x)$ are different properties can be explained by tracing their actual relationship, which may be displayed as follows. Start with the primitive predicable '$x=y$' and abstract the property $(\lambda x)(\lambda y)\,(x=y)$. That this is satisfied by a pair is recorded in our notation by $(\lambda x)(\lambda y)(x=y)$, $[w,z]$. To get a's own peculiar predicate $(\lambda x)(x=a)$ or $(\lambda w)[(\lambda x,\lambda y\,(x=y))$, $[w,a]]$ substitute a designation of a for z in the second free argument place in $(\lambda x)(\lambda y)(x=y)$, $[w,z]$ and bind the only free variable with λ. Or to get the simpler designation $(\lambda x)(x=a)$, take the constant a as a value of z in $(\lambda x)(\lambda y)(x=y)$, $[w,z]$ and apply λ-conversion to get '$w=a$'. Replace the variable w by the variable x and abstract on x to get $(\lambda x)(x=a)$. To get the universal predicate $(\lambda x)(x=x)$

or $(\lambda w)[(\lambda x)(\lambda y)(x=y), [w,w]]$ substitute the first argument for the second argument in the second argument place in $(\lambda x)(\lambda y)(x=y), [w,z]$ to get $(\lambda x)(\lambda y)(x=y) [w,w]$ and bind the free variable with λ. To get the simpler formula put t for both w and z in $(\lambda x)(\lambda y)(x=y), [w,z]$, apply λ-conversion to get '$t=t$', replace t by x to get '$x=x$' and abstract on x to get $(\lambda x)(x=x)$.)

2.7 Identity as relation continued: Wittgenstein's argument concluded

So much for the idea that '$a=b$', if true, says only that a is itself. If the machinery I have brought to bear to distinguish these predications seems overly elaborate, or seems question-begging, remember that it arises from the requirements upon a general theory of reflexive pronouns and draws support from everything such a theory has to explain.[6] As for the other side of the Wittgenstein dilemma: to say of two things that they are identical is not necessarily to say anything like 'these two things a,b are one and the same.' It is to say, where $a \neq b$, 'a is identical with b'—which is not at all the same message. If $a \neq b$ then the message is simply false. Falsity isn't nonsense. (If it were, so would its negation be.) No more than saying something true (even saying "a is itself") is saying nothing.

2.8 Hacking's other argument for his non-relational view of identity

So much for the argument Hacking has cited for the non-relationhood of identity. His other support for his view that identity isn't an attribute or relation is that he says *identical with Cicero* is type 1 level 2, in Church's terminology, whereas identity of individuals has to be defined in terms of predicates of type 1 and level 1 in the ramified hierarchy, and in terms of predicates not already presupposing individual-identity. What does this show? What I can't see it shows is either that a predicate of type 1 level 2 doesn't determine a property; or that the identity of a and b for which complete community of all type 1 level 1 predicates is allegedly[7] a sufficient condition is not such that $(a=b \supset (Fa \equiv Fb))$ for all extensional replacements of F. And of course Hacking has not tried to show that 'identical with Cicero' induces opacity in the subject term in the context 'x is identical with Cicero'. It is precisely this, the weakness of the antecedent, which makes the attempted Leibnizian definition of '$=$' so risky and so interesting. Again, if Hacking's interesting characterization of what it is to be a logical constant, does indeed bag '$=$' and settle that old dispute about its status, why not say that he has demonstrated that at least one logical constant is a dyadic attribute or relation-word? But here one begins to think: perhaps the exact characterization of the precise status of '$=$' does not matter. Let us go back to what makes Leibniz' Law itself true. We cannot conceive of how a could be identical with b, how a could actually be b, and a be F yet b be non-F. There is nothing in the natural dialectic which presents this argument to us to confine it to some seventeenth-century conception of property. Nor then, if my predicate-operator account of 'necessarily' is correct, can *necessarily F* escape it.

2.9 *Identity as a relation concluded*

I think we should distinguish three different theses:

(A) To define identity by $(F)(Fx \equiv Fy)$ we need to impose a restriction upon F and confine it to real properties: because otherwise the definition will only move us round and round in a circle. This is true, and *if* '$=$' is to be defined (which I think it isn't) by $(F)(Fx \equiv Fy)$, it is important.

(B) Once Leibnizian identity is defined, nothing forces us to allow that $(x=y \supset Fx \equiv Fy)$ holds for any extensional F whatever. But this is in no way a consequence of (A).

(C) In particular '$=$' is not a property at all, so it does not even need to be excluded by the operation of thesis (B) from counting as a case of F in $(Fx \equiv Fy)$. *A fortiori* the same holds of 'necessarily identical'. But this last follows neither from (A) nor from (B).

This concludes what I have to say about Hacking's first and

second parts. I find that I have still not touched upon the most challenging part of what he had to say about my original paper. This is his less general third section about the *de re* and the *de dicto*, and about the analogy between the scopes of necessity and negation. But for fear of leaving no room for Professor Marcus, who says things germane to both these questions, I must postpone all this for one section till I have moved leftwards and replied to her.

III

3.1 *Professor Marcus on being necessarily identical*

Ian Hacking finds almost every conceivable difficulty in the idea that there is a genuine property of being necessarily identical with Cicero. Ruth Marcus finds none at all. She has got me wrong, however, if she thinks I don't think that *necessarily identical* is a genuine relation. Indeed the λ-version I presented of her 1947 proof depends upon its being one. My whole purpose in that section of the paper was to gain favour for a distinction between different scopes of 'necessarily' and for a predicate-operator analysis of *de re* 'necessarily' which makes *necessarily identical with Cicero* absolutely unproblematic as a property. Much of the thrashing about concerned the unsatisfactoriness for this purpose of Kripke's dictum: 'Let us interpret necessity . . . weakly. We can count statements as necessary if whenever the objects mentioned therein exist, the statement would be true' (p. 137 op. cit., my footnote 2b). The relation *necessarily identical* was not, I was saying, to be had so cheap. Either I was wrong, however, or even now I seem not to have made myself clear enough about what I wanted to achieve. Nor, to my surprise, has Richard Cartwright entirely succeeded in conveying his message.

Professor Marcus says 'Cartwright is correct when he says you can't take any old sentence in English and replace any old singular term with a variable and place a . . . lambda operator in front and get yourself a predicate which denotes the very property that was being ascribed to the object. Try it for example with "Giorgione was so-called because of his size". If you want to use abstraction you've got to get the property out of the subject before it will work for you. And the same is true not just for abstraction, but for the principle of substitutivity of identicals, and just about any other logical principle. That's the sort of thing we do when we put sentences into logical form.... But I see no reason why the abstract formed from □ (Cicero=Tully)... isn't the most straightforward of properties. It's the property of being necessarily identical with Tully... a property is a function which takes... a possible world as an argument and a set of individuals as value, the property represented by $[\lambda x[\Box(x=\text{Tully})]]$ will take a unit set as value in each world where Tully exists, and (this is where necessity comes in) the member of each set will be Tully himself.' It is this kind of quick way with the point which will restore to the contingency theorist the illusion that he has a leg to stand on. The contingency theorist starts with a respectable intuition, that if 'necessarily' governs a context then (as one would expect with an operator well designed to introduce what Brentano or Frege would have called a thought) that renders the context an intensional context. The intuition finds support in the fact that supplanting one true sentence by another in the context may change the truth-value of the whole;[8] and further support in certain features of the behaviour of singular terms and predicates in 'necessarily' contexts. Nor is there any question of matters looking very obviously different after we have spotted rigid designators and/or 'put sentences into logical form'. For intensional idioms have come to stay. They are not an illusion to be dispelled from within the sanctum of logical form. If current theories of logical form do not represent intensional contexts for what they are, so much the worse for current theories. The contingency theorist may fairly add that if possible world semantics, with or without the theory of rigid designation, deals with intensional idioms by, amongst other things, denying (in effect) the opacity of 'necessarily' contexts, then possible world semantics is scarcely a neutral theory by which to resolve a disputed question about $(a=b) \supset \Box(a=b)$. (Indeed the only way to convince the contingency theorist of the acceptability of possible world semantics is to force him into (4) via my proof of (4λ).) Of course there may be all sorts of interesting differences to be established between (say) 'believes' contexts and 'necessarily' contexts. But bare assertion cannot avail against the real *prima facie* possibility that what Cartwright has shown about, e.g., *Philip believes that x denounced Catiline*, or *Probably x denounced Catiline*, applies equally, both before and after the 'putting into logical form', to $\Box$ (*x is Tully*). Perhaps it makes no more difference to the latter open sentence than it does to the former two open sentences that it is a rigid designator which the variable *x* supplants. This was what I thought in the paper. What the paper says, and it is on this that the discussion with Ruth Marcus and Saul Kripke at Bristol should have continued longer, is that a distinction between a sentence-scope and a predicate-scope for *necessarily* is what is required in order to legitimate the property (λ*x*) [Nec[*x* = Tully]]. Adapting a phrase of Professor Marcus, this is what is needed to get the subject out of the property. Casimir Lewy had even had the impression that a predicate scope 'necessarily' was what Kripke had always meant. But this was denied. Rather, rigid designators were meant to be the whole key to the problem. I do not understand how by themselves they can solve it. But, once the scope distinction which is needed is made, and once the *de re* is distinguished from *de dicto* by something better than a *fiat* against intensionality, the theory of rigid designation does no work; and the scope of 'necessarily' is even smaller than it is on the Russell–Smullyan approach which Kripke endorses. Of course, as Ian Hacking pointed out, this raises the question of the connection of the sentence-scope and the predicate-scope *necessarily*. But I am postponing that.

3.2 Rigid designators and substitutional quantification

I am said to have misunderstood rigid designators because I say that, if an object o, e.g. the first silicon particle I encountered on disembarking at Temple Meads, lacks a rigid designator, then all statements made by the use of a rigid designator for o and saying of o that it is identical with Cicero will be true. So (on the logician's reading of 'all') anything nameless will be necessarily identical with Cicero. But this was not the affirmative claim. The claim was that this was a *consequence* of the best amendment I could think of to repair the deficiencies of Kripke's linguistic definition of necessity weakly interpreted. 'We can count statements as necessary if whenever the objects mentioned therein exist, the statement would be true.' But I did not counsel the acceptance either of this or of the amended definition. I gave another non-linguistic definition which would not have this consequence and which was independent of rigid designation.

Ruth Marcus claims 'if Wiggins did in fact encounter a first silicon particle after alighting at Temple Meads, he could name it that, and mark the use with capitals. He could then say of that thing, ... that it wasn't identical with Cicero.' But my point was that I didn't in fact dub that particle; and even if I had done so that wouldn't have made much impression on the number of nameless things which would be left over in the world to plague the linguistic definition of *de re* 'necessarily'. It may be true that for any object o it is possible to name o. But it doesn't follow from this that it is possible to name all objects. To get over the defect which I was criticizing not only do we require the latter to hold, we also require that every object actually have a name or rigid designator. Otherwise it will be true that there is an object o non-identical with Cicero which is such that every statement with a rigid designator for o and saying of o that $o = $ Cicero is true: and it will be true therefore that something different from Cicero is necessarily the same as Cicero. The idea that we can hold off this disaster by pretending that all objects have names when they haven't is surely one of the most extraordinary to be encountered in modern philosophy of logic. Certainly, a formal language whose intended interpretation requires to be founded in such a myth is a strange candidate to be a neutral vehicle for the philosophical exploration of either ontology or indirect discourse. Professor Marcus calls her objection to my objection to the linguistic interpretation of *de re* 'necessarily' an aside, but some of her recent writings suggest that she does think of systems of substitutional quantification as just such a neutral vehicle.[9] I divine that in her mind the opacity questions touched upon above in 3.1 are not insulated from all interaction with the questions of this section. But if this guess is wrong, then I must apologize to her for replying at such length to what she meant as only an incidental remark.

3.3 *Rigid designators concluded*

The points I have just taken up in Professor Marcus' reply occur at the end of an extended inquiry into the rigid designation of higher order objects and into identity statements concerning these higher order objects, a level where 'there is no excluding identities even after analysis which are not flanked by rigid designators'. She is much more concerned with achieving this exclusion at the level of discourse about first order entities than I am or need to be; and she is much more ready than I am to say that 'rigid designators are required ... to establish ... identity'. I thought, and think, that on my reading of the *de re* 'necessarily' at least some of the questions need not arise. (See III *ad finem* (A).) What she says about higher order objects is, as one would expect, of independent importance and extremely interesting. If one were to comment upon it properly one would have to start where Frege left off in *Concept and Object*, consider the mutual relations of terms such as *husbandhood* and *husband*—surely they badly need to be distinguished—and scrutinize what might be meant by her identity 'husband = married male'.

But this is not the place to embark on that. Nor perhaps is the notion of rigid designation, as it applies to definite descriptions, sufficiently well understood yet at the level of first order languages. Kripke has, as remarked already, warned against certain extensions of his theory to definite descriptions.[10] It is an old idea that there are at least two semantically distinct manners of occurrence for definite descriptions and that Russell correctly characterized only one of them, the rarer one. See for instance David Mitchell's *Introduction to Logic*, written some time before Keith Donnellan published the article which has had such influence. But I find it interesting that Kripke has not sought to associate himself or his theory of rigid designation with that theory; and it is still far from obvious that the relevant distinct sets of truth-conditions can really be provided for first order sentences like 'the shortest man on the battlefield is the French general'; or that rigid designation, as opposed to Russellian scope, is the key to understanding sentences like one I saw in the *Times Business News* while I was composing this reply: 'A substantial contribution to a huge deficit is proposed by the present Government, who are actually proposing that the new capital transfer tax should tax timber crops several times before they are harvested—each time their custodian, the owner for the time being, dies.'[11]

3.4 *Possibility and relative possibility*

My final comment on Professor Marcus paper is that her way of expounding these matters of possibility, conceivability and identity involves her in the idea that necessity and possibility—the metaphysical modality involved in $(a=b) \supset \Box(a=b)$—are relative to our language, our culture, and our scientific knowledge. Here, if I understand either Ruth Marcus or Saul Kripke at all, I think she departs substantially from Kripke's own method of exposition. It is not so much that a conflation results between metaphysical and epistemic possibility and necessity—she could keep them apart in spite of the relativity to knowledge which she introduces here—as, that her account of possibility generates the paradox that the less you know the more metaphysical possibilities you can objectively postulate. If you ask yourself 'But is it really possible?' and go and find out some more facts and pursue implications, well, first you have gone beyond the call of duty—there was nothing in the relative notion of possibility to require you to do this—and second any possibilities you manage to discredit like that will be discredited relative to a different body of knowledge from that against which they counted as possibilities. That ignorance should not positively enlarge one's powers of conceiving in the philosophically interesting sense of conceive was pointed out by Arnauld. It is interesting in the present connection that it occurs in his objections to a Cartesian argument, cited with approval by Kripke, which uses the *cogito* in an attempt to prove the conceivability of mind without body.[12]

IV

4.1 *The semantical unity (or diversity) of sentence scope and predicate scope occurrences*

The point I have left over from Hacking's reply is his suggestion that the man he calls the *de dicto* philosopher must have an easier time than I can have in demonstrating via the open sentence 'necessarily ($x =$ Cicero)' that necessary identity with Cicero is a property. It will be clearer by this point why I doubt that, in the presence of the suspicion of opacity, open sentences are enough; and doubt that in the presence of this suspicion even open sentences formed by the deletion of certifiably rigid designators are enough. It is my fault, but Hacking is also mistaken in supposing that I am precluded from using open sentences to define necessary identity. On my view I can use open sentences if their extensionality is first ascertained. (What is more, if *de re* 'necessarily' is not to be artificially restricted in its occurrences I must use them.) For instance I use the open sentence '(Man (x))' to form the property (λx) [Man(x)], to which I can then apply a predicate operator 'necessarily' as in [Necessarily [(λx) [Man x]]]. By this method the scope of the 'necessarily' is explicitly limited to the predicate (λx) [Man (x)] in the statement that Cicero is necessarily a man—[Nec [(λx) [Man x]]], (Cicero). There is both this difference from Kripke's and Marcus's procedures, and also, as already claimed, a prior difference—that the open sentence which one begins with is demonstrably extensional. None of this syntactical material is enough of course in the absence of semantics, i.e. a systematic assignation of truth conditions for sentences involving 'necessarily' as a predicate operator. I must refer the reader to the place where this is attempted.[13] In the same place the analogy between 'necessarily' and 'not' is pursued in answer to one of Hacking's very questions. Hacking says that logicians tend to explain connectives which govern both sentences and predicates via the sentential case, and he wonders what my procedure would be. For definiteness let us consider one of these logicians' explanation which is not open to criticism, and which is a model of what is needed.

4.2 *The semantical unity of 'and'*

'And' figures between sentences, between predicates (as in 'the apple is red and round') and between terms (as in 'Jack and Jill ran up the hill'). The predicate-use is certainly important in understanding the truth conditions of quantified statements. If it is to be true that something is weak and mortal then weak-and-mortal is what some one thing must be. It is not enough, say, for there to be something weak and for there to be something mortal. It is notoriously impossible to see the component '(weak x & mortal x)' as a genuine *sentential* component of the formula (Ex)(Weak x & mortal x). Since 'x' stands for nothing in particular, neither 'weak x & mortal x' nor its smaller components are self-sufficient sentences. Of course all of these subformulae have to be evaluated in the process of evaluating the whole quantified formula; but since open sentences cannot have truth values the evaluation is in terms not of truth but satisfaction. *A fortiori*, the conjunction '&' cannot be understood in the context of the open sentence 'weak x & mortal x' as conjoining sentences.

How then are the functions of sentence-conjunction and predicate-conjunction to be plaited together? If at all, then by stipulating correct satisfaction conditions for a sign which performs both roles. Let s range over denumerable sequences of entities. Let overlining form names of expressions. Let ϕ, ψ range over well formed formulas of a language *whether open or closed sentences*. Then for all s, s satisfies the formula $\overline{(\phi \& \psi)}$ iff s satisfies ϕ and s satisfies ψ. And for all s, s satisfies $\overline{Ex_i \Phi x_i}$ iff some sequence unlike s in at most the ith place satisfies $\overline{\phi x_i}$. So a sequence s will satisfy say $\overline{(Ex_3)}$ $\overline{(\text{Mortal } x_3 \, \&}$ $\overline{\text{Weak } x_3)}$ iff some sequence s' unlike s in at most the third place satisfies $\overline{\text{Mortal } x_3 \, \& \text{ weak } x_3}$. This last holds iff s' satisfies $\overline{\text{mortal } x_3}$ and s' satisfies $\overline{\text{weak } x_3}$. ($s'$ satisfies $\overline{\text{mortal } x_3}$ iff its third item is mortal.) Finally let truth be satisfaction by all sequences. Then we may check that we have precisely what was required. And, inasmuch as we have got that, we prove to be justified in treating '&' as a single connective.

Fired by this success we may try to get rid of 'and' between terms by seeing 'Jack and Jill were six' as 'Jack was six and Jill was six'; 'Jack and Jill ran up the hill' as 'Jack ran up the hill *with* Jill and Jill ran up the hill *with* Jack'; and 'Jack and Jill built a house' as 'Jack helped Jill build a house and Jill helped Jack build a house'. If this is the best we can do with the second and third sentences, then 'and' is not straightforwardly univocal; but we are spared plural or conjunctive subjects, 'and' where it reappears in the analysis does so in the manner already explained, and there is a circumscribed limit to the interference we visit upon predicates. We may be encouraged in these moves by the fact that there are languages—Russian is one—where writing the word for 'and' between terms is actually ungrammatical. So far so good. But this strategy will scarcely work with 'Bread and milk is good for Jack'. (Compare *tripe and onions, fish and chips, whisky and milk*, *gin and tonic, wattle and daub.*) Here we are finally forced into postulating a fusing or compounding sense of 'and' between stuff-terms; but in this category the disruption to predicates is minimal. (This new sense will not correctly explain the previous examples. Jack and Jill are not a compound, or a four-legged complex.) Such as it was, we can prosecute the unification no further. We may see it as some symptom of the correctness of separating off this stuff-compounding sense of 'and' that there are languages, Russian again for instance, in which a correct translation of bread and butter is 'bread with butter'.[14]

So much for the paradigm of what can and cannot be done. But in the straightforward cases what has been done? Hacking would suggest that the predicate linking role of '&' has been explained in terms of a basic sentence conjunction role; and he would reiterate his suspicion that any analogous procedure applied to 'not' would in due course undermine the supposed distinction of sentence-negation and predicate-negation. It surely would. But I find it far from clear that the foregoing definition of satisfaction for '&' does take the sentential case as primary. How, if that be so, does 'and' occur in our meta-linguistic open sentence 's satisfies ϕ and s satisfies ψ'? It is true that this open sentence can be got by supplanting names with variables in a sentence where 'and' previously conjoined sentences. But the same could have been said about 'x is weak and x is mortal'. What matters rather (as before) is how, meta-meta-linguistically now, the truth-conditions of '$(s)(s$ sat ϕ & $\psi \equiv s$ sat ϕ and s sat $\psi)$', which the open sentence helps to constitute, are determined. For just the same reasons as before these cannot be determined via the truth-value of any constituent *closed* sentences, e.g., in terms of some sequence satisfying ϕ and some sequence satisfying ψ. What is required is that, for some sequence s, s satisfy ϕ and s satisfy ψ—which again involves conjunction in its open-sentence, or predicate-linking, role.

This problem is almost as old as modern logic. In a variant form, Russell and Whitehead perceived it; and they decided that the connectives were in effect ambiguous. But, if (as they said) the predicate calculus '&' cannot be explained in terms of the propositional calculus '&', it still remains to try the opposite procedure. Perhaps $\overline{\phi \& \psi}$, where ϕ and ψ are closed, is the limiting, or *zero*-free variables, case of $\overline{\phi \& \psi}$ where ϕ and ψ are open sentences with n free variables.

4.3 Not and Necessarily

Let us work out this idea with regard to negation. The phenomenon of predicate negation is deeply entrenched in natural language—'unregenerate', 'ignoble', 'involuntary', 'scortese', 'aorist', 'nekulturny'. None of these looks very happily reducible to sentence negation. There is something good then about being forced into the opposite assimilation. Suppose we think of a language with one negation sign and in which negations take the form

Not $[(\lambda x_i) [A]] [t]$

Where A is a formula and t is a singular term. In the case where λx_i is vacuous, because x_i does not occur free in A, t is some arbitrary fixed term: let us say '$\wedge$'. Thus the external negation 'Not (Cicero is bald)' has the form

Not (λx_i)[Cicero is bald] [$\wedge$]

and the internal negation 'Cicero is non-bald' has the form

Not $(\lambda x_i)[x_i$ is bald][Cicero]

The unifying interpretation is as follows

s sat $\overline{[\text{Not}(\lambda x_i)[A]][t]}$ iff (s') [((s' unlike s at most at i) & $s'^\star \overline{(x_i)} = s^\star(t)) \supset s'$ does not sat A]

Here $s^\star(t)$ is the interpretation for sequence s of the term t and $s^\star \overline{(x_i)}$ is the interpretation for s of the ith variables (i.e. the ith item in s). The conditions for the two sentences will turn out to be interderivable. But if we follow this view of the matter then the scope-difference on which we have insisted will correspond to two different *semantically interpreted* methods of building up two syntactically distinguishable structures. It amounts to seeing each *not* as a case of a single functor from predicates to predicates. In the case of predicate negation one is taken from the predicate to its complement. Similarly in the case of sentence negation one is taken from (e.g.) the universal predicate λx(Cicero is bald)—supposing Cicero is bald—to the null predicate Not[λx(Cicero is bald)].

The parallel with □ and *nec* is manifest. It is the tradition to use what is (in effect) the procedure Hacking commends, and to blur the difference between *necessarily Cicero is a man* and *Cicero is necessarily a man*. I should argue that (as with sentence connectives) the other view, the predicate or open-sentence based view, is to be preferred. The really difficult question is this. If one starts off with the *de re* 'necessarily' which I have characterized, and if one follows the recipe I have recommended for conjunction and negation, then in the limiting case where this 'necessarily' is applied to an open sentence with zero free variables, will one encounter a notion of 'necessarily' which coincides with the accepted meaning of *de dicto* necessarily or □? It is not certain. If one doesn't and if my characterization of the *de re* is correct, then 'necessarily' may be ambiguous between *de re* and *de dicto* senses. This would not be so strange, and the two senses would not necessarily be *unconnected*. But if one decided that in the limiting case the resulting notion of necessity was a good account of sentential 'necessarily', and if the semantics of *de re* 'necessarily' I have offered with Christopher Peacocke in the previously cited article are correct,[13] then in general only (4λ) would be forthcoming as a theorem.

NOTES

1. I remain unconvinced of the dastardliness of calling the converse $(a=b) \supset (Fa \equiv Fb)$, of the Identity of Indiscernibles, 'Leibniz's Law'. After all it is entailed by *eadem sunt quorum unum alteri substitui potest salvo veritate*; and Leibniz knew it was entailed, queer though his interpretation of the individual variables or constants might have been. And it is true moreover that $(a=b) \supset (Fa \equiv Fb)$. Let us give Leibniz credit for that.
2. Cp. my 'Individuation of places and things', *P.A.S.S.* (1963), vol. XXXVIII (reprinted in its unedited and correct form in Michael Loux, *Universals and Particulars*), section VI.
3. If the schema $Fx \equiv Fy$ is intended, as it usually is intended, to register a claim we want to make outside the context of some formal system, then the totality itself is no better defined than the totality of extensional predicates expressible in say, English.
4. Neither the *Investigations* passage nor the attack upon Ramsey in *Philosophical Grammar* (at p. 315 in the Rhees Kenny edition, Blackwell, Oxford, 1974) seem to improve upon it.
5. My italics. 'Naming and Necessity' Princeton Lecture III, ad init.
6. To mention but one thing, consider Wisdom's headscratch problem. Wisdom scratches his head and tells you to do the same. You can't comply. Either you scratch Wisdom's head, in which case you fail in at least one way to imitate Wisdom's performance, which was one of Wisdom's scratching his own head; or you scratch you own head—in which case you don't scratch Wisdom's. If Wisdom insists on being perverse and disallowing either performance, then nothing short of the lambda notation can finally clarify what is required of you. For some other desiderata

on the theory of reflexive pronouns, see Geach, *Reference & Generality*, Chapter Five.
7. I say 'allegedly', because 2.4 has already distanced me from this condition, and perhaps from fully or properly *defining* identity at all. Cp. footnote 9 of my *Identity and Spatio Temporal Continuity* (Blackwell, Oxford, 1967).
8. See Alonzo Church, *Introduction to Mathematical Logic* (Princeton, 1956), pp. 24–5. There may be a way round this argument, on which Quine, Davidson and Wallace have rested so much in other connections: but it is by no means easily controverted.
9. See, e.g., Ruth Barcan Marcus, 'Quantification and Ontology' in *Nous*, 1974. It is true that, by some method like the one Professor Marcus suggests in her reply, a language might be given a denumerably infinite number of interpreted constants or rigid designators (although the only very straightforward way to conceive of this is to take something like numerals as designators and the numbers or some other ordered totality as their interpretation). It may therefore be true that substitutional quantification can be designed as a formal system not to offend against our intuitions of validity. But the questions I was pursuing in the text were not these.
10. See footnote 9 of my paper.
11. It is worth noting the writer of the letter himself is a bit worried and tries to cover himself with the addition of 'the owner for the time being', which could still be misunderstood by a reader determined not to be parted from his amusement at the sentence. For all I know the precautionary move was prompted by some intuition corresponding to the theory of rigid designation.
12. Arnauld's Objection 'De Natura mentis humanae' against Descartes, p. 201 in Adam and Tannery *Œuvres de Descartes*, vol. 7.
13. See 'The *De Re* "Must": a note on the logical form of essentialist claims' with an *Appendix* by C. A. B. Peacocke

forthcoming in *Semantics* edited by Gareth Evans and John McDowell (O.U.P., 1975).

14. *Chleb s maslom*, using the same preposition '*s*' as is used to deal with the Jack and Jill case. If my argument for the distinctness of the 'Jack and Jill' problem and the 'bread and butter' problem is correct, then that is the beginning of the case for an ambiguity in the Russian proposition '*s*'. (On these questions see 'Sentence Sense, Word Sense and Difference of Word Sense' in Steinberg and Jacobovits, *Semantics: an Interdisciplinary Reader*, Cambridge, 1971.) Against this, it may be said that if bread and butter will not fit the 'Jack and Jill' analysis, Jack and Jill will fit the 'bread and butter' analysis. So '*s*' is not ambiguous, it may be held. But taking Jack and Jill as a complex would entail consequential changes in all the predicates which are applicable to them singly or jointly, an uninviting prospect in the extreme. It seems obvious that 'with' must in any case be ambiguous, on my view; for to carry through the Jack and Jill strategy, 'with' must carry a sense to be rendered by, e.g., a Latin *dative* in 'Jack fought/married with Jill and Jill fought/married with Jack' and a sense to be rendered by, e.g., a Latin *ablative* in 'Jack ran up the hill with Jill & Jill ran up the hill with Jack'.

IV / The Relation between Natural Languages and Formalized Languages

Frederic B. Fitch

A natural language is comprehensible as spoken or written, while a formalized language is ordinarily comprehensible only as written. We might even regard a written natural language as a different language from the spoken form of the language, but in the case of a formalized language we would not often want to distinguish a spoken form of it as distinct from a written form, since a formalized language is usually regarded primarily as written.

Yet there is no reason why a language could not be natural in the sense of being comprehensible as a spoken language and also be formalized in the sense of being defined precisely by use of rules specifying which strings of words and sentences and which strings of sentences are logical proofs. That is to say, there may be an overlap between natural languages and formalized languages, and the languages falling in this overlap would be especially interesting since they could be used for ordinary communication but would still possess all the advantages possessed by formalized languages. I will call these languages *normalized* languages or dialects. A normalized language is *natural* in the sense that it can be understood and spoken, and yet it is *formalized* in the sense that the written form of it (and perhaps also the spoken form of it) is formalizable in the usual way.

Rather than discuss in a general way the obvious differences between unformalized natural languages and formalized written languages, I will discuss some aspects of a particular normalized dialect of English, and without defining this dialect in detail I will make some remarks about its surface structure and its deep structure and the relation of these to quantification.

In this dialect a fundamental binary mode of combination is used called *application*. This is essentially the same operation which serves as the fundamental binary mode of combination in combinatory logic, but in combinatory logic the applicator is always written to the left of the applicand, whereas in this dialect the applicator is sometimes on the right side of the applicand. For example, if in this dialect an adjective is placed immediately to the left or right of a noun which the adjective modifies, we have a case of application of the adjective to the noun. Similarly, an adverb is said to be applied to a verb (or a verb phrase) which it modifies by immediately preceding or following. Other cases of application are involved in forming sentences from verbs and nouns and in forming prepositional phrases from prepositions and nouns, as will be indicated in more detail below.

A few of the many syntactic categories required in this dialect and serving to classify both individual words and phrases consisting of groups of words are: proper noun, common noun, adjective, intransitive verb, transitive verb, adverb (of various kinds), preposition. The application of an intransitive verb (or intransitive verb phrase) to a proper noun gives rise to a sentence. In this case of application, the applicator (the verb) is placed to the right of the applicand (the noun), as in the sentence, 'John runs'. The application of a transitive verb to a proper noun gives rise to an intransitive verb phrase. Thus the phrase, 'loves Mary' is an intransitive verb phrase. In this case the applicator is placed to the left of the applicand. If the intransitive verb phrase is applied to the proper noun 'John', we get the sentence, 'John loves Mary'.

In the notation of combinatory logic the application of 'a'

to 'b' is written as '(ab)'. Thus 'John runs' is written as '(runs John)', and 'John loves Mary' is written as '((loves Mary) John)'. The applicator is always written to the left of the applicand in combinatory logic.

Application is also used in applying modifiers to what they modify, as was noted earlier. Thus the phrase 'runs swiftly', could be expressed as '(swiftly runs)' in the notation of combinatory logic and the sentence, 'John runs swiftly', as '((swiftly runs) John)'.

A prepositional phrase, such as 'of France', is analysed as the result of applying 'of' to 'France' and so appears as '(of France)' in the notation of combinatory logic. Since 'of France' modifies 'king' in the phrase 'king of France', the latter phrase appears as '((of France) king)' in the notation of combinatory logic. Now this latter phrase is an adjective phrase, and any adjectural phrase may be converted in an intransitive verb phrase by applying the verb 'is' to it. Thus 'is king of France' appears as '(is ((of France) king))', and the sentence, 'Louis is king of France' appears as '((is ((of France) king)) Louis)'.

The sentence, 'Louis is king of France', may also be regarded as being of the same form as the sentence, 'Louis rules France', where 'France' is the direct object. In other words, 'is king of' may be viewed as a transitive verb phrase, and may be regarded as the result of applying 'is' to the phrase 'king of'. The latter phrase itself may be regarded as the result of applying 'of' to 'king', but this is a kind of backward application of 'of' since it gives the phrase 'king of' rather than the phrase 'of king'. When 'of' is thought of as applied in this backward way, we will call it 'of*' and when applied in the forward way, we shall call it simply 'of'. The two analyses of the sentence 'Louis is king of France' are then

1   ((is ((of France) king)) Louis)
2   (((is (of* king)) France) Louis)

There are operators 'C' and 'I' in combinatory logic which have the properties $(((Ca)b)c) = ((ac)b)$ and $(Ia) = a$. If these operators are included in our language, it is easy to show (using extensionality) that

$$\text{of}^\star = (C \text{ of})$$

and

$$\text{of} = (C \text{ of}^\star)$$

and that (1) and (2) above are equal to each other if 'is', in this context, is represented by the operator 'I'. This means that if 'C' and 'I' are present in the language, then the two analyses of the sentence are not ultimately different but give the same 'deep structure' for the sentence. By the 'deep structure' we mean the analysis of the sentence in the notation of combinatory logic, or the combination of concepts and individuals expressed by such notation. (Operators such as 'C' are not actually included in the normalized dialect itself, nor is combinatory notation included, but they are included in an extended form of the dialect that is used for analysing deep structure.)

This relatively simple way of analysing a sentence so as to give its deep structure cannot be used when quantifiers such as 'any man', 'some man', 'every woman', 'no house', 'the king of France', and so on, are present in the sentence.

Consider as an example, 'Every man loves any woman who loves that man.' Notice that we here use the phrase 'that man' instead of the pronoun 'him'. In general, we will avoid use of third personal pronouns except as mere abbreviations for phrases like 'that man'. This avoidance of third personal pronouns as primitive is analogous to the avoidance of variables as primitive in combinatory logic. Variables, as such, are primarily *symbols*, and are neither concepts nor names of concepts. So a logic or a language having sentences that express combinations of concepts and individuals should have no essential need for variables, but only for names of concepts and names of individuals and for modes of combining such names.

In dealing with quantification we will employ not only

quantifiers, such as 'every man', but also what will be called 'quantified phrases', such as 'that man', as in the sentence 'Every man loves any woman who loves that man.' In some cases we also need quantified phrases of the form 'that first man', 'that second man' and so on, as in the sentence, 'Any man likes every man who admires that first man.'

Quantifiers and quantified phrases act like noun phrases as far as the surface structure is concerned, and may be called 'surface noun phrases'. They may combine with adjectives, verbs and prepositions in the same way that proper nouns do, but only as far as surface structure is concerned, and the application of adjectives, verbs, prepositions, and so on, to them is not genuine or 'deep' application but will be referred to as 'surface application'. Furthermore, we can regard such words as 'every', 'any', 'some', 'no', 'the' as 'surface adjectives' which may be applied by surface application to common nouns to give quantifiers. Similarly 'that', 'that first', and so on, are surface adjective phrases that may be applied to common nouns to give quantified phrases. For example, the surface structure of the sentence, 'Jack loves every woman who loves Jack' may be expressed, '(Jack {loves {every (woman {who (loves Jack)})}})' where parentheses indicate genuine or deep application and braces indicate surface application; and the surface structure of the sentence 'Any man loves every woman who loves that man' may be expressed, {{any man} {loves {every {woman {who {loves {that man}}}}}}}. Here all applications are surface applications.

Relative pronouns may be regarded as surface pronouns which may be dispensed with in the deep structure, just as ordinary pronouns are also dispensed with in the deep structure. The procedure will be first to replace phrases beginning with relative pronouns by phrases beginning with 'such that' and then to express the latter phrases in combinatory logic by use of abstraction, which is obtainable in combinatory logic by use of such operators as 'B', 'C', 'W' and 'K' (or more economically by use of 'S' and 'K') and does not require use of variables. Thus the phrase, 'A thing which Jack knows' would first be rewritten as 'A thing such that Jack knows that thing', and then would be expressed in combinatory logic by use of abstraction.

In forming an abstract in combinatory logic the procedure is as follows: Suppose we wish to find the abstract of '$(((ab)c)b)$' with respect to 'b'. By using such operators as 'B', 'C', 'W' and 'K' where

$$(((Ba)b)c) = (a(bc))$$
$$(((Ca)b)c) = ((ac)b)$$
$$((Wa)b) = ((ab)b)$$
$$((Ka)b) = a$$

We move 'b' in '$((ab)c)b)$' to the right obtaining an expression of the form '(db)', where 'd' does not contain 'b' and is the required abstract. In particular,

$$(((ab)c)b) = ((((Ca)c)b)b)$$
$$= ((W((Ca)c))b)$$

Thus '$(W((Ca)c))$' is the abstract of $(((ab)c)b)$', with respect to 'b'.

'A thing which Jack knows' can be expressed in combinatory logic as 'a thing such that Jack knows that thing' and hence as the abstract with respect to 'a' of 'Jack knows a', that is, of '$((\text{knows } a) \text{ Jack})$'. Since

$$((\text{knows } a) \text{ Jack}) = (((C \text{ knows}) \text{ Jack})a)$$

the required abstract is '$((C \text{ knows}) \text{ Jack})$', and this latter abstract expresses the same concept as 'a thing which Jack knows'.

Consider next how the deep structure of a sentence such as 'Every woman loves Jack' is to be analysed by use of combinatory logic. We first form the sentence 'If Jill is a woman, Jill loves Jack' and note that it has the following deep structure, (where 'if p then q' is analysed as $((\supset q)p)$): '$((\supset((\text{loves Jack}) \text{Jill})) ((\text{is woman}) \text{Jill}))$'. We next form the abstract of the latter expression with respect to 'Jill'. Call this abstract 'a'.

Then by applying to 'a' the universality operator 'A', we get 'Aa' as the deep structure of the original sentence. In detail 'Aa' is '$(A(W(B(C((B \supset)$ (loves Jack))) (is woman))))'.

In lieu of giving a complete and detailed account of quantifiers in this language I will have to be content with asserting three points as follows because of limitations of space:

1. Rules for quantifiers are easily formulated as surface structure rules, and even as surface structure rules that avoid use of pronouns I have done this for several fundamental quantifiers of English in my paper, 'Natural Deduction Rules for English' (*Philosophical Studies*, vol. 24 (1973), pp. 89–104). Here the convention was adopted that leftmost quantifiers have the greatest scope.

2. Unrestricted quantification exists in any language within which the topic of unrestricted quantification can be discussed. In other words, there is no way to discuss unrestricted quantification without already using it. Since unrestricted quantification is discussible in English, it already exists in English. Consequently, I incorporate it in the normalized dialect of English that I have constructed. In any case, unrestricted quantification is philosophically important in the sense that philosophical discussion in one of its most typical forms, is characterized by that high degree of generality that can be expressed only by use of unrestricted quantifiers. Here 'anything' would mean 'anything at all' in the most general possible sense.

3. The correct analysis of quantification as within the form of combinatory logic that serves to express the deep structure of the normalized dialect of English is the standard one that is obtained by using abstraction and applying an operator for universality or existence to the resulting abstract, as has already been illustrated in one case.

Something should also be said about the possibility of the consistency of a combinatory logic that is to be used for expressing deep structure in the way I have indicated. This combinatory logic will indeed be inconsistent if it possesses both unrestricted excluded middle and unrestricted abstraction, since the Russell paradox will then arise in it as a genuine contradiction. I believe that it remains consistent, however, if a mild restriction is placed on excluded middle like the one used in system $Q\,D$ in the last chapter of my recently published book on combinatory logic (*Elements of Combinatory Logic*, Yale University Press, 1974). A corresponding mild restriction with respect to excluded middle also has to be placed, of course, on the normalized dialect of English. This would leave all ordinary sentences of the dialect as satisfying excluded middle, but it would impose limits on excluded middle in the case of sentences involved in formulating the Russell paradox and similar paradoxes.

It seems to me important to construct a normalized dialect of English which is powerful enough to handle philosophical discourse and discourse about all languages, including itself. Only in this way, I believe, can philosophical and linguistic issues be treated with an acceptable amount of rigour and with some hope of achieving scientifically satisfactory results, and only by use of combinatory logic, or some similar sort of logic, can a satisfactory account be given of the deep structure of such a dialect. Classical set theory and theories of types seem unsatisfactory compared to combinatory logic for representing the deep structure of languages having unrestricted quantification. This is mainly because unrestricted quantification is not permissible in these latter systems. For example, set theory lacks quantification over so-called *notions* and type theory restricts quantification to a specific type.

It might be supposed that the proposed dialect would violate results established by Tarski concerning the nature of truth. Elsewhere (in my paper 'Universal Metalanguages for Philosophy', *Review of Metaphysics*, vol. 17 (1964), pp. 396–402) I have argued that the approach I am taking in combinatory logic circumvents these results of Tarski. Similarly they will be circumvented in the normalized dialect that employs combinatory logic for its deep structure.

Comment

BY P. T. GEACH

Professor Fitch has brought together a number of topics; the connections between them are not always clear to me, and I must ask him to restore liaison between things I treat disjointedly.

I agree with him that a spoken language can in principle be as fully formal and formalized as a written language. Symbolic logicians who use unpronounceable symbols, or symbols with both superscripts and subscripts, show little consideration for those whose memory works auditorily rather than visually; but most logical symbols have conventional pronounciations—depending obviously on the reader's own vernacular. The difference of medium between written and spoken language is of course logically unimportant: with modern technique of recording, there is not even a difference in durability.

Fitch seems to confuse the difference between spoken and written language with the difference between natural and artificial language. Whether spoken or written, the sentence 'For some x, x is identical with x' is not standard English but artificial jargon: if we took it as English, 'x' could not be consistently parsed—it would need to be a mass term or count noun in the context 'for some x' and a proper noun in 'x is identical with x'. I marvel that the Friends of Ordinary Language have not seized on this to show the syntactical incoherence of quantification theory. Of course I do not think any the worse of quantification theory for its formulas' not being ordinary English; but it is not their being unpronounced that makes them not to be good English.

Fitch has shown in the only indisputable way—by himself doing what he claims can be done—that a fragment of English can actually be formalized: all the sentences of the fragment are undeviant, even if rather stilted, English sentences. This achievement, in the *Philosophical Studies* article Fitch cites, appears to me an important one. Various schools of thought, with one *parti pris* or another, have exaggerated the difference between natural languages and logical calculi; Fitch's results show on the contrary that you can do a lot of logic in standard English. This way of doing logic is not very convenient in logical practice—though its possibility might be helpfully brought to the notice of beginners in logic—but it gives great theoretical insight into the nature of ordinary syntax. (Cf. *Tractatus* 3.3421.)

With this article in mind, I was considerably surprised to find Fitch offering such crude and unsuitable analyses of English syntactical structures as he gives us in the paper we have just heard. He wishes to regard the sentences of his fragment of English as built up by successive performance of a binary operation, application. An example is that the phrase 'king of France' is built up by applying 'of' to 'France' and then applying the phrase 'of France' to 'king', or alternatively by applying 'of' backwards to 'king' and applying 'king of' to 'France'. (I am here ignoring a small complication about the copula 'is'; since Fitch compares it to an identity function, whose value is always equal to its argument, I think this is justified.) I shall return to the king of France in a moment. What I must now remark is that for quite simple English constructions an analysis in terms of binary combination is extremely unplausible if not manifestly wrong. Take a phrase ⌜A and B⌝—I use Quine's quasi-quotes, with capital letters as metalinguistic variables. Is this formed by applying 'and' to B and then applying ⌜and B⌝ backwards to A? or by applying 'and' backwards to A and then applying ⌜A and⌝ to B? or by applying A to B and then applying 'and' to the result, and finally using some device of combinatory logic to get 'and' into middle position? Any such solution would seem quite wrong. The connective 'and' does not logically go with one conjunct more than the other; and if A and B are two sentences, there is no good sense in speaking of applying one to the other.

I should thus claim that binary application gives a wrong

syntactical analysis even for the simple case of two-place symmetrical connectives. The idea works even worse for operators that can take a varying number of arguments. Consider an expression ⌜$A, B,$ or C⌝, where 'or' is read in the exclusive sense. This cannot be analysed in terms of a two-place exclusive 'or': ⌜$A, B,$ or C⌝ is different in force both from ⌜$(A$ or $B)$ or C⌝ and from ⌜A or $(B$ or $C)$⌝. Nor is there any two-place connective, say 'ϕ', such that ⌜$A, B,$ or C⌝ could be taken to be short for ⌜$(A\ \phi\ B)$ or C⌝ or for ⌜$A\ \phi(B$ or $C)$⌝. If we take A, B, and C to be sentences, a little manipulation of truth-tables shows this. Still less can ⌜$A, B,$ or C⌝ be analysed in terms of a binary application-operator. Nor does surface grammar suggest any such thing.

Let me now return to the king of France. Fitch's two suggested analyses do here more or less fit ordinary grammatical analysis in English and other vernaculars; some languages modify the word 'France', others modify 'king' to 'king of' (Hebrew grammarians speak of nouns in the construct state). But what grammarians find natural makes no sense at all in logic. There are no logical procedures by which the name 'France' is turned into an operator 'of France' that can operate upon the one-place predicable 'king' to yield the one-place predicable 'king of France', or by which a backwards operation of 'of' on the one-place predicable 'king' gives us the two-place predicable 'king of'. On the contrary, in logic the two-place predicable 'king of' is prior to the one-place predicable 'king', which Quine would call the result of *derelativizing* 'king of'.

Fitch's procedure in this part of his paper seems to be as follows. He takes over from ordinary grammar the idea of one expression's governing or agreeing with another: prepositions govern nouns, adjectives agree with nouns, subjects govern verb phrases, transitive verbs govern objects, etc. He then assimilates all these intuitively very different relations to one relation of binary application, and asserts that—so long as pronouns, quantifiers, and quantified phrases do not enter in—this is the whole of the law in syntax. But the assimilation appears arbitrary and unplausible; there are simple grammatical constructions that resist analysis in terms of binary application; and in such examples as 'king of France' the suggestions of conventional grammar run counter to the needs of logic.

Fitch's foray into grammar is in aid of a formal logic in which—apart from the parentheses of binary application—all well-formed expressions are of the same category. Obviously this logic can gain no support from even the crudest traditional grammar. Only a noun, noun-phrase, or pronoun can be subject of a verb, not an adverb, preposition, or conjunction; a preposition can govern only a noun or noun phrase or pronoun; and so on. I am not maintaining that the old grammatical categories are adequate; I have myself sketched out a reformed system of categories ('A Program for Syntax', in *Semantics of Natural Language*, ed. Donald Davidson and Gilbert Harman; Dordrecht, D. Reidel and Co., 1972). But total Gleichschaltung of the grammatical categories is just not on; grammarians would rightly ignore such a suggestion.

Fitch claims that in logic category distinctions can be abolished without paradox if we mildly relax the Law of Excluded Middle. This is not obviously true, since negation-free paradoxes, which cannot be dealt with by a deviant logic of negation, are well known, and indeed Fitch mentions one in his own *Symbolic Logic*. It will be relevant here to mention a comment on Frege relating to functional application, which I published some years since in *Three Philosophers* (Oxford: Basil Blackwell, 1961). I showed there that a theorem of Frege's *Grundgesetze*, containing neither negation nor quantifiers, leads to a paradox. Frege assumes that there is a function corresponding to Fitch's binary application, and for convenience I use Fitch's symbol for this; *this* assumption can give rise to no trouble, since it cannot be a matter of principle that a function is undefined for some arguments—one can always fill the gaps, as Frege insisted, by arbitrary stipulation. Frege further assumes that for every function there is an object that is the course of values, *Werthverlauf*, of the function: if we represent the function as '$F\xi$', where the Greek letter indicates the argument-place, the course of values will be $\lambda x F x$—to use a more familiar notation than Frege's. Frege's paradox-fraught theorem is:

$\vdash (\lambda x F x\ a) = Fa$

Now let us replace the functional sign '$F\xi$' by '$G(\xi\xi)$': we get

$\vdash (\lambda x G(xx)\ a) = G(aa)$

Finally, replacing 'a' by '$\lambda x G(xx)$' we get:

$\vdash (\lambda x G(xx)\ \lambda x G(xx)) = G(\lambda x G(xx)\ \lambda x G(xx))$

Thus for any arbitrary function $G\xi$ we can specify an argument, namely the object $(\lambda x G(xx)\ \lambda x G(xx))$, the result of binarily applying the object $\lambda x G(xx)$ to itself, for which we have $Gb = b$. But this cannot be right: for any number of functions Gb is *never* the same as b.

This paradox is easily reproduced in terms of Fitch's operators, as has long been known.

$((Wa)\ b) = ((ab)\ b)$
$\therefore ((W(BF))(W(BF))) = (((BF)(W(BF)))(W(BF)))$
But $(((Ba)\ b)\ c) = (a\ (bc))$
$\therefore (((BF)(W(BF)))(W(BF))) = (F((W(BF))(W(BF))))$
$\therefore ((W(BF))(W(BF))) = (F((W(BF))(W(BF))))$

So for Fitch—who apparently rejects Frege's distinction between function and course of values—the same unacceptable conclusion arises as arose from Frege's theorem: and I think his claim to avoid paradox is unfounded.

At least, he could make the claim good only by adding further restrictions which he has not specified: restrictions on the *tertium non datur* will not suffice.

Comment

BY JOHN MCDOWELL

Do we know enough about Professor Fitch's normalized dialect of English to be able to assess its philosophical utility? Thanks to the beautiful simplicity of its surface syntax, we have a pretty good general conception of that. Similarly with its deep syntax. As far as I can see, however, Fitch's paper tells us nothing about the relation between these two levels, or about the motivation for distinguishing them. On what principle do we decide that application of, say, a verb to a quantifier is not genuine or deep application but merely surface application? This question seems all the more pressing in view of the possibility, alluded to by Fitch, of formulating proof theory for quantifiers entirely at the surface level. It will not do to appeal, in a general way, to linguistics for answers to this and similar questions; for, notoriously, distinctions of syntactic level are, in different sorts of linguistic theory, justified in different ways. I am not suggesting that Fitch's distinction of levels is wrong, but simply that he has not said enough about it.

As for semantics, Fitch tells us nothing about how the strings of expressions which constitute sentences of his dialect mean what they do, apart from the implication that they 'express combinations of concepts and individuals'. (The 'propositions' of Russell's logical atomism?) Of course we understand his example sentences perfectly well, but that is because of their closeness to forms of speech with which we are familiar, and not because of anything he says about how the meanings of the parts contribute to the meanings of the wholes.

It may seem captious to insist on this. Surely, after all, the semantics of a language whose syntactic structure is that of combinatory logic should take virtually no work to construct. All that we need is the assignment of suitable objects and functions to the various primitive expressions; simple recursive clauses should deal with all the combinatory operators (assuming that the semantic description of the dialect would apply at the level of deep structure).

Nevertheless, Fitch's apparent lack of concern with semantics seems worth mentioning, for two reasons. First, if it is right to assume that the semantic description of the dialect would apply at the level of deep structure, the insufficiency of what Fitch says about the distinction of levels is further emphasized. Consider, for instance, the sentences

1   Jack wearily reached the door
2   Jack barely reached the door
3   Jack allegedly reached the door.

It seems inconceivable that any satisfying account of how the meanings of these sentences depend on the meanings of their parts could represent them as differing only in the identity of their parts and not at all in their mode of construction. Yet their surface syntactic forms seem identical. So it appears that semantical considerations compel us to view their syntax as diverging at a different level. Now, would that be Fitch's conclusion? Leaving us in the dark, as he does, about what the distinction of syntactic levels is for, he leaves us uninformed as to whether he regards semantical justifications for claims about syntax as being so much as permissible.

Second, by not even gesturing, as I did above, in the direction of an account of what a semantic description of his dialect might look like, Fitch leaves the unfortunate impression that he thinks there is some virtue in *syntactic* formalizability as such. But it is surely evident that syntactic formalization, in the absence of semantical rigour, is no guarantee of scientific respectability. A collection of strings of symbols may look scientific to the casual eye but be nonsense for all that.

What is the normalized dialect for? 'Only in this way', Fitch says, '... can philosophical and linguistic issues be treated with an acceptable amount of rigour and with some hope of achieving scientifically satisfactory results.' Does he mean that we ought actually to speak and write the dialect, or something similar, in discussing philosophical and linguistic issues? And which issues? As it stands, the claim seems to me to be too vague and sweeping to be sensibly assessed. We need a much more complex view of the role which formalization should play in philosophy.

It is arguable that the most fundamental issue in philosophy concerns the nature of meaning in general. (If that sounds too new-fangled, the issue can be described as that of the relation, in general, between language, or thought, and reality.) It seems plausible that this issue would be conclusively settled by a convincing description of the general shape which an adequate theory of meaning for any language would take, including an account of the place which such a theory would occupy in the theorist's general theory of how things are. Now, does Fitch mean to suggest that the works in which such topics have recently been most illuminatingly discussed—for instance Chapter Two of Quine's *Word and Object*, Davidson's seminal articles, Dummett's *Frege*—would have been in any way improved by being *translated into* his normalized dialect? The idea seems absurd. It seems obvious that, until we are agreed on these issues, there will always be room for a kind of philosophical discussion of them to which formalization would be no advantage; and if (*per impossibile*, no doubt) we come to an agreement, it will not be because we have arrived at something which we could improve by formalizing it. No doubt an ideal theory of meaning for a particular language, conforming to the envisaged general description, would be formalized; but the theory of theories of meaning, and its justification, seem quite another matter.

As this last remark suggests, formalization can be expected to have its primary role in the detailed and piecemeal construction of theories of meaning for particular languages, rather than in the head-on consideration of general issues concerning the relation between language and reality. Of course this is not to depreciate the philosophical importance of formalization. For, in the first place, any general specification of the shape which a theory of meaning for a language ought to take would be vulnerable to the actual impossibility of matching it, so that one could hardly interest oneself in the general specification to the exclusion of the work involved in the detailed construction; and it seems clear that something like normalization would be essential in constructing a manageable theory of meaning for any natural language. Second, all sorts of, broadly speaking, metaphysical questions would have to be faced in the course of the detailed construction, and it is at least arguable that at least some of them would be best handled by formal theories. For instance, a theorist of meaning who treats tensed discourse in terms of quantification over, and relations between, times incurs an obligation to construct a theory of times, and this would arguably be best done by means of axioms and definitions. Third, the perspicuity and satisfyingness of one normalization rather than another, in handling particular constructions and devices of particular natural languages, might cast light back on the general issues. For instance, the best recent work on referential devices in English suggests that referential relations between language and reality are best comprehended in the light of theories of meaning for formal languages containing individual variables. (But this is obviously not a suggestion to which Fitch would be sympathetic.)

In connection with the construction of theories of meaning for particular natural languages, there arise a number of difficult and fascinating questions concerning the relation between natural languages and the formalized languages devised for such purposes. In attempting to construct a theory of meaning for a natural language, with all its apparently chaotic variety, the obvious strategy is indeed to normalize or regiment the language; then we can envisage a relatively simple theory of meaning for the normalized or regimented language, together with an account of its relation to the original, unregimented vernacular, as constituting a theory of meaning adequate for the vernacular. But now, exactly what relation should there be between a vernacular sentence and its normalization or regimentation? Synonymy plus a traceable transformational route from regimentation to vernacular? In the context of the idea that a specification of what a theory of meaning, in general, is will tell us what meaning, in general, is, we ought to want to avoid appeal to notions like that of synonymy in our general description of the shape which an adequate theory of meaning would take; and it is not obvious what to put in its place. Again, if we use regimentations in a theory of meaning for a natural language, can we be committed thereby to any conclusions about the conceptual resources deployed by speakers of the language? For instance, if we deal with adverbial modification in Davidson's way, by regimenting sentences containing it into sentences which quantify over, and make appropriate predications concerning, events, are we thereby committed to the view that speakers of the language for which we are constructing a theory quantify, in some sense, over events? Or is it just we, the theorists, who do that? These and similar questions seem to me to be the crucial questions raised by the topic of the relation, in general, between natural and formalized languages. But they are not Fitch's concern, and I shall take them no further.

Given that, in order to produce a manageable theory of meaning for a natural language, we should need to normalize or regiment it, the question arises what should be the logical structure of the regimented language we employ. What reasons are there for preferring Fitch's normalization to other candidates, for instance first-order quantification theory or various possible enrichments of it? Fitch's reason for preferring his dialect is that it permits unrestricted quantification, but that seems inconclusive. Perhaps that feature might have been an advantage in a language designed for actual employment in discussing philosophical questions concerning the relation, in general, between language and reality, though even that seems less than obvious. In any case, it is far from obvious that the possibility of unrestricted quantification is any virtue in a language designed to normalize, say, English for the purpose of giving a theory of meaning for that language. Are there, then, other advantages in Fitch's dialect? For instance, can natural-language quantifiers be better handled? Not as far as Fitch's paper shows. Standard quantification theory cannot deal with, say, 'Most women love Jack'; but Fitch's way with 'Every woman loves Jack' will not extend to such sentences either. Perhaps it might be suggested that Fitch's normalization is superior to a regimentation into first-order quantification theory on the ground that, given the greater syntactic richness of Fitch's dialect, the forms into which natural-language sentences are regimented, for handling by a theory of meaning, could be closer, if we did it his way, to their actual surface syntax. But whether such syntactic similarity is a desideratum at all is itself a moot question: one, indeed, of those general questions concerning the relation between natural and formalized languages which Fitch, despite his title, does not consider.

Reply to Comments

BY FREDERIC B. FITCH

The first criticism by McDowell is that I have not sufficiently delineated the relation between surface structure and deep structure. But I surely have given examples that make quite clear the general method of going from surface structure to deep structure, and without writing a long treatise on the subject I could not possibly state all the specific rules involved. Geach apparently understood my brief account of this relationship well enough and summarized it clearly.

McDowell next expresses his dismay over the fact that I do not give a complete semantics for my normalized dialect of English. Again, I must reply that to do so would be to write a lengthy treatise. Yet McDowell seems to feel that my paper should, for example, leave no doubt in the mind of the reader as to the fact that, and as to how, the following three sentences differ in their mode of construction:

1   Jack wearily reached the door.
2   Jack barely reached the door.
3   Jack allegedly reached the door.

Without attempting to give a completely detailed answer to this problem, or to hundreds of other equally profound problems, I will at least say that I do not regard these three sentences as differing in either surface or deep syntactic structure, though they clearly differ in meaning, and in particular the first two imply that Jack reached the door, and the third does not imply this. I would say that (3) is logically equivalent to the sentence, 'It is alleged that Jack reached the door', while neither (1) nor (2) is logically equivalent to a sentence of exactly this form. The truth of (3), indeed, would be determined by first determining the truth of this latter sentence to which (3) is logically equivalent and from which it differs in syntactic structure.

In general, for really usable languages, semantics is far less scientific than syntax. For example, it is almost impossible to give an exact meaning for any common English word. The syntax of what I call a normalized language, on the other hand, can be formulated with complete scientific rigour. This is one reason for my paying more attention to syntax than to semantics. It may be that 'syntactic formalization, without semantic rigour, is no guarantee of scientific respectability', as McDowell asserts, but semantic rigour is so difficult to obtain in the case of usable languages that the onus of achieving scientific respectability must be assigned largely to syntax.

The claim that logical or philosophical treatises would not be clearer if written in a normalized language seems to me extremely dubious. Many sentences of English are ambiguous because of uncertainty regarding the scopes of quantifiers, while this uncertainty does not exist in the case of a normalized language. If even one such sentence occurs in a philosophical treatise, the treatise would be clearer if expressed in a normalized language.

McDowell raises an interesting point when he asks whether a vernacular language quantifies over the same things as a normalization of it does. My answer is that there really is no such thing as a normalization of a vernacular language. There are simply two different languages that are somewhat similar, one being a vernacular language and the other being a normalized language. The vernacular language might quantify over times and the normalized language might quantify over events, and this would be a difference between them, but unless the normalized language is treated as a more acceptable substitute for the vernacular language, we do not need to assume that temporal quantifications in the vernacular language are 'really' quantifications over events. In any case, the process of transforming a vernacular language into a normalized language need not involve any radical change of range of quantification. For example, vernacular English surely does contain unrestricted quantification (since otherwise unrestricted quantification could not even be discussed in vernacular English), and hence any transformation of vernacular English into a normalized language would not need to involve a rejection of unrestricted quantification. McDowell, however, asserts that 'it is far from obvious that the possibility of unrestricted quantification is any virtue in a language designed to normalize, say, English for the purpose of giving a theory of meaning for that language'. But if English already contains unrestricted quantification, as indeed it does, then any theory of meaning for English would have to be expressed in a language that also contains unrestricted quantification, and the same is true of any general theory of the relation of language to reality.

I turn now to Geach's criticisms of my paper. He appears to be favourably impressed by my demonstration in my

Philosophical Studies article that a fragment of English can be formalized in such a way that rigorous quantification rules are included without use of variables and so that the quantificational ambiguities of ordinary English are overcome. This shows, he says, 'that you can do a lot of logic in standard English'. On the other hand, he has no such commendation to make for my present paper, and he regards as 'crude and unsuitable' my use of basic binary operation in terms of which all syntactic structure is analysed.

One of his objections to the use of this binary operation is the alleged consequence that all well-formed expressions are of the same category. But this objection suggests that Geach is confusing surface structure with deep structure. As far as surface structure is concerned we can have a large number of different grammatical categories and, with respect to those categories, a severe limitation on the class of expressions that are accepted as well-formed surface-structure expressions. The mere fact that the same binary operation is used to join adverb to verb and to join preposition to noun does not entail that the results of such joining belong to the same grammatical category of surface structure and does not require, for example, that the use of this operation to join a proper noun to a proper noun need give a result that is a well-formed expression of surface structure.

In the case of deep structure, the situation is different. Here we have a system of combinatory logic, and all results of applying well-formed expressions of deep structure to well-formed expressions of deep structure are themselves well-formed expressions of deep structure. But we still can make any number of distinctions that we wish among these well-formed expressions, and thus have a very complex system of categories even for deep structure. The main difference is that at the level of deep structure the distinctions between categories cannot be used as a basis for ruling certain expressions as not well formed, while at the level of surface structure these distinctions can be so used.

I turn now to Geach's objections to using binary combination to analyse such expressions as "A and B". (Here double quotation marks are being used somewhat like Quine's corners.) This use of binary combination is well known in combinatory logic and has been employed there for many years without encountering any dire consequences. If what he wants is a primitive ternary operation, this could indeed be provided in an extended form of combinatory logic which would have a primitive n-ary operation for $n = 2, 3, 4$, and so on. (A student of mine, W. I. Grosky, has developed such a combinatory logic in his Ph.D. thesis, 'A Mathematical Theory of Constructible Automata', Department of Engineering and Applied Science, Yale University, 1971.) But this would be an added and unnecessary complication as far as the surface or deep structure of my normalized dialect of English is concerned, and not worth the trouble of introducing it.

Part of Geach's discussion of the representation of "A and B" in combinatory logic (or of "$[A$ and $B]$", as I shall write it below) shows a confusion between the use of expressions that denote ordered couples, on the one hand, and expressions that represent the result of binary combination, on the other. In combinatory logic as ordinarily formulated, "(AB)" is the application of "A" to "B" by way of binary combination and is not an expression denoting an ordered couple, and the expression "$[A$ and $B]$" is to be treated not as the result of the application of 'and' to "(AB)", that is, not as "(and $(AB))$", but either as "((and $B)A)$" or as "((and $A)B)$", depending on which convention one chooses to use. I prefer to treat "$[A$ and $B]$" as (an abbreviation for) "((and $B)A)$". In a sense it *does* appear that 'and' goes with "B" more than with "A" in "A and B" (that is, "$[A$ and $B]$"), at least where "A" and "B" are sentences. Thus we might write, "A; and B." But 'and' does not have to go with one more than the other in order to justify the procedures of combinatory logic in this situation.

Geach also objects to the usual techniques of combinatory logic in handling ternary operators, such as the ternary exclusive 'or' as applied to three sentences in "A, B, or C". He points out, rightly, that the ternary exclusive 'or' cannot be analysed merely in terms of repeated uses of the binary exclusive 'or', but nothing in combinatory logic requires any such analysis. There is no difficulty in giving a correct analysis of the ternary exclusive 'or' in the notation of combinatory logic.

In his discussion of the phrase, 'king of France', Geach becomes unusually assertive without giving much in the way of supporting arguments. He admits that my treatment of 'of' conforms somewhat to the views of various grammarians, but then states that 'what grammarians find natural makes no sense at all in logic'. I fail to agree. He then goes on to say, in effect, that my treatment of 'of' as an operator is simply wrong, but he does not say why, unless his final sentence on this topic is supposed to say why. This final sentence, however, asserts that 'in logic the two-place predicable "king of" is prior to the one-place predicable "king", which Quine would call the result of *derelativizing* "king of".' I agree with this statement, but I do not regard it as evidence that my treatment of 'of' is faulty. This is because I consider the one-place predicable as short for 'a king', and 'a king' as short for 'a king of something'. Thus the two-place predicable 'king of' is prior to the one-place predicable 'king', but 'king' in 'king of' is not the one-place predicable 'king'. It is rather something more fundamental that can be operated on (from the right) by 'of France' to give 'king of France', and that can be operated on (from the right) by a backward application of 'of' to give 'king of'. A forward application of 'of' to 'France', operating on it from the left, gives 'of France'.

The so-called 'paradox' that Geach points out asserts that for every function f in combinatory logic there is an argument a such that that $fa = a$. This is actually no paradox except in the sense that some people may be surprised by it. A similar result in a much more general form was published by me eight years before Geach (*Actes du XIème Congrès International de Philosophie*, 14: 121–7). This result perhaps appears to be a paradox because, outside of combinatory logic, functions are not usually defined over all functions as arguments, so an argument *a* of the requisite sort often cannot be found. It is part of the strength of combinatory logic, however, that such an argument can always be found, and this fact makes it possible to represent computer circuits in combinatory logic by a novel and powerful method, as I show in my book, *Elements of Combinatory Logic* (Yale University Press, New Haven, 1974).

If the so-called paradox were a paradox in a serious sense, a straightforward contradiction should be derivable in combinatory logic. But many systems of combinatory logic in which the so-called paradox is derivable are known to be consistent.

V / Quantifiers in Logic and Quantifiers in Natural Languages

Jaakko Hintikka

1 THE PROBLEM OF NATURAL-LANGUAGE QUANTIFIERS

Once upon a time most logicians believed that their quantifiers were obtained from the quantifiers of natural languages by abstraction or regimentation. (In this paper I shall restrict my attention to logicians' existential and universal quantifiers plus their counterparts in natural languages.) This belief was expressed in so many words time and again in textbooks and treatises of logic and in discussions of the philosophical problems of logic.[1] When the syntax and semantics of natural languages began to be taken seriously by contemporary linguists, it nevertheless soon became clear that there are all sorts of subtle problems about natural-language quantifiers which have no counterpart in logicians' so-called quantification theory. Nor were most of these problems touched, let alone solved, by ordinary-language philosophers.

This has by no means destroyed the belief that there is a close connection between the two kinds of quantifiers. However, in the last few years the traffic seems to have been moving mostly in the opposite direction. Generative semanticists like George Lakoff have proposed using formulas of formalized quantification theory not only as semantical representations of natural-language sentences but as the basis of their syntactical generation as well.[2] If this view were correct, a poor logician like myself would have no business poking his nose into the topic indicated by the title of my paper. In that eventuality, the relationship between the quantifiers of formal logic and the quantifiers occurring in the surface structures of natural languages would be determined by the syntactical transformations which are supposed to take us from the former to the latter. And the investigation of these transformations, prominently including the restraints they are subject to, is on this view a major task of linguists, not of logicians.

It is easy enough to pick holes in this Lakovian programme. Some indirect indications of its insufficiency will be given in the sequel. It is considerably harder, however, to propose a more satisfactory overall view of ordinary-language quantifiers. In another paper, I have in fact shown that first-order logic (lower predicate calculus), logicians' 'quantification theory', is insufficient as a semantical representation of English quantifier sentences.[3] In this sense, the received view of quantification theory as a regimentation of natural-language quantifiers is demonstrably false. Where, then, can we turn to for a better theory of natural-language quantification?

There exists one particularly natural way of looking at quantifiers which has never been put to use entirely satisfactorily before. It is to consider quantifiers as *singular terms*. It is plain even to a linguistically naked eye that quantifier phrases like 'some man', 'every woman', 'a girl', and even phrases like 'some boy who loves every girl' behave in many respects in the same way as terms denoting or referring to particular individuals. They can sometimes be used to report the same events as proper names. We can apply to them many such notions (e.g. the notion of coreference) as are primarily applicable to noun phrases which denote particular individuals. In fact, linguists have recently indulged in such applications to no end (and, according to some commentators, to no good purpose). Quantifier phrases can occur in most of the same grammatical constructions as noun phrases denoting particular individuals.

One can also apply to certain quantifier phrases the same distinction between the referential and the attributive reading which Keith Donnellan and others have claimed to exist in the case of certain denoting phrases of a different sort, viz. definite descriptions.[4] (I can say 'I saw a pretty girl walking by' and refer either to some particular female in perambulatory motion, or just make an impersonal existential statement concerning what I witnessed.) In view of such obvious facts, it seems eminently desirable to try to treat quantifier phrases both syntactically and semantically in the same way as singular terms.

This is what the late Richard Montague tried to do in his treatment of quantification in English.[5] The idea was not original with him, however. Bertrand Russell had already in *The Principles of Mathematics* tried to treat quantifiers as denoting phrases.[6] Russell's theory is quite interesting in several respects, one of which is that he tries to describe the semantical differences between different quantifiers in English, such as 'all', 'every', 'any', 'some', and 'a'. (As Russell was aware, the differences between those quantifiers is a feature of natural languages which has no obvious counterpart in formal logic. Hence it is an interesting task to account for those differences in precise logical terms.) However, I shall not discuss Russell's theory here. In spite of its interest, this theory is not strong enough to capture many crucial facts about English quantifiers.

Montague's idea was to treat quantifier phrases on a par with singular denoting terms not only syntactically but also semantically. The usual explanation as to how he did this is to say that he reversed the usual interpretation of predication. Instead of reading 'John is clever' as expressing the membership of John in the class of clever people, he took it to express the membership of cleverness in the class of John's attributes. Then a quantifier sentence like 'every Welshman is clever' can be understood in the same way, as expressing the membership of cleverness in the class of attributes all Welshmen have. Thus the semantical entity correlated with 'every X' will be the class of attributes all X have, and analogously for 'some X'.

I cannot try to evaluate this treatment here.[7] A few remarks on Montague's theory are nevertheless in order. Obviously it cannot make great claims to pragmatic or psycholinguistic plausibility. What is more important, in the real development of Montague's semantics little use is made of the correlation of 'every X' with the class of attributes all X have. For instance, the semantic interpretation of 'every boy loves some girl' or 'the lover of every woman' will have to be obtained by a more complicated process into which 'every boy', 'some girl', and 'every woman' do not enter just through the semantical entities correlated by Montague with them. Thus Montague does not really treat of quantifier phrases like singular terms except in a Pickwickian sense.

Neither Russell's nor Montague's treatment of quantifiers is thus fully satisfactory. Although quantifier phrases are very much like ordinary singular terms there are important differences between the two, differences which perhaps explain why earlier treatments of quantifiers as singular terms have not been successful. Intuitively, one is tempted to say that quantifier phrases denote, but that they just do not denote any particular constant individuals in the way ordinary singular terms do. This is among other things reflected by the fact that quantifier phrases do not even obey the usual laws of identity, in the sense that different occurrences of the same unambiguous quantifier phrase have to be treated differently in one's semantics. What I mean is illustrated, e.g., by the fact that in the sentence

1   John saw a warbler yesterday, and Bill saw a warbler, too

the two occurrences of 'a warbler' cannot be understood as referring to the same bird.

The same puzzling phenomenon appears in connection with reflexivization and pronominalization. For instance,

2   every man hates every man

says something quite different from

3   every man hates himself.

Likewise,

4   Some boy believes that Mary loves him

differs in meaning from

5   Some boy believes that Mary loves some boy.

These examples are of particular interest in that they show that the most natural rules for reflexivization and pronominalization fail to preserve meaning in the presence of quantifiers. (Cf. Barbara Hall Partee's essay on the alleged meaning preservation of transformations, pp. 9–10.)[8] The same goes for equi–NP deletion, as shown by the non-synonymy of the following sentences.

6   Every contestant expected to come in first.
7   Every contestant expected every contestant to come in first.

This marks another contrast between quantifiers and singular terms, for the following sentences are synonymous.

8   John expected to come first.
9   John expected John to come first.

The same can be said of the most straightforward rules of relative clause formation, as illustrated by the fact that (10) – (11) are non-synonymous while (12)–(13) are synonymous.

10   Every Democrat who voted for a Republican was sorry.
11   Every Democrat voted for a Republican, and every Democrat was sorry.
12   John who voted for a Republican was sorry.
13   John voted for a Republican, and John was sorry.

As emphasized by Barbara Hall Partee, these phenomena present problems of more than casual interest for our ideas of linguistic semantics at large.

For any satisfactory semantics of quantifiers, these phenomena pose interesting problems. How can quantifier phrases be in some respect so like singular terms and in other respects so unlike? Traditionally, such discrepancies between quantifiers and singular terms are often dealt with by saying that quantifier phrases stand for 'arbitrarily chosen' or 'random' individuals. However, it is scarcely satisfactory just to say this. Who is supposed to make this arbitrary choice? When? Why has the 'arbitrary choice' to be repeated for each occurrence of one and the same phrase? Moreover, not all these 'arbitrary choices' are comparable. What is the difference between the choices associated with 'some man' and 'every man', respectively? Traditionally, this line of thought has also led to difficult philosophical problems about *ekthesis*, 'general triangles', etc.[9]

The 'arbitrary choice' suggestion is an attempt to keep what is good in the analogy between quantifier phrases and singular terms and reject what is bad. What is bad is (among other things) that the analogy easily commits us to treating quantifier phrases as if they referred to constant individuals. What we have seen is enough to show that the 'arbitrary choice' idea does not avoid this difficulty and that it gives rise to others as well.

Formal logic offers no instant solutions, either. There are important discrepancies between logicians' quantifiers and quantifiers in English. One of them is the presence of several existential and several universal quantifiers in English which nevertheless exhibit subtle differences in their behaviour, for instance 'every' and 'any'. As we saw, Russell already tried to spell out some of the differences between the members of such pairs of quantifiers, but without much success. It is also clear that the 'arbitrary choice' idea does not help us here at all.

Another peculiarity of English quantifiers is the use of the indefinite article 'a', which obviously is in its typical employment an existential quantifier, in an apparently different function in the construction '— is a(n) . . .' to express predication.

The main obstacle to applications of quantification theory to the study of natural-language quantifiers is nevertheless the difficulty of giving explicit translation on transformation rules to connect the two. Generative semanticists' claims notwithstanding, nothing remotely like a satisfactory set of such rules can be found in the literature.

Such discrepancies between the quantifiers of logic and the quantifiers of natural language require explanations. The task of supplying them is neither a problem in formal logic alone nor yet a merely linguistic problem, it seems to me.

2 GAME-THEORETICAL SEMANTICS AS A SOLUTION

The game-theoretical semantics of quantifiers I have recently developed can be viewed as a way of overcoming the problems of these very kinds.[10] In the game-theoretical approach, the semantical properties of a quantified sentence S are determined by a two-person game $G(S)$ correlated with it.[11] In any actual round of this game $G(S)$ (the usual game-theoretical term for my 'round' is of course 'play') the quantifier phrases of S are replaced by proper names of individuals chosen one by one by the one or the other of the two players. We might almost say that in such a round of the game, quantifier phrases are interpreted as standing for these chosen individuals. This explains the partial similarity of the semantical behaviour of quantifier phrases with that of singular terms, indeed with that of proper names. Quantifier phrases do indeed function precisely like proper names, although not absolutely but only in each particular play of a semantical game. Since these games determine the semantics of quantifiers (in my approach), small wonder that quantifiers are easily and naturally thought of as a curious kind of singular denoting phrases not unlike proper names.

My approach nevertheless does not commit us to treating quantifier phrases semantically as if they stood for constant individuals, for the semantical properties of S can be characterized in terms of the overall characteristics of the correlated game $G(S)$, for instance in terms of the existence of different kinds of strategies for the two players. Such characteristics of $G(S)$ are independent of what happens during any particular play of $G(S)$, while the quantifier phrases of S are related to specific individuals only in some particular round (play) of that abstract game. For this reason, quantifier phrases cannot absolutely speaking be understood as picking out definite individuals, however 'arbitrarily selected'.

Some of the precise rules for the games $G(S)$ will be given below in section 4. There the reader will also find detailed examples of what may happen in these games.

We can nevertheless see already at this stage of discussion, that is to say without knowing anything more of my semantical games, how the game-theoretical idea allows us to overcome several of the difficulties mentioned earlier.

The choices of individuals for which quantifier phrases stand which are made in the different rounds (plays) of the abstract game $G(S)$ are indeed arbitrary in the sense that they are not determined by the general properties of the game $G(S)$. (Of course they are *not* arbitrary if each of the two players is actually trying to win.) Since the choices of individuals whose names are to replace quantifier phrases are made one by one, different occurrences of the same phrase may be replaced by different proper names, thus explaining the failure of the usual identity principles and also the failure of the usual pronominalization and reflexivization rules. (The same goes *mutatis mutandis* for equi-NP deletion and relativization.) Choices associated with different kinds of quantifiers (existential vs. universal) can be separated from each other in that they are made by different players.

This suffices to explain some of the puzzles mentioned above. The others, for instance the precise semantical difference between 'every' and 'any' and the relation of the copulative phrase '— is a(n) —' to the uses of the indefinite article as a quantifier, can also be explained in the game-theoretical semantics, but only after it has been developed somewhat farther.

The general interest of these semantical games is shown by the fact that they are tantamount to the language-games of seeking and finding whose philosophical implications are studied in my book, *Logic, Language-Games, and Information* (Clarendon Press, Oxford, 1973). Their connection with the Wittgensteinian idea of language-game is obvious. Now we are beginning to see that they are also directly relevant to the semantics of natural languages.

3 GAME-THEORETICAL SEMANTICS FOR FORMAL LANGUAGES

Game-theoretical semantics can nevertheless be applied also to formal quantificational (usually called 'first-order') languages and not only to natural languages. Indeed, they are probably appreciated more easily by first seeing how they can be set up for formal first-order languages.

These languages are of course to be thought of as *interpreted* languages, which means that we are given a domain of individuals D on which all the predicates of the language in question —call it L—are interpreted. (We also assume that the only free singular terms of L are proper names of members of D.) This in turn means that each atomic sentence built up of the predicates of L and of the names of the members of D has a definite truth-value, true of false. Since the crucial concept of all semantics is that of truth (on an interpretation), what our task is is essentially to extend the notion of truth from these atomic sentences to all the sentences of L, no matter how many quantifiers and sentential connectives they contain.

The games $G(S)$ that serve to accomplish these may be thought of as idealized processes of verification in which one of the two players, called 'myself' or 'I', is trying to show that S is true, and his opponent, who is called 'Nature' and who is perhaps best thought of as a Cartesian *malin genie*, is trying to show that it is false. My purpose in the game $G(S)$ is in fact to produce a true atomic sentence. If that happens, I have won and Nature has lost. If the game ends with a false atomic sentence, I have lost and Nature has won. Since the verification of an existential statement requires the searching for and the finding of a suitable individual, these verificational games are essentially games of seeking and (hopefully) finding.

At each stage of the game, a sentence S' is being considered. (This S' will belong to L or to a slight extension of L obtained by adding to it a finite number of names of members of D.) From the basic idea on which the game $G(S)$ is based we can at once gather what the game rules must be. What happens at a certain stage of the game is determined by the form of S'. We can distinguish the following cases depending on what this form is.

(G.E) If S' is $(Ex)F(x)$, I choose a member of D, give it a proper name (if it does not have one already that can be used), say 'b'. The game is then continued with respect to $F(b)$.

(G.U) If S' is $(x)F(x)$, the same happens except that Nature chooses b.

(G. $\vee$) If S' is $(F \vee G)$, I choose F or G, and the game is continued with respect to it.

(G. $\wedge$) If S' is $(F \wedge G)$, the same happens except that Nature makes the choice.

(G. $\sim$) If S' is $\sim F$, the roles of the two players (as defined by the rules (G.E), (G.U), (G. $\vee$), (G. $\wedge$), (G. $\sim$), and (G.A)) are reversed and the game is continued with respect to F.

Although (G. $\sim$) is formally unobjectionable, it is a somewhat unintuitive rule. For many purposes, it is more natural to replace this rule with a number of others dealing with the different kinds of negated sentences, or else to introduce a set of obligatory rewriting rules which serve to push negation-signs deeper into our sentences. An example of the former kind of rule is the following.

(G.$\sim \vee$) If S' is $\sim(F \vee G)$, Nature chooses $\sim F$ or $\sim G$, and the game is continued with respect to it.

An example of the latter kind of rule is the following.

(N.E) If S' is of the form $\sim(Ex)F(x)$, it is to be rewritten as $(x)\sim F(x)$.

In a finite number of moves an atomic sentence A is reached containing solely predicates of L and names of members of D. Winning and losing are defined with respect to it.

(G.A) If A is true, I have won and Nature lost; if A is false, vice versa.

If each type of negated sentence is dealt with by means of a special rule instead of (G.$\sim$), we also need the following rule.

(G.$\sim$A) If the game has reached the sentence $\sim A$, A atomic, I have won and Nature has lost if A is false; if A is true, vice versa.

The crucial point here is of course to be able to define truth independently of what happens in any particular play of these semantical games. The intuitive idea is of course that if S is true, it can be verified. This idea is captured as follows:

(G.T) S is true if and only if I have a winning strategy in $G(S)$.

Here 'strategy' is to be understood in the precise sense of the mathematical theory of games.[12] The idea it embodies is nevertheless so natural that it can be understood without any familiarity of game-theoretical results or conceptualizations. A player has a winning strategy if he can choose his moves in such a way that, no matter what his opponent does, he in the end wins the game. (Of course his choices will in general depend on the opponent's earlier moves.)

It is most easily seen that if S is indeed true in the traditional sense, I can make my moves so that all the sentences S produced during the game are (apart from switches of roles induced by (G.$\sim$)) true in the traditional sense. Since this includes the outcome, I have a winning strategy. Conversely, if I have a winning strategy in $G(S)$, it is easily seen that S is true in the traditional sense. Hence what (G.T) defines is indeed equivalent with the traditional concept of truth.

In spite of this equivalence, game-theoretical semantics has interesting uses already as applied to formal languages. One of them is discussed elsewhere at some length. In showing the equivalence of what (G.T) defines with the traditional concept of truth, we have to assume that our semantical games are games with perfect information. (Intuitively speaking, either player always comes to know and never forgets what has happened at the earlier moves.) If this requirement is given up, we obtain semantics not only for ordinary quantificational logic but for the logic of what are known as finite partially ordered quantifiers as well. Although their theory is much more powerful than that of ordinary (linearly ordered) quantifiers, I have argued that it has to be resorted to in order to interpret English quantifiers. This line of thought will not be developed here, however. It is taken up in my paper, 'Quantifiers vs. Quantification Theory', *Linguistic Inquiry*, vol. 5 (1974), pp. 153-77.

4 GAME-THEORETICAL SEMANTICS FOR A FRAGMENT OF ENGLISH

Game-theoretical semantics can be extended easily from formal languages to a fragment of English. The two players can be kept intact and so can the given domain D. (The fact that many English quantifiers range over some specifiable subclass of D, for instance the class consisting of persons, does not cause any difficulties in principle.) In English, there are admittedly no variables which could be replaced by the names of individuals chosen in the course of a game. However, what we can do is to substitute such a name for the whole quantifier phrase. This phrase will then have to be taken care of somehow, in the sense that it imposes certain conditions on the individual chosen.

This motivates, for instance, the following special case of the game rule for the English quantifier 'some'.

(G. some) If the game has reached a sentence of the form

X–some Y who Z–W

then I may choose an individual, give it a name if it does not have one already, say 'b'. The game is then continued with respect to

X–b–W, b is a(n) Y, and b Z.

It is being assumed here that the 'who' in 'who Z' occupies the subject position and that the main verb in Z is singular. The context X–W is so far allowed to be an arbitrary one, except that 'who Z' must of course be an entire relative clause. Certain restrictions on the context will later be imposed by the principles that govern the order of application of our rules. They will not be studied in this paper, however.

For instance, when applied to the sentence

Some man who loves her promised Jane to marry her

(G. some) yields a sentence of the form

John promised Jane to marry her, John is a man, and John loves her.

Here we have X = empty, W = 'promised Jane to marry her', Y = 'man', and Z = 'loves her'. The special case of (G. some) just formulated is readily extended to all the other special cases in the singular and also to plural uses of 'some'. No general formulation is attempted in this paper, however. Its uses with mass terms are in any case disregarded here.

The only real difference between the special case of (G. some) just formulated and others is that in general we have (so to speak) to watch out to see where the wh-phrase comes from. For instance, in addition to the sentence of the form

> X–some Y who Z–W

we may want to consider also sentences of the form

> X–some Y where Z_1–Z_2–W

where

> where Z_1–Z_2

can be thought of as being formed from

> Z_1–in d–Z_2.

Applied to them, (G. some) yields, through my choice of a place b, the sentence

> X–b–W, b is a(n) Y, and Z_1–in b–Z_2.

For instance, when applied to

> Some town where Bill lived as a child is located in Holland

(G. some) might yield

> Dubbeldam is located in Holland, Dubbeldam is a town, and Bill lived in Dubbeldam as a child.

Here X = empty, Y = 'town', Z_1–Z_2 = 'Bill lived — as a child'. and W = 'is located in Holland'.

The other special cases of (G. some) are equally straightforward to formulate.

An analogous game rule for the English indefinite article will be called (G. an). Generic uses of the indefinite article must of course be excused from its purview. It might seem that another exception is needed here for the situation in which 'is a' expresses predication. However, no distinction is needed between the uses of 'is a' to express predication from the ones in which the 'is' expresses identity and 'a' is an existential quantifier. For instance, the sentence

> John is a boy

can be parsed either as

> Boy (John)   (predication)

or as

> John = a boy   (identity).

In the latter case (G. an) applies, yielding a sentence of the form.

> John is Jack, and Jack is a boy

where again the 'a' may be given either interpretation without any embarrassment. Thus we need a special rule for the so-called predicative uses of 'is a' only as a stopping rule, to avoid regress. We can for instance stipulate that if the only rule that applies to

> a is a(n) X

(where X does not contain relative pronouns and where 'a' is a proper name) is (G. an), then here 'is a(n)' is treated as expressing predication.

This observation solves one of the problems posed earlier in section 1 of this paper. It also goes a long way towards explaining how a natural language like English can use the same word 'is' both for identity and (in the combination 'is a') for predication without any ambiguity resulting therefrom.

A special case of the game rule for the English universal quantifier 'every' can likewise be formulated in my approach.

(G. every) If the game has reached the sentence

> X–every Y who Z–W

then Nature may choose an individual and give it a proper name (if it did not have one already), say 'b'. The game is continued with respect to

X–b–W if b is a(n) Y and (if) b Z.

It is assumed here that the 'who' in 'who Z' occupies the subject position. The second (bracketed) 'if' is clearly an idiomatic peculiarity which merely serves to make the punctuation of the sentence clear.

This rule is easily extended to other uses of 'every', and parallel rules for 'any' and 'each' (we shall call them (G. any) and (G. each)) are easily formulated. The rule (G. any) can also be extended to plural uses of 'any'. For 'no', occurring (say) in

X–no Y who Z–W,

a similar rule (G. no) can be formulated. Nature chooses now an individual, call it 'b', and the game is then continued with respect to

neg + (X–b–W) if b is a(n) Y and if b Z

Here 'neg +' indicates the process of forming a (sentential) negation in English.

Our game rules for quantifiers are also readily extended so as to cover the 'absolute' quantifiers 'anyone', 'somebody', 'everyone', 'anybody', 'nobody', 'anything', 'everything', 'something', etc.

The extension of our earlier game rules for formalized sentential connectives to English connectives is straightforward. The earlier rules are easily transformed into rules for the English particles 'or', 'and', and 'not'.

The resulting game rules will be called, unsurprisingly, (G. or), (G. and) and (G. not). In addition to them, a special rule (G. if) for 'if' will be considered.

A few remarks are in order concerning these rules.

(i) The applicability of (G. and), (G. or) and (G. if) will be ruled out whenever there are pronominal cross-references between conjuncts, disjuncts, or the consequent and the antecedent, respectively. However, the rules do apply when the pronominal reference is to a proper name. Then (G. and),

(G. or) and (G. if) must also have the effect of replacing the pronoun by this proper name (depronominalization).

(ii) The rule (G. if) applies (with the restriction just indicated) to sentences of the form

X if Y

allowing me to choose either X or neg + Y. The latter alternative means that suitable rules for forming sentence negations must be built into my game rules.

A further development of the game-theoretical semantics would show how such rules can be motivated and formulated. In this paper, we shall just take them for granted.

(iii) Phrasal 'and' must of course be excused from the scope of (G. and). For a sentential 'and' binding terms, we must have some rule of the following kind.

(G. conj) a_1, a_2, ... , and a_k X may be replaced by a_1 X', a_2 X', ... , and a_k X' where X' is like X except that the main verb is in the singular. (In X it must of course be in the plural.)

It is assumed here that the conjunction in the original sentence occupies the subject position. The rule (G. conj) is easily extended to cover the other cases as well.

An analogous rule (G. disj) is needed when 'or' is used to bind terms (NP's).

(iv) Instead of (G. not), it is much more natural to introduce a number of obligatory rewriting rules which serve to define the operation 'neg +' of forming a sentential negation in English. What these rules will look like in the case of quantified English sentences can nevertheless be determined only by means of a further inquiry which will not be attempted here.

(v) Pronominalization will in fact occasion certain qualifications to our game rules for quantifiers, for the reshuffling of X, Y, Z, and W which takes place in these expressions can sometimes disturb pronominalization relations between them. In this paper, I shall nevertheless disregard this problem.

If we follow the crude first-approximation rules for English pronominalization which have been proposed by Langacker and others,[13] we can safeguard rules like (G. some) simply by requiring the pronominalization relations between Z and W to be reversed when (G. some) is applied. However, this does not yet amount to a satisfactory analysis of the situation. Such an analysis will not be attempted in this paper.

It is easy to extend game-theoretical semantics to epistemic, modal, and doxastic concepts, at least in some of their typical uses. The basic idea is a straightforward combination of possible-worlds semantics for these notions with our game-theoretical principles.[14] What is being defined then is the truth of a sentence S in a world ω. Since we are dealing with an interpreted language, a set of possible worlds (with the appropriate alternativeness relations defined on it) must be given. At each stage of the extended games, the two players are considering a sentence S' and a world ω', beginning with S and ω. The game rules for epistemic and other modal notions (in the wide sense of the term) can then be formulated as rules for stepping from one world to another. The following rules are cases in point. Others are easily formulated by anyone familiar with possible-worlds semantics.

(G. knows) If the game has reached a world ω' and a sentence of the form

a knows that X,

where 'a' is a proper name, Nature may choose an epistemic a-alternative ω'' to ω'. The game is continued with respect to ω'' and X', where X' results from X by replacing all pronominal cross-references to the initial 'a' by 'a'.

(G. knows not) If the game has reached the world ω' and the sentence

a does not know that X'

where 'a' is a proper name, then I may choose an epistemic

a-alternative ω'' to ω'. The game is continued with respect to ω'' and neg +X′, where X′ is like X except for the replacement of pronouns referring back to 'a' by 'a'.

Sentences of the form

a does not know that X

will of course have to be exempted from the scope of (G.not), if it is being used.

Only the part of English which can be dealt with by means of these rules is what will be considered in this paper. This fragment of English could be delineated more clearly, but such an enterprise is not necessary for most of my observations. In any case, several of the results to be obtained I believe to obtain more widely than this fragment.

Selected examples may perhaps help to illustrate the game rules. It is for instance of interest to see how the validity of well-known logical principles of logic appears in the game-theoretical semantics. As an example, consider the self-contradictory sentence

14   John loves himself, but nobody loves him.

Here (G. and) applies ('but' here being but a stylistic variant of 'and'), enabling Nature to choose between

15   John loves himself

or

16   nobody loves John.

If the former is false, Nature can defeat me by choosing it. If it is true, Nature can choose the latter and have the opportunity of choosing an individual whose name is to be substituted for 'nobody' in (16) (in accordance with the absolute version of (G. no)). Among others, Nature can choose John, this choice resulting in the sentence

17   neg +(John loves John)

which obviously is synonymous with

18   John doesn't love himself.

But this is false by hypothesis, making Nature the winner and myself the loser.

In neither case can I defeat Nature, which means that I cannot have a winning strategy in any domain. In virtue of (G.T), this means that (14) is logically false.

As another example illustrating also the epistemic rules, consider the sentence

19   Some clever boy who loves every pretty girl believes that he is lucky.

Although we have not yet discussed the order in which the game rules are to be applied, in this particular case the order is easy to guess. An application of (G. some) to (19) yields a sentence of the form

20   John believes that he is lucky, John is a clever boy, and John loves every pretty girl.

Here Nature may choose any conjunct in virtue of (G. and), for there is no pronominalization between them. If Nature chooses the last one, then Nature's further application of (G. every) may yield

21   John loves Mary if Mary is a pretty girl.

If Nature chooses the first conjunct in (20), she may then select, in virtue of a doxastic analogue (G. believes) to (G. knows), a doxastic alternative ω' (with respect to John) to the world ω in which we are evaluating (20). The game then continues with respect to ω' and the sentence 'John is lucky'.

Such examples also illustrate a useful moral about our semantical games. First, from the set of all different sequences of applications of our game rules to a given English sentence S (in the fragment we are studying), we can obtain a representation of S in a suitable logical notation. How this is to be done is indicated here only informally. For instance, when (G. some) is applied to a sentence, the new name may be replaced by a variable bound to an existential quantifier which is invented immediately after the quantifiers which have likewise resulted from earlier applications of (G. some), (G. every), (G. an), (G. any) or (G. each). The bound variable is subsequently treated in the same way as the substituting name.

We shall use this translatability only unsystematically in this paper without studying its precise limits.

The solutions to our initial puzzles which were described earlier in informal terms in section 2 above, can now be confirmed by means of our precise game-theoretical rules. For instance,

2   Every man hates every man

is correlated with a game in which Nature has two different choices by (G. every) which typically result in a sentence of the form

21   Tom hates Harry if Tom is a man and Harry is a man.

This means that the original sentence is of the form

22   $(x) [x$ is a man $\supset (y)(y$ is a man $\supset x$ hates $y)]$.

In contrast, in

3   every man hates himself

Nature has only one choice by (G. every). It results in a sentence of the form

23   Tom hates himself if Tom is a man.

The correlated logical structure is clearly

24   $(x)(x$ is a man $\supset x$ hates $x)$

Likewise one can deal with such sentences as

4   some boy believes that Mary loves him

and

5   some boy believes that Mary loves some boy

as well as with

1   John saw a warbler yesterday, and Bill saw a warbler, too.

as distinguished from

25 John saw a warbler yesterday, and Bill saw it, too.

For instance, when applied respectively to (4) and (5) (G. some) yields entirely different results, in the former case for instance (if John is my choice)

26 John believes that Mary loves him, and John is a boy

and in the latter

27 John believes that Mary loves some boy, and John is a boy.

Applied to the first conjuncts of (26)–(27) (G. believes) takes us to a doxastic alternative of the original world and yields respectively

28 Mary loves John

and

29 Mary loves some boy,

thus illustrating the difference in meaning between (4) and (5).

In a similar way, the failure of equi-NP deletion and of relative clause formation (in their customary formulations) to preserve meaning becomes easily explainable in our game-theoretical semantics.

This still leaves unexplained the differences between such apparently similar natural-language quantifiers as 'every', 'each', and 'any'. The precise differences between their respective meanings can nevertheless be explained in the game-theoretical approach, it seems to me. This requires a closer examination of the consequences of an important difference between the games associated with the sentences of a formalized first-order language and those associated with English quantifier sentences. In the former, the order in which the several game rules are brought to bear is completely determined by the form of the sentence which has been reached in the game. In the latter, the order has so far been left largely arbitrary. As was pointed out earlier, for instance in (G. some) X–W can be any context in which the quantifier phrase 'some Y who Z' may occur.

Far from being a defect of our game-theoretical semantics for a fragment of English, this freedom is a tremendous asset. It allows certain important types of further conceptualization. It serves to explain certain ambiguities in English. What is even more important, it allows us to develop an account of the ways in which other ambiguities are avoided in English. For they must of course be avoided (if they are avoided) by imposing further restraints on the order in which the game rules are applied (over and above such trivial restraints as the *ceteris paribus* preference of the left-to-right order). It seems to me that a full account of the semantics of such special quantifiers as 'any' can be given in this way, that is to say, given in terms of the order of application of (G. any) with respect to other game rules.

Furthermore, the same ordering principles show how the negation-forming operation must function in English, thus giving us important insights into the semantics of English quantifiers as distinguished from logicians' formalized quantifiers and at the same time filling a gap in my presentation so far. For reasons of space, these ordering principles cannot be examined here, however.

In general, it seems to me that the game-theoretical approach gives us a powerful and flexible theory of the semantics of quantifiers in natural languages. A comparison between the games associated with formalized first-order sentences and those associated with English sentences will then show the difference between logicians' quantifiers and natural-language quantifiers.

NOTES

1. Cf., e.g., W. V. Quine, *Mathematical Logic* (Harvard University Press, Cambridge, Mass., 1955), pp. 1–8; P. F. Strawson, *Introduction to Logical Theory* (Methuen, London, 1952), *passim*; G. H. von Wright, *Logical Studies* (Routledge and Kegan Paul, London, 1957), pp. 1–6.
2. Cf. George Lakoff, 'Linguistics and Natural Logic', in Donald Davidson and Gilbert Harman, eds., *Semantics of Natural Language* (D. Reidel, Dordrecht, 1972), pp. 545–665; 'On Generative Semantics', in D. D. Steinberg and J. A. Jakobovits, eds., *Semantics: An Interdisciplinary Reader* (Cambridge University Press, Cambridge, 1971), pp. 232–95.
3. 'Quantifiers vs. Quantification Theory', *Linguistic Inquiry*, vol. 5 (1974), pp. 153–77.
4. Cf. Keith Donnellan, 'Reference and Definite Descriptions', in D. D. Steinberg and J. A. Jakobovits (note 2 above), pp. 100–14 (appeared originally in *Philosophical Review*, vol. 75 (1966), pp. 281–304); 'Proper Names and Identifying Descriptions', in Davidson and Harman (note 2 above), pp. 356–79.
5. See the papers collected in Richmond Thomason, ed., *Formal Philosophy* (Yale University Press, New Haven, 1974), especially 'The Proper Treatment of Quantifiers in Ordinary English', first printed in Jaakko Hintikka, Julius M. E. Moravcsik, and Patrick Suppes, eds., *Approaches to Natural Language* (D. Reidel, Dordrecht, 1973), pp. 221–42.
6. Bertrand Russell, *The Principles of Mathematics* (George Allen and Unwin, London, 1903), pp. 56–65.
7. For a few critical remarks, see my paper 'On the Proper Treatment of Quantifiers in Montague Semantics', in Sören Stenlund, ed., *Logical Theory and Semantic Analysis* (D. Reidel, Dordrecht, 1974), pp. 45–60.

8. Barbara Hall Partee, 'On the Requirement that Transformations Preserve Meaning', in C. J. Fillmore and D. T. Langendoen, eds., *Studies in Linguistic Semantics* (Holt, Rinehart and Winston, New York, 1971), pp. 1–21. I am relying heavily on this important paper in several respects.
9. Cf. Jaakko Hintikka, *Logic, Language-Games, and Information* (Clarendon Press, Oxford, 1973), pp. 109–11.
10. It was nevertheless foreshadowed by the informal uses several logicians made of game-theoretical ideas for their own purposes. Cf., e.g., A. Ehrenfeucht, 'An Application of Games to the Completeness Problem for Formalized Theories', *Fundamenta Mathematicae*, vol. 49 (1960), pp. 129–41; Leon Henkin, 'Some Remarks on Infinitely Long Formulas', in *Infinitistic Methods* (Pergamon Press and Państwowe Wydawnictwo Naukowe, Oxford and Warszawa, 1961), pp. 167–83. (This latter paper was accidentally omitted from the bibliography of my 'Quantifiers vs. Quantification Theory', see note 3 above.)
11. For the basic ideas of game theory, see for instance R. D. Luce and H. Raiffa, *Games and Decisions* (John Wiley, New York, 1957).
12. Cf. Luce and Raiffa, op. cit., p. 43.
13. See Ronald W. Langacker, 'On Pronominalization and the Chain of Command', in David A. Reibel and Sanford A. Schane, eds., *Modern Studies in English: Readings in Transformational Grammar* (Prentice-Hall, Englewood Cliffs, New Jersey, 1969), pp. 160–86; John Robert Ross, 'On the Cyclic Nature of English Pronominalization', in *To Honor Roman Jakobson* (Mouton, The Hague, 1967), vol. III, pp. 1669–82; reprinted in Reibel and Schane, pp. 187–200.
14. For possible-worlds semantics, see for instance my book, *Models for Modalities* (D. Reidel, Dordrecht, 1969).

Comment

BY ROBERT J. FOGELIN

The paper that Professor Hintikka has presented to this conference is an attempt to apply game-theoretic techniques to quantifiers of natural language. The essay is, in fact, an extension of an earlier paper, 'Language Games for Quantifiers', where these techniques were first applied to the standard quantifiers of formalized languages.

The first thing I wish to notice is that Hintikka's appeal to game theory is philosophically motivated. By this I mean he is not borrowing a batch of mathematical machinery merely because it seems to work—as one might borrow, say, topology and be content with good results in the total absence of psycholinguistic plausibility. In the present essay Hintikka touches only lightly on the philosophical foundations of his approach, but since I think these matters important I have followed his references back to earlier writings where these issues are discussed directly.

Why, then, should quantifiers of either a natural or a formalized language have anything to do with game theory? In answering this question, Hintikka appeals specifically to Wittgenstein's notion of a language game. Wittgenstein, of course, employed this notion in a variety of ways for a variety of purposes, but Hintikka gives prominence to the idea that the employment of language—as a game—is an *activity*. With this in mind, he goes on to suggest that the use of a word (or family of words) will often have a verb associated with it that indicates the distinctive character of this activity.

> Actions and activities are in our language typically represented by verbs. As a consequence, an answer to the question: 'What activities constitute the natural environment of a word?' may sometimes be reformulated as an answer to the question: 'What verbs are there to which the word in question has an especially intimate connection.'[1]

As an example of this, Hintikka notices that the word 'good' has associated with it such verbs as 'to evaluate', 'to praise', 'to commend', etc. With respect to quantifiers, Hintikka suggests that they are associated with such verbs as 'to search', 'to look for', and 'to find'. This is exhibited in the verification procedures appropriate to quantified statements where our task, typically, is to look for (and hopefully find) individuals that satisfy certain specifications. But these very procedures, as it turns out, can often be treated by game-theoretic techniques, so by examining the games (broadly defined) that we play with quantifiers, we discover that they are games (narrowly defined) that fall into the province of game theory.

Whatever there is to be said of the use of the Wittgensteinian term 'language-game' in general, here the word at any rate sits especially happily. This happiness is not due only to whatever informal similarities there are between games proper and those activities which Gilbert Ryle has called 'the game of exploring the world'. It is primarily due to the fact that in the case of quantifiers, the relevant 'language game' can also be formulated as Games in the precise game-theoretical sense of the word.[2]

I think that most Wittgensteinians will find this closing remark unpalatable. I do not say this to criticize Hintikka's approach. He is not writing commentary on Wittgenstein's notion of a language game. Nor do I think that the measure of agreement with Wittgenstein is the measure of truth. Yet I do think that there is a deep disagreement between Hintikka and Wittgenstein concerning the character of language games, and an examination of this difference raises interesting questions—none of which I can answer.

I have remarked that Wittgenstein uses the notion of a language game for a variety of purposes. First it helps us to see that employing language is something we do—it is an activity. Furthermore, if we examine these activities, we will notice, in Hintikka's words, 'The multiplicity and variety of the different language-games which are involved in the use of language....'³ But there is another feature of Wittgenstein's doctrine of language games that Hintikka does not take over (at least in the present context): Wittgenstein draws our attention to the similarities between the uses of language and the playing of games in order to *dispel* the idea that 'if anyone utters a sentence and *means* or *understands* it he is operating a calculus according to definite rules.' (PI.§81.) If we look, we will see that the ordinary games we play are not everywhere bounded by strict rules, yet we play them nonetheless. The rules governing ordinary games are not complete in the ideal sense in which logicians employ this idea. There is no obvious reason why our language games should meet this standard either, and Wittgenstein gives a number of examples where our rules would simply leave us at a loss what to say. (e.g. PI§80).

'But at the very least, the rules governing games must be *consistent*!' Perhaps Wittgenstein's most notorious heresy was to call this assumption into question as well:

> 'We take a number of steps, all legitimate—i.e. allowed by the rules—and suddenly a contradiction results. So the list of rules, as it is, is of no use, for the contradiction wrecks the whole game!' Why do you have it wreck the game? (*RFM*, p. 167.)

A little later, Wittgenstein muses in the following way:

> We say that the contradiction would *destroy* the calculus. But suppose it only occurred in tiny doses in lightning flashes as it were, not as a constant instrument of calculation, would it nullify the calculus? (*RFM*, p. 169.)

It might be that those areas where the use of the calculus will lead to the contradiction (or other forms of incoherence) simply lie off the main path of regular application. Wittgenstein seems to make this sort of suggestion about Russell's Paradox:

What Russell's '-f(f)' lacks above all is application, and hence a meaning.

. . .

Here one is looking at language without looking at the language game. (*RFM*, p. 166.)

In what language game outside of logic (in mufti) will the Russell property find application? If none, it will not interfere in the actual employment of language and, if it generates paradoxes in some idealization of our language, this need not, it seems, concern us.

Now it has been my experience that philosophers are impatient—and often explicitly angered—when ideas of this kind are ventured in public. It often calls forth heavy rhetorical retaliation. Yet inconsistency is neither being recommended nor condoned: we are simply concerned with how the rules governing our language actually work. It seems to me that we can *imagine* a situation of the following kind. Our language is governed by a set of syntactical and semantical rules which, if applied without constraint, lead to inconsistency or unacceptable results of some other kind. I am supposing that these are the *actual* rules governing the language—rules with psycholinguistic relevance—rules, for example, that we might acknowledge when they are pointed out to us. I shall represent the sentences generated by these rules by a square. The square will contain, as we have said, sentences that are declared anathema and so marked with an asterisk front and back.

Inside this box is another set of sentences composed of those that human beings find occasion to employ in daily life.

Although many non-deviant sentences will fall outside this inner box, we are to imagine that no deviant ones fall inside of it. These are sentences that arise within actual language games. We do not have to suppose that there is a sharp boundary between the inner and outer box, and, of course, the contents of this inner box may change over time, reflecting man's changing concerns.

Now let us suppose, for a moment, that this description does, in fact, characterize natural languages: the syntactical and semantical rules that govern our language do not meet the logician's standards even of consistency, yet this never, or rarely, comes to the surface. There is, after all, no practical point in constructing such curiosities as the Russell Class. Next we are to imagine the logico-linguist attempting to characterize the syntactical and semantical rules of this language. He will probably begin with common-sense rules—rules, for example, that the native speaker will acknowledge or, at any rate, find plausible as characterizations of the rules he follows. These initial rules will, however, prove formally unsatisfactory. Yet the feeling can persist that there must be some formally correct set of rules that characterizes non-deviant everyday discourse and if these rules are not revealed in the surface grammar that we can all understand and acknowledge, then it must be contained in a deeper grammar that only the expert can ferret out and evaluate. This is the fundamental move of the *Tractatus*. In fact, over the last twenty years a development of this kind seems to have taken place. The formatives of Chomsky's early theory were not English sentences, but they were rather like English sentences. The deep grammar was sufficiently like the surface grammar to still be called a grammar. In contrast, some of the recent product of generative semantics could as well be schematic diagrams for the synthesis of DNA.

Let me bring this ramble to a close. One assumption that underlies much work in contemporary linguistics is that there must be some formally acceptable system of rules that generates the sentences we employ. The first point I have made—following Wittgenstein—is that this *need* not be true in order for the actual rules that govern our language to be serviceable. The second point is that if natural languages lack formal correctness, then the attempt to impose these standards upon natural languages will yield the characteristic Tractarian development of a deep structure lying beneath and supporting the messy manifold of everyday speech.

But if the rules that govern our language do not form a coherent system, what methodology will be appropriate for studying them? I think that this is an important question which if taken seriously will challenge our standard notions of explanation. In any case, I do not know how to answer it.

There is one way of answering these abstract cavils: produce a coherent set of rules that accurately characterizes a natural language or at least some interestingly large fragment of a natural language. This Hintikka attempts with respect to a set of standard quantifiers of English. Hintikka's approach is motivated by a comparison between quantifiers and singular terms (e.g. proper names). He gives a list of ways in which quantifiers function like a singular term and then he gives a list of ways in which their functions differ. He then sets a high standard for success in treating quantifiers: any account should exhibit both the source of these similarities and the source of the differences. Hintikka claims that this can be done using the game-theoretic techniques originally used for quantifiers in formal languages.

To illustrate Hintikka's procedures, let me go through a simple example using his rules. We can take a tidy world where all objects have names and all basic propositions are enumerated. A basic proposition is an atomic proposition or its denial, whichever is true. (By the way, these restrictions are *not* needed on Hintikka's approach.)

Objects: a, b, c, d
Functions: Mx, Fxy, Lxy

Basic Truths: $Ma, Mb, -Mc, -Md$
$-Faa, Fab, Fac, -Fad$
Fba, Fbb, Fbc, Fbd
$-Faa, Fcb, -Fcc, Fcd$
$Fda, Fdb, Fdc, -Fdd$
The same pattern holds for the function Lxy.

We can now play a game against nature with the following proposition as our starting point: $(Ex)(Mx \& (y)(Fyx\ Lyy)$

I. My move: $Ma \& (y)(Fyx \supset Lyy)$
II. Nature's: $(y)(Fya \supset Lyy)$
III. Nature's: $(Fba\ Fbb)$
IV. Rewrite: $-Fba \lor Fbb$
V. My move: Fbb

A brief study will show that here I have a winning strategy against nature, so the original proposition is true for the envisaged world. Now for formal languages at least, this procedure brings out both the similarities and differences between quantifiers and singular terms. In each play of the game, the quantifier phrase is treated exactly like a name—this is brought out by replacing it with a name. Thus in a particular play of a game we can cash in the previously vague idea that quantifiers stand for arbitrarily chosen individuals. But quantifiers do not have the status of an arbitrarily chosen name *simpliciter*: instead the quantifiers are related to individuals through a series of choices governed by game-theoretic rules.

The final step is to adopt these same procedures for quantified expressions as they occur in natural languages. Thus instead of moving directly from an expression in the formal language to an expression in the natural language, we pattern the game-theoretical rules for natural language upon the previously developed rules for the formal language. That is, we do not first translate the sentence of the natural language into symbolic notation and then apply semantic methods to this derived expression. Instead, we construct a system of semantic rules for the fragment of the natural language itself—patterning them after rules already developed for formal languages.

Formal Language	Natural Language
Semantical Rules	Parallel Semantical Rules

These semantical rules, on Hintikka's approach, are game-theoretical procedures for verification. It is at this level that the semantics of a formal language and the semantics of a natural language meet.

I really have no specific criticisms of this approach. Hintikka has completed what we might call a feasibility study for a game-theoretic approach to the semantics of natural language by applying it to a set of standard quantifiers. He has also been careful not to exaggerate the extent of his accomplishments by including a long list of extensions to be made and problems to be solved. My informants—in this case not native, but professional—suggest that Hintikka still has to tackle some of the more intractable problems, the interaction between pronouns and quantifiers, for example. But Hintikka, of course, knows this. Nor has he faced up to the problem of specifying the order in which rules are applied. Here he seems to rely on a knowledge of the order that the quantifiers have in a translation into a formal language, but perhaps I am wrong about this. Again, however, Hintikka acknowledges that this job has to be done in a non-intuitive way. So with Oliver Twist, what we want is more, for, unlike Oliver Twist, the fare has been to our taste.

Finally, before closing, I wish to point to an interesting parallel between Hintikka's approach and one developed by my colleague, Frederic Fitch. Their general programmes are different: Hintikka is attempting to produce a semantics for a fragment of English whereas Fitch is attempting to produce a set of natural deduction rules for (roughly) that same fragment, i.e. Fitch has developed a system of rules for the quantifiers of English that is patterned after the natural deduction rules for first order logic. I can give only a single example of this since the more exotic cases take some explaining. The natural deduction rule for the introduction of a universal quantifier of a formal language has the following form:

1. a

      ϕa

$n.$ $(x)\phi x$

Here Fitch uses what he calls a subproof technique. To introduce a universally quantified statement as a step in a proof we construct a subproof general with respect to an arbitrarily chosen individual whose name flags the subproof (in this case 'a'). Being general with respect to a given letter means that we may not reiterate anything into the subproof or take it out again if it mentions this letter. This is Fitch's method for allowing us to use proper names in developing a logic of quantifiers while at the same time guaranteeing their arbitrariness in the required sense. Just for an object of comparison, let me put two Fitch-style proofs side by side—one for a formal language, the other for a natural language. The argument in question is:

> John is a man.
> <u>Any woman is a mystery to any man.</u>
> ∴ Any woman is a mystery to John.

Formal Language
1. Mj
2. $(x)(Wx \supset (y)(My \supset Mxy))$
3. a Wa hyp.
4. $(x)(Wx \supset (y)(My \supset Mxy))$ Reit.
5. $Wa \supset (y)(My \supset May)$
6. $(y)(My \supset May)$
7. $Mj \supset Maj$
8. Mj Reit.
9. Maj
10. $Wa \supset Maj$
11. $(x)(Wx \supset Mxj)$ Universal Quantifier Introduction

Natural Language
1. John is a man.
2. Any woman is a mystery to any man.
3. Jane is a woman.
4. Any woman is a mystery to any man.
5. Jane is a mystery to any man.
6. John is a man.
7. Jane is a mystery to John.
8. Any woman is a mystery to John.[4]

It now seems to me that we can make the same claims for the Fitch approach that Hintikka makes for his own. It too brings out the similarities and differences between quantifiers and proper names by showing how quantifiers can be *handled* by a system of rules where names are put in the place of quantifiers under given constraints. For Hintikka these rules concern the methods for verifying a proposition: Fitch concentrates on rules of deductive inference. But the similarity remains deep: on the Hintikka approach, the names chosen have only temporary standing in a particular play of a game. In the same way, the chosen name in the Fitch system only has status in the sealed off environment of a subproof, and proofs never end within subproofs.

It seems to me to be possible, then, that Hintikka and Fitch are working out a single insight in alternative modes. They bring out the relationship between quantifiers and singular terms by showing how singular terms can play a role in the rules that govern quantifiers. They then make the connection between the quantifiers of formal languages and the quantifiers of natural language by an extension of these rules from the first area to the second. Given the state of the art, it is impossible to say whether the game-theoretic of the natural deduction approach will, in the end, prove more fruitful. Hintikka claims that the game-theoretical approach to semantics is more powerful than the standard approach, for the former yields the latter on the assumption that our semantical games are games with perfect information. He also claims to have shown that this more general theory must be resorted to in order to interpret English quantifiers. This argument occurs in his paper, 'Quantifiers vs. Quantification Theory', which I am afraid that I have not been able to secure during the brief time that I have had to prepare these comments. But setting this issue aside, it seems to me that the similarity of these approaches are more impressive than their differences and the progress that has already been made using each of them is mutually reinforcing and suggests that the Wittgensteinian maunderings of the first part of this paper may, at any rate, be premature.

NOTES

1. Jaakko Hintikka, *Logic, Language-Games and Information* (Clarendon Press, Oxford, 1973), p. 57.
2. Ibid., p. 63.
3. Ibid., p. 57n.
4. Frederic B. Fitch, 'Natural Deduction Rules for English', *Philosophical Studies*, 24 (1973), pp. 92–3.

Comment

BY TIMOTHY C. POTTS

Professor Hintikka introduces his subject-matter as the universal and existential quantifiers of modern logic together with their counterparts in English, claiming that first order logic 'is insufficient as a semantical representation of English quantifier sentences'. This assumes that we can recognize an English quantifier sentence independently of logic, for if it were defined as a sentence whose logical structure could be represented by a formula containing at least one quantifier, his claim would be false by definition. Equally, then, it must be possible to recognize what he calls a 'natural language quantifier' without recourse to the logical quantifiers and then to raise the question in what sense, if any, the latter have counterparts in English. The paper does not, so far as I can see, squarely face either of these fundamental issues; our only recourse is to derive such enlightenment upon them as we may, by reading between the lines.

The notion of a semantic representation also contains an ambiguity which must be brought out into the open. A semantic representation of a proposition is, presumably, a representation of the meaning of that proposition; and to this we may add, that to understand the meaning of a proposition is to know what would be the case, if it were true (Wittgenstein, 1922, 4.024), for Hintikka makes it clear that he regards truth as the key to meaning. Now first order logic has never pretended to offer a complete semantic representation of propositions, only a partial one; the reason for this is that its formulas always contain some schematic symbols. A schematic symbol is one for which we may substitute any linguistic expression of a given category; we shall, of course, obtain different propositions with different meanings according to the substitutions which we make, so a formula of first order logic will, at best, represent only what is common to the meanings of a whole class of propositions.

Each formula delimits a class of propositions by exhibiting a structure and thereby representing any proposition which has that structure. Now the formation rules for first order logic determine what structure each formula exhibits, but a general-purpose language is not presented to us complete with explicit formation rules. We are offered only the language in use and, if we want to specify its formation rules, must work backwards. Furthermore, there is more than one possible starting-point for this enterprise: we can begin by asking for a structure in terms of which the *meaning* of a proposition can be explained, or for a structure in terms of which the peculiar features of *this* language, as opposed to the special features of other languages, may be explained. These two questions will lead to different answers, for if two propositions, whether of the same or of different languages, have the same meaning, then the structures in terms of which their meanings are to be explained will be the same, but the structures in terms of which the special features of a particular language are to be explained will be different; while, conversely, if one proposition has two meanings, then two different semantic structures will be assignable to it, but only one structure of the other type.

Logic is concerned with an aspect of meaning, with what we understand about the meaning of a proposition when we know what logical consequences may validly be inferred from it, etc. So in claiming that a given proposition has a certain logical form, we are, in effect, saying: 'If you see this proposition as having such-and-such a structure, we can explain why certain other propositions may validly be inferred from it.' In order to see something as a structure, we must see it as having elements which are inter-related; furthermore, the elements may be of different kinds. In first order logic, it is laid down in the formation rules what the elements of formulas are to be, what their kinds and the manner in which they may be combined; in the last step, essential use is made of the distinctions between kinds of element. Thus, in order to see a logical formula as exhibiting a semantic structure of a proposition, we also have to see the latter as composed of elements or constituents of different kinds or categories, combined in a particular way.

One sense, therefore, in which first order logic might be inadequate as a semantic representation of certain English propositions is that the system of categories which it employs is not adapted to giving an explanation of the meanings of the latter. This must be what Hintikka has in mind when he suggests that ordinary-language quantifiers are 'singular terms'. For first order logic draws a sharp distinction between quantifiers and proper names. It does not, indeed, contain any proper names, which belong rather to language, but it does contain schematic symbols for each of which any proper name may be substituted. Quantifiers, by contrast, are second level functions of one argument—I follow Frege here, who invented the quantifiers and assigned them to this category. Frege thought that formulas containing quantifiers could be used to represent logical structures of propositions of German; if, however, both proper names and the expressions which he correlated with his quantifiers are sub-categories of a single super-ordinate category of singular terms, then such formulas are the wrong kinds of structure for the purpose.

Even supposing, however, that the categories of first order logic provide us with structures in terms of which the meanings of certain propositions can, in part, be explained, there still remains a second sense in which logical formulas may be inadequate semantic representations; for the quantifiers are not schematic symbols: we cannot substitute for them any second level function of one argument that we choose. Their meanings are supposed to be defined, either by a recursive specification of the circumstances in which any formula containing at least one of them will be accounted true, or by the rules of inference of the logical system. So it would be quite possible for the categories of first order logic to be the ones we need, but the meanings given to the quantifiers to be at fault. And these are two separate issues, which have to be clearly distinguished if it is said that first order logic is insufficient as a semantic representation of English quantifier sentences.

In order to apply this distinction, we still need to know how to identify English quantifier sentences and hence, presumably, English quantifiers. Hintikka suggests that they are singular terms, i.e. 'terms denoting or referring to particular individuals'. This will only be of help to us if we are first able to pick out something as a 'particular individual' and, even then, 'denote' and 'refer to' are used so variously both in ordinary language and philosophy that we should need a more exact account of the matter in order to proceed with any safety. For example, if someone says that John was afraid of dying, is he referring to a particular individual emotion which John underwent? In one sense, as contrasted with saying merely that John was moved by the thought of death, yes. I think it is evident, upon a little reflection, that it is hopeless to try to identify singular terms *via* particular individuals; rather, we shall have to work the other way round and get at particular individuals *via* singular terms. Frege, of course, saw this difficulty and used proper names to explain what objects are, but unfortunately he did not tell us how we are to pick out a proper name when we encounter one.

Perhaps, then, we shall do better to fall back upon Hintikka's list of examples. First, he cites 'some man', 'every woman', 'a girl' and 'some boy who loves every girl' as quantifier phrases; then 'every', 'some', 'no', 'all', 'any' and 'a' as English quantifiers; and finally 'anyone', 'somebody', 'everyone', 'anybody', 'nobody', 'anything', 'everything' and 'something' as 'absolute' quantifiers. Now we should at once notice that any attempt to explain what an English quantifier is by enumeration of English words contravenes one of Frege's cardinal rules of method, never to ask for the meaning of a word except in the context of a proposition. The relevance of this rule can be illustrated by the following examples:

1   John has something to do before he goes home.
2   There is something to drink in the refrigerator.
3   Something moved in the corner of the room.

Only in example (3) does 'something' occur as a function of second level; in example (1) it is a function of third level, while an example like (2) at present defeats logical analysis.

Frege overcame this problem by citing linguistic expressions in a form which showed how they could be combined with other expressions in order to yield a proposition, that is, by including, as integral parts of the expressions, schematic symbols. Thus, if we write 'something$_x$ ϕx', where the Greek letter 'ϕ' is a schematic symbol for which any first level function of one argument may be substituted, we have a second level function of one argument, quite distinct from 'something$_f$

'$\mu_\alpha f\alpha$', which is a sign for a third level function of one argument, since only a second level function can be substituted for '$\mu_\alpha \phi\alpha$'. The sub-script letters of the notation, together with their counterparts, are required in order to show how a function of second or higher level combines with its argument; I assume that the reasons for employing them will be familiar (cf. Wittgenstein, 1922, 4.0411). The device of including schematic symbols in the citation of a linguistic expression, however, presupposes a method for analysing the semantic structures of propositions, so it is not open to Hintikka to use a similar device until he has committed himself to a method of analysis.

Frege's method was recursive and may be summarized thus: if, from an expression of category α, we remove one or more occurrences of an expression of category β, the category of the *remaining* expression is $1\alpha\beta$. The method thus generates a system of categories each of which is of the form $n\alpha\beta_1 \ldots \beta_n$, for $n \geq 0$. Being recursive, it must, of course, have a starting-point in the form of at least one basic category, expressions belonging to which can be recognized independently of the categorization procedure. Frege used a single basic category, proper name (N), accounting propositions as complex proper names; this will not sustain a correct account of the concepts of truth and falsity (cf. Wittgenstein, 1922, 4.431) and it is widely accepted today that a second basic category, proposition (P) is also necessary. The category of 'something$_x$ ϕx' then comes out as 1P1PN, but of 'something$_f$ $\mu_\alpha f\alpha$' as 1P1P1PN.

We could quite well have, in a formal system, schematic symbols for which any linguistic expression of category 1P1PN migth be substituted, e.g. '$O_x\phi x$' and '$Q_x\phi x$', but the logical quantifiers represent two particular linguistic expressions of that category, namely 'everything$_x$ $\phi\chi$' and 'something$_x$ ϕx'. What Hintikka calls 'quantifying phrases' also belong to this category, since we can have, e.g., 'A girl fell' just as well as 'Something fell'. In these cases, a count noun replaces 'thing' and so, too, with 'everybody$_x$ ϕx' and 'someone$_x$ ϕx', 'body' and 'one' being equivalent, in this context, to 'person'. It is interesting to note that the schematic letters appear to be redundant in the case of quantifying phrases, as against quantifiers, the count noun determining the category of the whole phrase.

The words 'every' and 'some', however, which are parts of these phrases, belong to a different category and so should not, if confusion is to be avoided, be called either quantifiers or quantifying phrases. Many of the logical consequences of propositions containing quantifying phrases can be expounded if their count nouns are treated as disguised functions of first level, which allows us to paraphrase, e.g.

4   A girl fell

by

5   Something both is a girl and fell.

'Some' will then correspond to what is left of proposition (5) when the two first level functions have been removed from it, viz.:

6   Something$_x$ both ϕx and ψx,

which is thus an expression of category 2P1PN1PN, a second level function of *two* arguments. This will also be the category of 'every$_x$ ϕx ψx' and 'some$_x$ ϕx ψx' and we can only represent these in first order logic by using a propositional connective in combination with a quantifier, in 'Polish' notation '$\Pi_x C \phi x \psi x$' and '$\Sigma_x K \phi x \psi x$' respectively; of course, we could always replace these by single symbols, given an appropriate system. Thus logic sometimes pushes us into componential analysis and does not necessarily mirror the word boundaries of language.

The notation of first order logic was built, as a matter of historical fact, upon a method of analysing the structures of propositions; we tend to forget this nowadays, when first order logic seems much less mysterious to us than language, but, nevertheless, the intended meanings even of its schematic symbols can only be explained by recourse to propositional analysis. It is true that the ordering convention employed in formulas does not always correspond to that observed by languages, but this should not be a matter of major concern. If the formulas of first order logic fail to represent the semantic structures of propositions, this can only be due to one of two factors. Either the recursive categorization procedure, i.e. the analysis of expressions into function and argument, is mistaken; or the wrong choice of basic categories, together with the assignment of expressions to them, has been made.

Frege very deliberately rejected the grammarians' distinction between subject and predicate, claiming that his replacement of it by the distinction between function and argument would stand the test of time. Hospitable as he was in his use of 'proper name', he also excluded quantifying phrases from the category of proper names; that quantifying phrases should be accounted functions of second level was then inevitable. His analysis stands or falls by its success in elucidating the validity of logical consequences and it should by now be well known that medieval logicians, in spite of their brave attempts in theories of *suppositio*, were unable to construct a viable theory of consequences for propositions containing multiple quantifying phrases, whereas Frege succeeded. If we are now to disown Frege's innovation, we must at least demand an alternative method of analysis which will deal as well as his does with consequences for this type of proposition; otherwise we should indeed be selling our birthright for a mess of pottage.

Though Hintikka's remarks about singular terms are far too sketchy to fulfil this requirement, it may be that the relevant rules of his two games, (G.U) and (G.E) from the first and (G. every) and (G. some) from the second, will reveal an implicit theory of analysis. Indeed, Hintikka appears to be claiming just this when he says:

> In any actual round of this game ... the quantifier phrases of S are replaced by proper names of individuals chosen one by one. ... We might almost say that in such a round ...,

quantifier phrases are interpreted as standing for these chosen individuals (p. 214),

a remark which is endorsed by Professor Fogelin in his comment:

> In each play of the game, the quantifier phrase is treated exactly like a name—this is brought out by replacing it by a name (p. 239).

But now let us look at the rule (G.U). It says that if the proposition in question is of the form '$\Pi_x Fx$', Nature may choose any member of the domain of quantification, give it a name if it does not already have one, say 'b', and that the game may then be continued with respect to 'Fb'. In stating this rule, Hintikka has used the notation of first order logic, in which '$\Pi_x \phi x$' is an expression of category 1P1PN but 'b' an expression of category N. Furthermore, in '$\Pi_x Fx$', '$\Pi_x \phi x$' is the function and '$F\xi$' the argument, whereas in 'Fb', '$F\xi$' is the function and 'b' the argument. So the two formulas have quite different, though related structures and, in applying the rule, we construct a new proposition from the schematic symbol of category 1PN which occurs in '$\Pi_x Fx$' and another schematic symbol of category N. There is no warrant here for saying that the quantifier is treated as a proper name, for the notation itself would belie us. The rule is in no sense a rule of substitution; placed in the context of the game and of the point of the game, it is clearly a rule of inference: '$\Pi_x Fx$' will be false if 'Fb' is false because '$\Pi_x Fx$' entails 'Fb'.

This argument from the notation cannot be extended to (G. every), which is exactly parallel to (G.U) except that the starting-point is a proposition of the form 'X–every Y who Z–W' and the proposition with respect to which the game is continued of the form 'X –b–W if (b is a Y and b Z)'. The question here, however, is whether we can even understand this rule. In order to be able to use it, we must be able to recognize a proposition of the form 'X–every Y who Z–W'

when we encounter one, and this demands that we know the range of possible substitutions for the schematic symbols which it contains. On this score, we are told nothing about X, Y and W; 'who Z' must be an entire relative clause and 'who' must occupy the subject position within it. Even this partial information relies upon the categories of traditional grammar, but Hintikka has no right to appeal to them at this point unless he has first shown by what method expressions are assigned to them. There is so much preliminary work to be done before (G. every) even gets off the ground as a possible rule that no conclusions can be drawn from it about how it treats quantifying phrases. I find, then, no argument either in Hintikka's games or in the earlier part of his paper which should lead us to abandon Frege's function and argument analysis or his assignment of quantifying phrases to category 1P1PN. Frege's analysis also shows how traditional grammarians were misled, by the method of substitution classes, into assigning quantifying phrases to the same category as proper names.

The meanings of the logical quantifiers, however, are fixed by the rules of inference for first order logic, together with the fact that it is consistent, not by the meanings of 'everything$_x$ ϕx' and 'something$_x$ ϕx'. It may well be, therefore, that the meanings of the two pairs do not coincide. For example, '$\Sigma_x \phi x$' has the sense 'There is at least one ϕ', whereas something$_x$ ϕx' may mean 'There are at least two ϕs'. Again, if '$\Sigma_x \phi x$' is used to represent 'a thing$_x$ ϕx', it will not accurately cover contexts in which 'a' means 'exactly one'. Finally, 'anything$_x$ ϕx' is correctly represented by '$\Pi_x \phi x$' in some contexts, e.g. 'Anything which ...', but by '$\Pi_x \phi x$' in others, e.g. 'If anything ...'.

Here, at last, we come to a genuine problem; but Hintikka's games do not contribute to its solution, for, so far as the meanings of 'everything$_x$ ϕx' and 'something$_x$ ϕx' are concerned, his rules do not differ from those which he gives for the quantifiers. Indeed, the position is still worse than this, for his explanation of the meaning of the universal quantifier relies upon our understanding of 'everything$_x$ ϕx', which is covertly smuggled in through the choice allowed to Nature. For (G.U) amounts to saying that if '$\Pi_x Fx$' is true, then everything$_x$ (within the domain of quantification) Fx. This criticism, of course, applies equally to what the logic text-books call a 'semantic' definition of the quantifiers; it, too, says only that '$\Pi_x \phi x$' is true just in case everything$_x$ ϕx. Anyone who adopts this account is precluded from the start from even asking whether '$\Pi_x \phi x$' represents 'everything$_x \phi x$'.

Hintikka's rule runs into an additional difficulty. Any substitutional theory of quantification requires that every object in the domain of quantification shall have a proper name. Hintikka tries to get round this by allowing us to baptize *ad libitum*. But how do we pick out an object within the domain if it does not already have a proper name? Only by means of the concept whose extension the domain is. That would limit us to restricted quantification, for there is no concept which defines the domain of 'everything$_x$ ϕx' and 'something$_x$ ϕx': their domain is, literally, everything. But the quantifiers which he uses in (G.U) and (G.E) are those of first order logic, which are not restricted and, in that case, no substitution theory, however extended, will suffice to explain their meanings. At the moment, we do not have any viable account of the meanings of the quantifiers which is independent of language.

REFERENCE

Wittgenstein, L. (1922), *Tractatus Logico-Philosophicus*, London, Routledge and Kegan Paul.

Reply to Professor Fogelin by Jaakko Hintikka
'Who's Afraid of Ludwig Wittgenstein?'

I find Professor Fogelin's comments on my paper perceptive and congenial in many respects. However, when he proposes to drive a wedge between my semantical games and Wittgenstein's language-games, I cannot accept his arguments. Professor Fogelin thinks 'that there is a deep disagreement between Hintikka and Wittgenstein concerning the character of language games'. The basis of this alleged disagreement in Wittgenstein is, according to Fogelin, Wittgenstein's appeal to 'the similarities between the uses of language and the playing of games in order to *dispel* the idea that "if anyone utters a sentence and means or *understands* it he is operating a calculus according to definite rules"'. Fogelin also recalls Wittgenstein's interesting related claim that the rules of our actual language-games need not even rule out contradictions.

In these Wittgensteinian strictures against calculi with sharp rules one can distinguish at least two different aspects. It seems to me that it is absolutely vital to keep them apart, even though they are clearly distinguished neither by Professor Fogelin nor, for that matter, by Professor Wittgenstein.

The first and by far the most important point Wittgenstein is making is to criticize the idea that using a language—more specifically, speaking a language (cf. the words 'if anyone utters a sentence . . .' in the quote above)—is a self-contained, self-explanatory activity comparable with a calculus with definite formal rules. In other words, the second Wittgensteinian point to which Fogelin calls our attention is perhaps merely a further continuation of the first one. This first point is calculated to connect the use of language with certain human activities. The second thesis develops this idea further and spells out what kind of activities go into these language-games which form the basis of our understanding any language. Or, rather, Wittgenstein spells out what these activities are *not*.

They are not the activities of manipulating a self-contained calculus, interpreted or not, nor are they comparable with such activities. They are not games played in language, but games played by means of language. They are games of using language to some actual non-linguistic purpose. This is strikingly brought out by Professor Fogelin's own references to Wittgenstein. For instance, the trouble with Russell's '$\sim f(f)$' is not that one cannot develop a game-like calculus—perhaps even an interpreted one—which can be played in accordance to some rules or others and in which this expression occurs. Rather, such a self-contained game remains unconnected with the real uses of language. In it, we would literally be 'looking at language without looking at the language game'—that is, at a language-game in the proper Wittgensteinian sense calculated 'to bring into prominence the fact that speaking of language is part of an activity, a form of life'.

I am tempted to generalize and to exaggerate here. A whole generation of philosophers have been misled by Wittgenstein's unfortunate terminology, I would like to say. The very point of his term 'language game' is to signal that these games are *not* purely linguistic, in the sense of involving language only. Wittgenstein's language games are precisely non-language games in that they transcend the boundaries of language only. I am afraid I do not find Fogelin's comment completely free from confusion in this matter.

This is for me a vital point, for if it is not appreciated, the philosophical thrust of my approach is easily misunderstood. My language-games of seeking and finding are not any old games people play with words and sentences. A comparison with certain games actually described in the literature may be instructive here. Paul Lorenzen has described certain kinds of games one can play with sentences containing logical constants.[1] Are my games different from his in any important respect? Yes, precisely in the way Wittgenstein's language-games differ from the self-contained games of a logician. Lorenzen calls his games dialogical, and they are precisely that—games of verbal challenges and responses. They are parlour games, not outdoor games. They cannot serve as the basis of genuine semantics. If they are not meaningless exercises, they in effect already presuppose a connection between our language and the reality. They are therefore not the language-games where our logical constants are at home but are rather parasitic on such primary games. Lorenzen cannot define the all-important notion of truth (truth *simpliciter*) in his approach, only the philosophers' artificial notion of so-called 'logical truth', which never ought to have been assimilated to the plain truth of an ordinary man in the first place. And even with respect to logical truth Lorenzen's success may be more limited than first appears. Lorenzen's games are incapable of being extended to certain types of logic which are actually needed in the semantics of natural-language quantifiers. Such a logic, called the theory of finite partially-ordered quantifiers, is studied in my recent paper, 'Quantifiers vs. Quantification Theory'.[2]

Unlike Lorenzen's dialogical games, my games of seeking and finding are outdoor games, played among the very objects our language speaks of (the members of our 'universe of discourse'). As indicated in my paper, they can be used to define the ordinary honest notion of truth for quantified sentences.

For essentially the same reason as led me to emphasize the difference between Lorenzen's games and mine, I am likewise led to decline the comparison which Professor Fogelin draws between my approach and that of Professor Fitch. Saying this is of course not to criticize the latter in the least. Nor are the two approaches, Professor Fitch's and mine, unrelated to each other. However, their aims are clearly different. As Fogelin points out, Professor Fitch aims at a proof technique while I am dealing with semantics. For this reason, his games of natural deduction are much more unlike my semantical games than Professor Fogelin apparently realizes. Deduction, whether natural or not, is after all a game played with expressions.

(Whether they are interpreted or uninterpreted formulae or natural-language expressions does not matter here.) Fitch is not outlining an 'outdoor' game that can serve as a backbone of semantics. This leads to the certain important interpretational differences between the two types of games. These differences are of the same sort as are discussed in my essay 'Quantifiers, Language-Games, and Transcendental Arguments', otherwise known as Chapter V of *Logic, Language-Games, and Information*.[3] Having shot my arrow there, I will only refer you to that earlier discussion. I feel very strongly that a distinction between the different kinds of language-games, viz. those of verification and those of logical proof, is the real beginning of wisdom in the philosophy of logic.

A couple of remarks may nevertheless be in order to clarify the situation. It is only by equivocation that Fogelin can bring the two approaches, Fitch's and mine, under a common denominator by speaking of 'the rules that govern quantifiers'. In the one type of game, viz. Fitch's, the rule in question might involve an introduction of a new name into an argument written down on a paper by a stipulatory *fiat*. In the other, the relevant rule might involve an arduous search for an actual object out there in the real world. I just wonder what bitter scorn Wittgenstein would have heaped on an attempt to assimilate these two unlike activities to each other.

In this important matter of opposition to merely linguistic games, I thus find myself on the side of angels, or at least on the same side as Ludwig Wittgenstein. Compared with this problem, the other points raised in Wittgenstein's theses appear to me of much smaller significance. The most general of them is the claim (if it really is Wittgenstein's claim) that ordinary language is not subject to precise rules. This thesis I will not discuss at length here. For one thing, it is not clear to me that it implies anything at all about my approach. It remains to be shown, it seems to me, that the alleged imprecision of our language makes it impossible or inadvisable to use precise formal tools for the purpose of philosophical clarification and understanding of its workings. The onus of proof is on others here, it seems to me. Notice, incidentally, that my semantical rules operate (in their syntactical component) on the *surface* forms of English quantifier sentences, not on those deep structures whose complexity Professor Fogelin despairs of.

Secondly, the degree of precision that the rules of our language are subject to is an empirical matter. Before the full returns of Chomsky's transformational grammars, of Montague semantics and Montague grammars, and of my own approach are in, a philosopher is simply presumptuous if he claims to be able to predict, sight unseen, what the truth about our actual language is like. Let me only say here that the signs I have seen point to a greater underlying regularity than one might expect *a priori*.

There is also no real connection between the precision problem and the question of consistency. The real foundation of a logic lies in pragmatically based semantics, such as my game-theoretical semantics. That is what enables logic to stand on its own feet, not conformity to this or that conventional formal rule or criterion. Now in this very matter of consistency there already exists a dramatic demonstration of my point in the literature. In his excellent dissertation,[4] Veikko Rantala last year put to interesting and important uses certain logical expressions (formulae) which are in the usual sense of the word self-contradictory (inconsistent). This Rantala accomplished by indicating (in effect) the mildly non-standard language-games which serve to connect these self-contradictory expressions with the world (more generally, with a given model). Thus these technically self-contradictory expressions were not only employed in some formal calculus, but given a perfectly good semantical (interpretational or model-theoretical) sense. Rantala's games are essentially games of seeking and finding played in a universe which may change in a certain way between the moves.

After Rantala's work, I can thus afford to remain completely unshocked by Wittgenstein's strictures against consistency, only regretting that Wittgenstein's somewhat shrill arguments do not seem to betray the real model-theoretical basis of what I take to be his very keen insight.

There is another reason why it seems to me important to stress the differences between my approach and an approach like Fitch's. When everything is said and done, we are in the latter approach basically still applying more or less familiar logical notation and more or less familiar logical proof techniques to natural language. How far can we get by means of such methods? Some interesting (albeit partial) light is shed on this problem by a study that I am in the process of carrying out. It concerns multiple questions in English. It turns out that the very powerful and flexible epistemic logic which can be used to analyse the semantics of English questions does not after all yield a satisfactory semantical theory for these questions. Among other problems, it fails to predict what the acceptable and unacceptable readings of multiple questions in English are.

In contrast, when my game-theoretical approach is applied to natural language directly, without going by way of traditional formalizations, it yields an eminently satisfactory treatment of multiple questions in English. It thus proves superior to the conventional applications of logical techniques to the study of natural language.

NOTES

1. See, e.g., Paul Lorenzen and Oswald Schwemmer, *Konstruktive Logik, Ethik und Wissenschaftstheorie* (Bibliographisches Institut, Mannheim, 1973), and the references given there.
2. *Linguistic Inquiry*, vol. 5 (1974), pp. 153–77.
3. Clarendon Press, Oxford, 1973, especially pp. 107–14.
4. *On the Theory of Definability in First-Order Logic* (Reports from the Institute of Philosophy, University of Helsinki, No. 2, 1973).

Reply to Dr. Potts by Jaakko Hintikka

'Back to Frege?'

Taken one by one, Dr. Potts' criticisms of my paper probably strike many readers—certainly readers coming from the kind of tradition to which I belong—as irrelevant to my main purpose and perhaps even pointless. To take but one example, why should I be under any obligation to display a method by which to 'recognize an English quantifier sentence independently of logic'? It is surely enough for me to concentrate on a few specific English words—'some', 'any', 'every', 'no', 'a' and 'each' (and their obvious derivatives) already suffice for my purposes—and on a few constructions in which they may occur. These present enough important problems for anyone to cope with in a single paper. And both the English quantifier words in question and the constructions in which we are allowing them to occur can be specified by enumeration. (In fact, these constructions can be specified precisely *post facto* by reversing the syntactical component of my game rules for English quantifiers and by using the resulting rules as transformations which create certain types of English quantifier sentences.) Potts objects to the specification of my subject matter by enumeration by saying that it 'contravenes one of Frege's cardinal rules of method, never to ask for the meaning of a word except in the context of a proposition', but if we also specify (albeit by enumeration only) the constructions (types of propositions) we are studying, this objection loses all force.

It is true that in my paper I spoke rather optimistically as if my theory covered all uses of English quantifiers. This is because I believe that it can be extended from the constructions I originally dealt with to virtually all others. (Of course there will always be idioms which are not amenable to a treatment as straightforward special cases of a general theory. For instance, I am not going to be upset if my theory does not automatically assign the right meaning to the Gilbert and Sullivan line, 'when everybody is somebody, nobody is anybody'.) Some of the extensions are pretty straightforward, and in no direction can I see serious theoretical problems which would bear on the basic ideas of my approach.

My optimism in this respect is handily illustrated by means of the very examples (1)–(2) Potts tries to use against me. In both of them the alleged difficulties have to do only with the nature of the entities we are quantifying over. This is a problem on any theory, and has no specific bearing on mine. Once these entities (and our ways of speaking of them) are fixed, my game rules apply even to these putative counter-examples. My rules might, for instance, take us from (1)–(2) through an appropriate choice by Myself to the sentences

1*   John has yesterday's dishes to do before he goes home.

and

2*   There is that bottle of beer to drink in the refrigerator.

Ironically, I am quite interested in the general problem of locating quantifiers even in a radically foreign language, and I have gone as far as to offer some ideas as to how this might be accomplished by means of considerations not unrelated to my semantical games.[1] But the paper I actually presented seemed to me—and still seems—as unlikely an occasion for that problem to matter as one can reasonably find. Only the White Knight and Professor Alonzo Church are on guard against *everything*.

Another strange thing about Potts' note is that he clearly assumes that my theory of quantifiers is a *substitutional* one.[2] Of course it is not, as is already shown by the demonstrable equivalence of the truth-definition it yields with the usual (objectual) one. The players do not look for substitution-values for open sentences, but for real objects to satisfy them. And truth is not defined for quantifier sentences in terms of the existence of suitable substitution-values, but in terms of the existence of strategies for finding such real individuals. Thus there is some fundamental misunderstanding somewhere underlying Dr. Potts' comments on my semantics.

Notice also that it is misleading of him to say that 'Hintikka tries to get around this [difficulty of having enough names of individuals] by allowing us to baptize *ad libitum*'. Not only is there no need for me to have a name for each individual in the domain; I do not in fact allow dubbings *ad libitum*. For in each game $G(S)$ there is only a definite finite number of name-givings in which we have to indulge in any actual play of $G(S)$.[3]

Furthermore, although I have not discussed this matter in print, it is not clear that the substitution-values introduced in the course of my games of seeking and finding have to be (logically) proper names. It may be enough that they only pick out contextually (demonstratively) individuated individuals, i.e. it may be that demonstratives like 'this individual', 'that one', etc., serve my purposes.[4]

Behind many of the individual criticisms Potts presents there nevertheless are certain important presuppositions which differ from mine. Most of his criticisms are little more than symptoms of this syndrome of assumptions. I do not know how to characterize it briefly, but it is clearly connected with the assumption van Heijenoort has called the conception of 'logic as language'.[5] According to this idea our language, with its characteristic logic, is in the last analysis the inescapable medium of all discourse and all communication. Even if we introduce new modes of expression, their definitions will have to be formulated in the same old native tongue. We cannot (on this view) step back and look at our language and its logic as it were from the outside, as if it were a calculus which could be arbitrarily reinterpreted. This is what we can do on the contrasting view, labelled by van Heijenoort 'logic as calculus'.

One of the best known adherents of the view of logic as language was Frege. It is no accident that he is the main authority Potts refers to.

One of the most important consequences of the idea of logic

as language is a denial of the possibility of a systematic model theory—or perhaps rather a denial of its philosophical importance. This is in fact the tacit axiom on which most of Potts' criticisms are based. When it is dragged into the open, his unhappiness with my paper becomes understandable. For I do not only espouse model theory (logical semantics) wholeheartedly, but the thrust of my paper is to go one step further and to analyse the language-games which connect our language with the world it can be used to speak of. These language-games serve to constitute those very representative relationships between language and reality that are taken for granted in ordinary model theory.

It seems to me that the idea of logic as language is fruitless and outdated. However, it is not so easy to provide short, telling arguments to that effect. Perhaps the most convincing proof is in the last analysis the success of logical semantics, either alone or pragmatically backed, in elucidating the linguistic, logical, and philosophical problems of language, especially problems arising in natural languages. Since the purpose of my paper was to outline a new method of solving such problems and since I did not have time enough to provide any extensive *essais de cette methode*, I can only assert here that it has already proved its mettle in this department, although not yet often in print.[6] However, there are plenty of applications of the older methods of model theory in the literature to show the tremendous value of model-theoretical methods in the study of language, it seems to me. I just do not see any future for an approach to semantics which does not take these model-theoretical methods into account. Hence I am tempted to say that once the tacit premisses are acknowledged on which Dr. Potts' criticisms are based, there is scarcely any need for me to present any other reply.

It is nevertheless of interest to see how Potts' presuppositions are connected with the specific remarks he makes either on my paper or on the general logical problems of language. At one point he writes: 'I think it is evident, upon a little reflection, that it is hopeless to try to identify singular terms *via* particular individuals; rather, we shall have to work the other way round and get at particular individuals *via* singular terms'. Of course this is 'evident' only if one rejects the whole idea of model theory, for it is part and parcel of any specification of how our language represents the reality it in fact represents to tell which terms stand for particular individuals, i.e., are singular terms.

Perhaps the clearest sign of Potts' presuppositions is his statement that 'logic is concerned with an aspect of meaning, with what we understand about the meaning of a proposition when we know what logical consequences may validly be inferred from it'. As I have repeatedly emphasized elsewhere, notions like validity (logical truth), entailment (logically valid consequence), etc., are neither self-sufficient nor self-explanatory. Both systematically and as a matter of research strategy, we must base such notions as logical truth and valid consequence on semantical (model-theoretical) concepts, which ultimately means basing them on the notion of truth (plain truth, or truth *simpliciter*, not the ill-named 'logical truth' of philosophers).[7] (In case you want an example of the difficulty of associating sufficiently sharp 'intuitions' with the notion of logical truth directly, without going by way of plain truth, several expert logicians' repeated failure (recorded in print) to distinguish what I have called deontic consequence from logical consequence, as diagnosed in my paper 'Deontic Logic and Its Philosophical Morals',[8] offers an instructive object lesson.) One is almost tempted to turn the tables completely on Potts here and to say that inferential relations between propositions do not yet tell *anything* about their meaning, at least not before their deeper model-theoretic backing is specified.

A typical part of the 'logic as language' syndrome is thus a confusion between questions of plain truth and 'logical truth'. Thus Potts is dead wrong when he tries to press my approach to the Procrustean bed of his own and claims that my rule (G.U) 'is clearly a rule of inference'. Clearly it is not, and cannot be, for it is a part of a definition (characterisation) of the notion of (plain) truth. One vivid way of seeing the tremendous difference between rules of inference (rules characterizing logical validity and logical truth) and my game-theoretical characterization of truth (truth *simpliciter*) is to observe that in the theory of finite *partially ordered* quantifiers (for it, see my 'Quantifiers vs. Quantification Theory'), unlike ordinary first order quantification theory, one cannot give a complete set of rules (complete axiomatization) for *logical* truths. Yet my game-theoretical definition of (plain) truth which includes rules like (G.U) works there just in the same way as in the old (linear) quantification theory.

Of course there may be rules of inference that go naturally together with the different clauses of a game-theoretical truth-definition (or with those of some other kind of truth-definition). Thus (G.U) is clearly related rather closely with the rule of inference known as universal instantiation. Similarly, (G.E) is related to existential instantiation. Their relationship is nevertheless more complicated than might first appear. (For a brief discussion of this relationship, see my paper, 'Quantifiers, Language-Games, and Transcendental Arguments'.)[9]

Now we can also understand—if not approve of—Potts' insistence on the question whether expressions of a certain category can or cannot be 'identified' in a natural language. If one assumes that we can do model theory, there is no problem here. One simply looks what kinds of entities the different expressions stand for. But if one assumes that one cannot really get outside one's language, one must base the identification on intrinsic linguistic evidence, which makes the problem much harder. Hence the identification problem Potts attributes to me are difficulties only within his approach, not mine.

A slightly different kind of answer is called for in response to Potts' remarks on the difficulty of 'understanding' rules like (G. every). Now the only presupposition of the applicability of tihs rule is that we can recognize when a string of English words of the form

> every Y who Z

occurring in the context

> X–W

is a quantifier phrase. Any half-way satisfactory treatment of English syntax must clearly be able to accomplish this. Assuming that some such treatment is possible is surely not a tall order. Moreover, in practice we do not seem to have any difficulties whatsoever in recognizing English quantifier phrases. Hence I cannot help finding Potts' criticisms of my paper on this score intensely puzzling and irrelevant.

There are in fact well-known problems in formulating the precise restrictions that are needed in forming relative clauses in English and hence needed in forming what I have called quantifier phrases. But I do not think that these precise difficulties are what Potts has in mind. And even if they are, my semantics is not any worse for them. As I have pointed out elsewhere,[10] my semantical rules turn out to apply also to the ungrammatical sentences formed in violation of these elusive restraints. (In other words, the restrictions are purely syntactical, and hence do not imply anything about the semantics of English quantifiers.) Hence the problem of formulating these restraints need not worry me in the least.

Dr. Potts would clearly defend his rejection of model theory by arguing that this theory involves a circularity. When we discuss the inter-relations of one language to reality, we have to use some language (metalanguage) or other. This language will have to be explained ultimately in terms of our original familiar home language, this objection goes.

This line of thought is not without some force and certainly it is not without interest. For instance, Potts points out, quite correctly, that those clauses of the usual 'truth-definitions' which deal with quantifiers themselves employ quantifiers.

But this observation is not nearly as conclusive as Dr. Potts obviously assumes. Even if we define the quantifiers of one language in terms of the quantifiers of another language, we are not necessarily moving in a useless circle. The circle is useless only if the two sets of quantifiers are of the same type. If they are not, even formal truth-definitions can yield valuable new insights.

Even if we think of the truth-definition which my approach yields as a purely formal one, it does not move in the kind of circle Dr. Potts thinks. It was already seen that my various game rules are steps towards a characterization of the notion of plain truth (truth *simpliciter*), not such rules of inference as serve to capture *logical* truths. However, they do not do even that by themselves. (They are not even assertions, but permissions. How could they possibly be truth-definitions or parts of truth-definitions?) Furthermore, Potts' claim that they involve quantifiers is most unclear. The rules for existential quantifiers, for instance (G.E) and (G. some), are of precisely the same form as the corresponding rules for universal quantifiers, for instance the rules (G.U) and (G. every), respectively. Hence the same quantifier, existential or universal, must be involved in both kinds of rules. But which one? Surely you cannot characterize existential and universal quantifiers of one language precisely in the same way in terms of precisely the same metalinguistic quantifier. Hence there is something very unclear indeed in Potts' claims.

The answer is that my game rules become vehicles of truth-definition only through the rule (G.T) which connects the semantical games with the notion of truth. (As I pointed out in my paper, it is this particular way of bringing in the notion of truth that is largely responsible for clearing up messy problems about the semantical behaviour of natural-language quantifiers.) Now this rule (G.T) defines truth in terms of the existence of winning strategies. There are quantifiers unmistakably present here, not only in the form of the *existence* of a suitable strategy, but also in the guise of the concept of a *winning* strategy. For such a strategy is to be defined as one which *none* of Nature's strategies will defeat.

A strategy is constituted by a *function* that tells a player how to carry out his moves, depending on those earlier ones he knows of. The quantifiers that are used in my truth-definition are therefore in effect *second-order* (function) quantifiers. (Whether or not Potts is technically right in saying that 'the quantifiers he (Hintikka) uses in (G.U) and G.E) are those of first-order logic', this statement is now seen to carry an entirely wrong suggestion in that the operative quantifiers of my truth-definition in the end turn out to be second-order ones.) Even from a strictly formal point of view, I am not moving in a circle. At worst, I am characterizing arbitrary first-order quantifiers in terms of a rather specific sort of higher-order quantifiers. The interest of an enterprise of this sort is amply shown by such studies as Gödel's 1959 paper[11] and my recent paper 'Quantifiers vs. Quantification Theory'.[12]

But there is really no reason to think of my approach as being geared to a truth-definition formulated in some particular language. The whole idea of my approach is not to speak of one language in another, but to get at the activities ('language-games') which connect a language with reality.[13] Of course, *if* these games are described verbally, they have to be described in some language or other. But this tautology does not make my enterprise circular, for one can get at these activities also by learning (being taught) them by example and training. The question whether my approach is circular is thus not at all the question whether quantifiers are needed if the rules of my semantical games are formulated in some language or other. Rather, the real problem is whether such a formulation is necessary in the first place or whether the games in question can be taught, learned, and mastered directly, without explicit verbal formulations of the rules. And the overwhelmingly obvious answer to this question is *yes*, it seems to me.

Thus it is precisely the pragmatic (game-theoretic) backing which I give to model theory that enables us to avoid the charges of circularity which may be levelled at the usual types of model theory. These charges are defeated even in their stronger form in which also truth-definitions for quantifier sentences in terms of quantifiers of a different type is allegedly found objectionable. It is thus doubly disappointing for me to see such circularity charges raised against the very first explicit treatment of quantifiers to which they do not apply at all, even if all that these charges really show is the inadequacy of the Fregean framework for dealing with game-theoretical ideas. Instead of trying to backtrack our steps to Frege and to the idea of 'logic as language', surely we ought to forge ahead to the promising land of game-theoretic semantics.

NOTES

1. See 'Behavioral Criteria of Radical Translation', Chapter IV of my book, *Logic, Language-Games, and Information* (Clarendon Press, Oxford, 1973).
2. For the contrast between substitutional and objectual interpretations of quantifiers, see, e.g., W. V. Quine, *Philosophy of Logic* (Prentice-Hall, Englewood Cliffs, N.J., 1970), pp. 91–4.
3. This number is at most equal to the depth of the sentence in question (in the sense defined, e.g., in my *Logic, Language-Games, and Information* (note 1 above)).
4. For the distinction between demonstrative and descriptive methods of individuation (cross-identification), see, e.g., my paper 'Knowledge by Acquaintance—Individuation by Acquaintance', in David Pears, ed., *Bertrand Russell* (Modern Studies in Philosophy, Prentice-Hall, Englewood Cliffs, N.J., 1972), pp. 52–79, reprinted in my recent collection of papers, *Knowledge and the Known* (D. Reidel, Dordrecht and Boston, 1974), pp. 212–33.
5. Cf. Jean van Heijenoort, 'Logic as Language and Logic as Calculus', *Synthese*, vol. 17 (1967), pp. 324–30.

6. Cf. nevertheless my 'Quantifiers vs. Quantification Theory', *Linguistic Inquiry*, vol. 5 (1974), pp. 153-77.
7. Cf. the methodological essays in my *Models for Modalities* (D. Reidel, Dordrecht, 1969).
8. See *Models for Modalities*, last chapter.
9. See *Logic, Language-Games, and Information* (note 1 above), Chapter V.
10. In a forthcoming work *The Semantics of Questions and the Questions of Semantics*.
11. Kurt Gödel, 'Über eine bisher noch nicht benützte Erweiterung des finiten Standpunktes', in F. Gonseth, ed., *Logica: Studia Paul Bernays Dedicata* (Editions Griffon, Neuchatel, 1959), pp. 76-83.
12. Note 6 above.
13. Cf. 'Behavioral Criteria' (note 1 above).

Index

Ajdukiewicz, K., 5
applicator, 184
Aristotle, 1-4, 9, 49, 85

Baumgarten, A.G., 2
Beth, E., 88
Bretano, F., 169

Cantor, G., 13, 54
Cartwright, R., 109, 110, 141, 168, 170
Chomsky, N., 237
Chwistek, L., 88
combinatory logic, 184-90, 196, 204-7
concretism, *see* reism

deep structure, 184, 186-90, 196-7, 204
Descartes, R., 120, 143
Donnellan, K., 210

Euclid, 3, 9, 28, 44
excluded middle, 3, 89, 190, 194-5
existence, *see* ontology

formal language, ontologically neutral, 15-16, 21, 22, 26, 27, 45, 50, 51-2, 54-5, 62-3, 171-2; construction of ontologically neutral formal language, 21-6; as tool in philosophy, 66, 171-2, 190, 197-9, 202-3. *See also* normalized language
formal logic, ontology and, 12, 26, 28, 42, 44, 45, 46, 62-3, 96-7; ontologically neutral, 15-21, 27-8, 40, 44, 45-50, 62-3. *See also* formal language, logic
foundations of mathematics, ontology and, 2, 3, 4, 13, 45, 46, 50, 54, 89. *See also* intuitionism

Frege, G., 13, 31, 32-5, 45, 126, 164, 169, 172, 194, 195, 246, 247, 250, 252, 262

game theory, and many-valued logic, 70-3, 84-5, 92-5; and normalized language, 240-2; and natural semantics for quantification, 214-16, 233, 242-3, 255-6, 268-9; and quantification for fragment of English, 219-26, 230; for formal language, 216-19, 229-30; for modalities, 225
Gentzen, G., 90, 154, 155

Hájek, P., 90
Heyting, A., 89
Hobbes, T., 122
Husserl, E., 14

'identicals are necessarily identicals', truth of, 97, 99-100, 132-3, 147, 151; derivation, 97, 99, 108-14, 147; dependence on possible world semantics, 102-7, 112, 136-40, 169-70; applications, 115-22, 142-6, 147; counter examples, 133-6, 147, 160; Kripke's account, 97-101, 101-4, 133-40
identity, notions of, 152-9, 160-7; Leibnizian, 152; Kantian, 152; as link between ontology and logic, 3, 10, 26, 147
intuitionism, 45, 64-5, 89

Kamlah, W., 89
Kant, I., 152, 158
Körner, S., 90, 150
Kotarbiński, T., 4, 5
Kripke, S., 97. *See also* identicals

Lakoff, G., 208
Lambert, K., 53, 54
Leibniz, 104, 150, 152–3
Leibniz Law, 97, 109, 117, 152, 157, 158, 164, 167, 180
Lemmon, E.J., 109
Leśniewski, 13, 14, 23, 24, 49, 52, 53
logic (science of), ontology and, 1, 3, 9, 10, 11, 12, 13–14, 26, 28, 35, 42, 46, 50; views of, 10, 12, 44–6. *See also* formal logic, many-valued logic, modal logic, natural language, quantification
Lorenzen, P., 89, 94, 255–6
Łukasiewicz, 64, 67, 68, 69, 73, 74, 76, 78, 79, 80, 83, 84, 86, 88, 95

many-valued logic, significance of, 12, 64–6, 70, 82, 88–9, 91; formalism of, 65–6, 85; logical consequence in, 66, 75, 82–8, 90; as a theory of degrees of truth, 66–70, 75–82; as a theory of degrees of commitment, 70–3, 92–5; as a logic of probability, 66, 75–6
meaning, theory of and reism, 5; and propositional logic, 10–12; and natural language, 198–200
modal logic, formalism of, 66. *See also* possible worlds, identicals
Montague, R., 210, 211
Moore, G.E., 4, 9

natural language, role in logic and language, 41–2, 62–3; and formal language, 183, 191–2, 199–200, 237–8, 257–8, 268; as an activity, 233, 268; and logic, 262–3, 268–9; logically standardized, 14, 15, 20. *See also* meaning, normalized language, quantification
normalized language, 183, 203; use of, 190, 197–8, 202–3, 238; construction of normalized fragment of English, 184–9, 191–2. *See also* natural language, meaning

ontological commitment, 55. *See* Quine, quantification, formal language, formal logic
ontology, etymology, 1–2; and context of natural science, 2, 3, 45; nature of, 1–4, 9, 10, 26, 43, 44, 46, 49; need for, 2, 3, 4, 13, 26, 28, 44–5, 49–50; origins, 1–4; and methodology, 3. *See also* logic, formal language, platonism

pansomatism, *see* reism
Partee, B., 212–13
platonism, bicategorial, 8, 9, 20, 21, 22, 26, 27, 45, 49; multicategorial, 8, 49; unicategorial, 6, 8, 9, 21, 22, 26, 27, 45, 49
(all) possible worlds, 12, 66, 73, 97, 99, 100, 102, 103–7, 110, 111–12, 116, 136, 140–3, 150–1, 225
propositional logic, as underlying ontology, 10, 18. *See also* meaning

quantification, in logical and natural language, 187, 189–90, 191, 196, 203, 208–10, 213–14, 229–30, 233, 243–5; quantifying, 16, 18, 22–4, 26–7, 28–43, 52–3, 210, 213, 229; and ontological commitments, 15–17, 18, 23, 26–7, 28–43, 48–63; and singular terms, 209–13, 238–9. *See also* formal logic, games
Quine, W., 29, 30–4, 41, 55–7, 103, 110, 111, 192, 193, 206

Ramsey, F. P., 99, 154, 163
Rantala, V., 258
reism, description, 4–5, 26, 45, 47; discussion, 6–9. *See* platonism
rigid designator, 99. *See also* possible worlds
Russell, B., 13, 14, 18, 34, 45, 49, 98, 124, 153, 173, 177, 196, 210, 211, 213, 236

semantic category, 14
surface structure, 184, 187–9, 196, 204, 209

Tarski, A., 84, 190

van Heijenoort, J., 262

Wittgenstein, L., 99, 154, 155, 161–4, 166, 192, 216, 233–5, 237–8, 248, 254, 258–9
Wolff, C., 1, 2–4, 9, 28

Zermelo, E., 1